Endorsements

Working on *Doubtless* with Alyssa will forever be one of the highest honors and crowning achievements of my life. Watching the way the Holy Spirit equipped and empowered her to write during the darkest season of her life in the midst of an unprecedented pandemic was nothing short of miraculous.

This book was birthed in the depths of a holy, sacred space of total reliance and dependency upon Christ. Alyssa's voice is refreshingly unpretentious as she bares her heart and soul with vulnerability, courage, and humility. Throughout the pages of *Doubtless*, she describes excruciating levels of physical and emotional pain, most of which have been unknown or unnoticed by others.

As Alyssa's friend for over six years, I experienced a greater level of understanding and revelation of the daily struggles she endures, as well as learned about the tremendous weight of traumatic experiences she has survived in several life-altering situations through her own account. Seeing the strength, joy, and endurance she has gained through her relationship with Christ is a testament to His power and love working in and through her on each step of her journey.

Through reading this book, I discovered that Alyssa is a living miracle. Most individuals who suffer from GAN do not live long enough to see early adulthood. Gaining a greater understanding of this disease has given me an appreciation for the severity of Alyssa's condition and an even greater awe and wonder at God's power in preserving her health. She has been able to accomplish more than many of the most able-bodied people I've met!

Whether you personally suffer from a physical disability or not, every person who reads this book will walk away changed for the better. The wisdom Alyssa has gained from her life experiences is rich and profound, and she generously shares her story so we may all reap the rewards of her steadfast pursuit of Christ despite impossible circumstances and receive a greater hope for the eternal life He paid for us all.

Lauren Steffes
Founder & CEO, Consecrate

Alyssa's ability to describe her experience as a disabled person is honest and raw, unlike anything I have ever read. She describes the struggles but also highlights the positive lessons that she has learned. Everything she has written and her storytelling makes her relatable, even to a person without a physical disability. Her account of overcoming adversity, finding herself, and growing up all while facing the reality of having a disability is inspiring for anyone, and packed full of wisdom and positivity. She beautifully articulates her thoughts and feelings as she navigates her life as it deviates from the "normal" path.

As the manager of a cafe that employs adults with disabilities, I am surrounded by people with disabilities who share their life experiences. Alyssa's account of her life through diagnosis and growing up through adversity is beautiful and real. Her positive outlook on hard circumstances and her ability to overcome is so empowering. You need this book as a reminder to take everything that happens in life and turn it into a weapon for a positive life. It is an inspiring read!

Isabelle Rudd
Cafe Manager, BrewAble

Alyssa is a young woman of great faith and confidence. She faithfully shows up to every prayer meeting and church event with a smile on her face and doesn't let anything stop her. I'm honored to know her and to witness her continuous perseverance and courage. Her book *Doubtless*, along with her beautiful artwork, is a powerful testimony of what overcoming looks like. Her creativity is an outlet of such depth and beauty that comes from a life of trials and healing. Alyssa's life and story are proof of God's faithfulness and provision!

Dr. Trudy Simmons
Counselor
Award-Winning TV Host & Executive Producer, *The Christian View*

Alyssa is wise beyond her years with a heart of gold. That's how I felt about Alyssa when I met her when she was 12 years old and how I still feel about her today. She has a strong quest for knowledge and truth. Her actions have always reflected her desire to grow physically, emotionally, and spiritually and to share this knowledge and truth with the rest of humanity. She is such a strong person with a message that can help heal the world.

Dr. Deborah Pearson
Sports & Family Chiropractic

Doubtless is a lovely, authentic story about overcoming adversity. I have known Alyssa for some time and have appreciated witnessing her transformation into a warrior. *Doubtless* will inspire others to look past their disabilities and find their purpose in life. Alyssa has found her purpose.

Stephen Taylor
Executive Director, SNs360 Inc

You will be a witness to the power of God after reading *Doubtless*. Alyssa Kumle gives us a unique perspective on a rare disease and how she found the strength and faith to live with it all!

Gelse Tkalec
Co-Founder & Executive Director, All In For Ethan: Helping Kids With GAN

Alyssa's book demonstrates a very courageous and life-giving servant of the KING. This book is inspired by the Holy Spirit!

Patricia Reeves
Executive Director, Art of Living Ministries

Alyssa's story brings Romans 5:3-4 to life. Through deep faith, her life is a living testimony of how sufferings can lead to hope. With great humility, she exemplifies strength and joy as she shifts the focus from her disabilities to her capabilities. Her story is worth reading.

Rick Thompson
Coach, Titans Wheelchair Sports Team

Doubtless: Walking By Faith, Not By Sight is a story of grit and grace. Alyssa takes the reader through an honest journey into living with limited mobility and finding courage through her faith. This book is not about disability but about limitless adventures and discoveries. It is a book of hope.

Aarti Sahgal
Founder & CEO, Synergies Work

Have you ever doubted God or yourself? Have you ever received news or a diagnosis that changed your life? Have you ever felt lonely, rejected, or like an outcast? Have you ever experienced pain or suffering you couldn't see purpose in? Have you ever lost hope or struggled with your faith? If you answered 'yes' to any of those questions then *Doubtless* by my sweet friend, Alyssa Kumle, is a must-read. This book will teach you how to find passion and purpose in your pain. It will encourage you and give you hope that will set you free from doubt and strengthen your faith as you learn to celebrate the adventure you are on.

Alyssa is a dear friend who has impacted my life in the way she lives her life with love, light, and joy. She has a powerful story and testimony of the power of Jesus's love to help you overcome anything in your life. She is wise beyond her years and shines the light of Christ to all those she encounters. This is a great book to give as a gift to those who are in need of learning how to walk by faith and not by sight.

Julie Davies
Author & Speaker

Alyssa's heart and story have impacted my life. She has used every single one of her days to love Jesus more and share Him and the fulfilling life that we all have available in Him. I love her transparency on overcoming things that could be viewed as setbacks and understanding what it's like for her daily to be the incredible friend, author, artist, coffee shop-lover, and foodie that we love her to be. Her words are empowering because this is her story and she's letting us into the good days, the bad days, and all the days in between. Thank you Alyssa for giving us a book I want my daughter to read.

Corrie King
On-Air Announcer, Victory 91.5

I first met Alyssa in 2015, when I was a vendor at my very first art show. She had a big smile, and I felt such a sense of joy from her that superseded her circumstances. As Alyssa wheeled around my booth in her wheelchair, she took her time looking at the art and asked thoughtful questions regarding my work. Her passion for art was very clear. She told me she too was an artist, and I asked to see her work. I loved the brightly colored artwork she showed me, which exuberated the same joy as Alyssa. When she left, I watched as she continued to visit other vendors' booths.

Alyssa spread her joy as she wheeled along in fascination with the art that surrounded her. I continued to see her at other shows. As always, after a brief conversation with Alyssa and a hug, I couldn't help but feel inspired and joyful. Alyssa embodies perseverance and touches everyone with whom she comes in contact.

Whether struggling with a disability or not, I know many people will be inspired, strengthened, and encouraged by Alyssa's book, *Doubtless*.

Kristin Repogle
Author & Artist

Alyssa Kumle's *Doubtless* is pure refreshment! She shares the courageous, overcoming power of a life that birthed itself from deep disappointment. The anointing in these pages will transform you to see challenges as a positioning for breakthrough power that never ends! Her transparency will leave you feeling seen in your own hidden struggles and give you fortitude! This book comforts the soul, energizes the spirit and brings light and glory to our Creator whose plans are greater than we could *even* imagine!

Melissa Row
Author, *Little Golden Tickets*

As a job coach for Lionheart WORKS participants, Alyssa brought her energy, warmth, and passion for people. Our young adults thoroughly enjoyed her enthusiasm and attentiveness to their needs and abilities. She led by example and inspired them to reach their full potential. She inspires people and encourages them well. We at Lionheart WORKS are so proud of Alyssa and her writing this book. We cannot wait to read it!

Heather H. Wagner, BSW, MA
Director, Lionheart WORKS and The Lionheart Life Center, Inc.

Alyssa's story is sure to inspire and encourage you no matter what season of life you are in. Take courage as you read her testimony of steadfastness and pursuit, believing in the goodness of God in the face of disappointment and difficulty.

Travis Gay
Pastor, The Awakening (Athens, Georgia)

I first met Alyssa and her parents in line at the cafeteria at the National Institutes of Health. I was awestruck by how high functioning she was for a patient with Giant Axonal Neuropathy. Thankfully, Alyssa has a slower progressing form of this horrific disease. As I got to know her, I was also filled with awe when I observed how mature and inspirational she is. There is no doubt Alyssa will continue to inspire and touch the lives of others with this book and many more to come.

Lori Sames
Founder, Hannah's Hope Fund

Alyssa shares her hope in a way that changes how you see any adversity. She lives what she shares and displays the beauty of not only overcoming insecurity but also how being hidden in her life has led to a purpose beyond what she could have dreamed.

Rachel Faulkner Brown
Director, Be Still Ministries

Alyssa's journey of faith beautifully unfolds as she bares her struggle with a life-altering condition. The message of hope in the midst of unforetold circumstances is infused into every page. Her story shows that there is beauty in suffering. Alyssa has been a good friend of mine for nearly 10 years and has always inspired me in the way she never lets her disability stop her or get her down.

Mary Jenna Nixon
Founder & Director, Uprooted Heart

With her big, beautiful smile and starry eyes, Alyssa rolled up on her trusty steed and ushered in a ray of sunshine! This is just how I saw her on the first day we met!

Alyssa's story is full of real and heartfelt emotions as she found the heart of God while searching for her significance and understanding of His purpose for her life, despite her physical disability. Her heart for God and her passion to serve Him through her art and creativity are beautifully revealed as Alyssa shares her journey. I have been blessed and encouraged by her story of hope, courage and perseverance.

Laura Maxwell
Founder & Director, One Heart Ministries

It is difficult to put into words what a treasure Alyssa is. The life she lives daily is a true testament to hope for all who read her journey. The joy Alyssa exudes while carrying the cross she has makes any person want to know the source of her radiant glow and contagious smile!

As you journey through these pages, Alyssa beautifully walks you through the battles and victories of her life since birth and you can't help but see where this joy she emanates finds its source! Her life laid out in these pages will bring hope and a brighter perspective on anyone's own struggles and hopefully lead all to share that through their own life to others, just as Alyssa has.

Kim Zember
Author, Restless Heart: My Struggle with Life and Sexuality

Alyssa Kumle has written a beautiful must-read about her journey of faith and overcoming adversity. I met this amazing girl when she was 11 years old, and have seen her struggle with some very challenging circumstances, knowing that God had a bigger plan for her life. With each difficult step she has chosen to trust God. Her remarkable story will encourage anyone who has had their faith tested with obstacles and hardships.

Karen Witkowski
Mentor & Friend

I have had the joy of knowing Alyssa deeply for the past five years and have encouraged her with writing her first book, *Doubtless*. I have never witnessed the faith and the endurance of such a young woman. She is a role model for anyone who has a serious disability. She never gives up and is always there for anyone who needs to talk. I highly recommend this book for anyone who struggles or knows someone who struggles with a disability.

Jan Sharpe
Mentor & Friend

Consecrate.

Published by Consecrate
www.consecrate.co
@consecrateco

© 2024 by Alyssa Kumle. All rights reserved. No part of this publication may be reproduced, stored in a retrieval system, or transmitted, in any form or by any means—electronic, mechanical, photocopying, recording, or otherwise—without prior written permission. The only exception is brief, cited quotations in printed reviews, blogs posts, or books.

International Standard Book Number: 978-0-33231-4

Consecrate is a trademark of Consecrate and is registered in the U.S. Patent and Trademark Office. All rights reserved.

All Scripture quotations, unless otherwise indicated, are taken from the Holy Bible, New International Version®, NIV®. Copyright ©1973, 1978, 1984, 2011 by Biblica, Inc.™ Used by permission of Zondervan. All rights reserved worldwide. www.zondervan.com The "NIV" and "New International Version" are trademarks registered in the United States Patent and Trademark Office by Biblica, Inc.™

Scripture quotations marked (ESV) are from The ESV® Bible (The Holy Bible, English Standard Version®), copyright © 2001 by Crossway, a publishing ministry of Good News Publishers. Used by permission. All rights reserved."

Scripture quotations marked (NKVJ) are taken from the New King James Version®. Copyright © 1982 by Thomas Nelson. Used by permission. All rights reserved.

Scripture quotations marked (NLT) are taken from the Holy Bible, New Living Translation, copyright ©1996, 2004, 2015 by Tyndale House Foundation. Used by permission of Tyndale House Publishers, Carol Stream, Illinois 60188. All rights reserved.

Scripture quotations marked (NLV) are taken from the New Living Version®. Copyright © Christian Literature International. Used by permission. All rights reserved.

Book Coach and Content Editor:
Lauren Steffes

Copy Editor:
Christine Kieti

Cover Photography:
Christian Garcia
www.cologarcia.com
@cologarcia323 @edenstudiosatl

Cover Design:
Lauren Steffes

Interior Book Design:
Sarah Sercombe
www.sarahalison.com.au
@sarahalison

Janina Victoria
www.janinavictoria.com
@janinavictoria

WALKING BY FAITH,
NOT BY SIGHT

ALYSSA KUMLE

consecrate

For my sister, Jaime

Table of Contents

Foreword — xv
Prologue: Diagnosis of Doubt — xvi

Part 1

1. The Beginning — 1
2. Diagnosis — 9
3. Hidden — 15
4. Buried Treasure — 23
5. Heartache — 29
6. Blank Canvas — 35
7. Divine Deliverance — 41
8. Uphill Climb — 47
9. A New Diagnosis — 55
10. Outcast — 63
11. Breaking Point — 73
12. Sustaining Grace — 83
13. Kingdom Family — 91
14. Selah — 99
15. Unexpected — 109
16. Trust Triumphs — 117

Part 2

17. Wild Heart — 129
18. A New Kind of Adventure — 139
19. Walk It Out — 145
20. Beautifully Broken — 151
21. Mended — 163
22. Royal DNA — 171
23. New Authority — 179
24. Way Maker — 187
25. Hindsight 20/20 — 195
26. Doubtless — 203

Epilogue: Healing Awaits — 213

Foreword

I am humbled and honored to call Alyssa a friend, fellow member of the Young Suffering Club, and part of our beloved Hope Heals Camp Community. Her story has moved me deeply because it is so similar to my own in a multitude of ways, and yet, her journey is painful and heartbreaking in a way I cannot fully imagine. Alyssa inspires me and gives me strength and perspective.

After a debilitating diagnosis as a seven-year-old, she has lived with a progressive, incurable disease in a world not made for her body. I get that. As I read her words, I wept as I have experienced so many similar emotions in a body that doesn't fully work.

She has difficulty balancing and has impaired coordination just like me. It is difficult to put into words the frustration when your body won't do simple tasks such as getting dressed or grabbing a cup of coffee. She writes of crawling in her closet to get clothes to wear to start the day.

As I have engaged so many in the disability world, there is a permanent, low-grade resentment and annoyance with the disabled body. You feel betrayed by your own flesh. The anger and frustration require a level of perseverance that few need to cultivate.

And yet, this unique story of suffering and disability also captures every able-bodied heart because we all want to know how to keep living in and even finding gratitude for the hardest parts of our lives. Alyssa's book and hard-won lessons learned remind us that our most difficult challenges can also be our most powerful assignments in life. She has chosen faith over fear and guides her reader toward a perspective of hope and radical peace.

What a powerful guidebook you hold in your hands. May it be part of your own story of acceptance of life's deepest pain.

Katherine Wolf
Co-Author, *Hope Heals, Suffer Strong, and Treasures in the Dark*
Co-Founder, Hope Heals Camp and Mend Coffee & Goods

PROLOGUE

Diagnosis of Doubt

Growing up I always dreamed of who I would be in life. Exploding with creativity, dreams, and wild ideas, I saw myself as a dancer, an athlete, a world traveler, confident and bold, fearless and unstoppable. Childhood was simple and sweet, and a safe time to explore and be free. But, in many ways, my childhood was cut short. Stolen. Robbed by a sinister foe. An enemy that would torment my heart, mind, and soul entered my life, when I was given an unfavorable diagnosis of a crippling nerve disease. This diagnosis opened the door to a demon called Doubt, who worked incessantly to derail my desires and dismantle my dreams.

With new physical limitations, I had to learn to live differently than I had ever envisioned, which reshaped the hopes and plans I had for my future. In an attempt to protect myself against disappointment and pain, I allowed Doubt to construct a stronghold, which then led me to become an avid worrier, always living with a sense of foreboding fear and needless caution. Over years of adversity and trials, I doubted myself—my intelligence, my beauty, my worth, and my abilities. I doubted others—to be trustworthy, empathetic, accepting, or understanding. And I especially doubted God—to be good, to be loving, and that He would grant me a life worth living despite my disease.

Even through pain or a seemingly impossible and unclear path ahead, my commitment to say yes and show up in faith is when Doubt began to break off in pieces, loosening its grip as I began to let Faith flood my soul. Through a journey of lots of refining and testing of my trust in God, my hope for this book is to encourage those of you who may be going through a trial or unfavorable circumstance that God really is a good and faithful Father when we choose to trust Him. He is the one who makes a way when there seems to be no way. He transforms brokenness into beauty and pain into purpose.

Even when Doubt kept me in a place of stagnancy and discouragement, I pushed through and kept going anyway until Faith demolished the stronghold that had kept me in bondage for so long. Believing for the best and refusing to let any limitations stop me, I can truly say that my trust in God is now unshakable. He has empowered me to live a *Doubtless* life through His powerful love that sets us all free from fear.

Through sharing my story, my hope is to shine a light on the common belief that suffering and disabilities are setbacks and to re-introduce them as blessings in disguise. I've learned that we can do all things through Christ who gives us strength (Phil. 4:13). I've learned that the power of Christ is truly perfected in weakness (2 Cor. 12:9). And I've learned that we can always make the choice to push Doubt aside to make room for the *Doubtless*.

PART 1

1

The Beginning

I never thought this would be my story. I pull up at the local coffee shop, hoping there will be a handicapped space available since they are often hard to come by or further away from the entrance than is convenient. Using hand controls to drive, my braced legs have more room to spread out on the floor of my car, and I have to lift them with my hands to get out. I cling to the side of my car as I thrust my folded walker out and fill it with what I will need for my morning of writing.

I wonder what my legs will feel like as I start my day, as every morning comes with new levels of weakness and muscle stiffness. I navigate the frustrating speed bumps on many parking lot ramps that only make going up more difficult while pushing against resistance—as if going up an incline isn't already hard enough. As I move forward, it feels like each step requires the strength of climbing a small mountain. I am careful not to trip since my legs can't keep up, lunging forward to push my cart as it gets ahead of me. My flat feet turn outwards and my collapsing knees counteract each other with each step.

At last, I get to the door and brace myself to tightly grip my walker with one hand in order to pull the heavy door open with the other and meet with a bump in the doorway that my walker gets stuck on while the heavy door starts to close on me. Sometimes people come running when they hear the banging in my attempt to get inside, but usually, it's just a startling, attention-grabbing moment in an often peaceful environment. I make my way over carpets or around chairs, and finally reach the cash register and place my order.

Doubtless

When my coffee is ready, they hand it to me while my two hands are still clutching my walker handles... really? Since most able-bodied baristas are often oblivious to the plight of the handicapped person, I often have to ask them to carry the coffee cup to my table. But when it's a busy morning, and there are multiple coffees ready to be claimed on the counter, I have to fend for myself. I practically hold my breath while heading to my table with a full, hot drink on top of a rolling surface.

Walking slowly is a tedious task, as I am used to thrusting forward as quickly as possible to get around. I finally reach my table with my coffee miraculously intact (on a good day) and settle into my chair. It's a relief to finally sit down. I open my laptop and begin to write...

Through all the challenges of my mundane routine, I think back to how easy life seemed during my early childhood years, with no known hindrances or stressors and a world full of opportunities for the future ahead of me. I begin to reflect and recall the tale of what pushed me to be set apart on a path of unexpected adversities. A time when I wasn't always rushing forward on weak and crooked legs in an attempt to remain on the go. A time when everything didn't take me five times as long as everyone else. A time when I wasn't exhausted by doing the littlest things. A time when I was just a normal, regular, healthy girl. A time when I was simply "me"—not "the girl with a disability."

Special memories begin to flood my mind of a carefree and sweet childhood within the quiet and safe suburb of Naperville, Illinois, where I grew up. At that stage in my life, I hadn't yet begun to live with these heavy burdens or disappointments but rather lots of fun activities and time outside where I felt truly free and filled with wonder, as children often are. I ran and played and was just like everyone else, and life hadn't shown its complexities yet.

We lived in a great neighborhood with a close-knit community and an open-door policy. All the neighbors knew each other and could go to each other's houses at any time, for any reason. I had my three best friends living right down the street, and we all would run through the yards, play on swing sets and in sprinklers, or spend time in each other's driveways drawing with chalk, playing hopscotch, tossing the basketball around, jumping rope, or rollerblading. With an abundance of adventure, friendship, and freedom, childhood was pretty awesome.

My best friend, Joanie, had a big trampoline in her yard where we would bounce each other in the air and laugh when we were thrown about, trying to stay as still as possible while the other one or two of us were determined to "crack the egg" that the person being bounced around was curled into. The days seemed to last forever as there wasn't a huge to-do list except to play with my friends and be spontaneous, with the anticipation of the ice cream truck jingle in the afternoons. Summers featured slip-n-slides and spraying each other with the hose, sending an unusual sensation of crisp,

THE BEGINNING

cool water flowing over my feet, contrasting with the dry, hot pavement.

I remember running to avoid the hot sting of burning my feet at the local community pool while waiting in the snack bar line during Adult Swim. Wednesdays were "Noodle Night," where noodles and rafts were allowed in the pool, and it seemed like such an exciting and rebellious action to take them in the water. On occasional weekend evenings, we played night games in one of the neighbor's yards, where a group of the neighborhood kids would play freeze-tag or capture the flag and chase fireflies in the grass as dawn approached.

It was such a magical time in the summer, with the fresh cool of the night air and darkening sky bringing a new level of awakening and a sense of aliveness within. Trying to fit activities in before our soon-approaching curfew of 9 o'clock brought a new level of excitement to the experience. Every day was an adventure as my few close friends and I would play with our toys, build things, and make up our own games with our own rules. You know life is good when the highlights involve macaroni and cheese and chicken fingers or trips to jungle gym play areas with the slippery, multi-colored tubes to crawl through at McDonald's.

Our neighborhood in Naperville was very flat, making it the perfect area to play games in the yards or ride bikes and Razor scooters through the street. I felt so cool when I drove my pink Barbie Jeep up and down the sidewalk, hardly able to imagine what actually driving a car would be like. The smell of fresh cut grass seemed new every day, and each house was close to the next, with the very sparse hills around. It seemed like you could see straight into every yard and into every detail of the landscape, which gave the neighborhood and the ones surrounding it a strong sense of safety and security.

People were frequently out doing yard work, maintaining and beautifying their spaces, something companies are mostly paid to do for people where I currently live in the South. Yard work was my dad's hobby. He and his best friend across the street had a running competition over who had the best yard. Spending so much time outside was refreshing, and I was bound to pass by a neighbor or two planting flowers or mowing the grass on my little walks or scooter rides down our neighborhood street.

The grass was especially green and soft up North, and it was perfect for sitting in and discovering the little lady bugs and creatures around. My friends and I would lay in the grass for hours, engaging in the world around us, sprawling out and breathing in the world. I miss the feeling of being barefoot in the soft grass or on the warm cement driveways and cracks in the sidewalks. There were the occasional tiny, pellet-like pebbles you'd step on, bringing shocking pains in your feet, yet it was neat feeling the direct connection with the different aspects of the earth. In the summertime, crisp and cool water misted from the sprinklers, and we would try to leap through

Doubtless

them without getting wet, while aiming for a shady spot of grass on the other side to collapse on. It was a sacred world, and I felt so alive.

I can still smell the burgers and hotdogs cooking on the grill at the neighbor's summer parties as the kids would be swinging on their swingset and hear the voices and laughter from the adults sitting on the deck upstairs eating and drinking, engaging in many conversations and laughs. I can still feel my boots sink into the blanket of thick, white snow that covered our world in the brutal winters and see the majestic wonderland that we would play in all day long as if it wasn't the slightest bit cold.

Our backyard had the only "hill" in the neighborhood where kids could sled down, though we often yelled at them to leave when they weren't our immediate, close friends. The hill was our territory, and my sisters and I were protective of our private slope. Snow days involved a whole process: suiting up in snow pants, boots, multiple coats, and all the skin-covering gear. But the more thick layers we wore, the more prepared we were to fearlessly dive into the frozen, white powder. It took hours to later dethaw all of our frozen limbs.

Snowmen and forts of different sorts could be found in every yard, and the blizzard-filled sky seemed unending when the adults would have to shovel the driveway clear multiple times a day. The winter wonderland was fun during recess at school as my classmates and I hovered by the brick building searching for icicles and comparing who's breath was the most visible. The thick snowfall was always so peaceful to look at, as the many flat fields were covered in miles of unending white.

Holidays and changes of the seasons brought about new and exciting festivities that gave every year special things to plan and look forward to. Our picture frames featured years of group photos from the neighborhood kids all trick-or-treating together and coordinating costumes with our yearly competitions of who counted up the largest number of candies at the end of the night. My two best friends and I would sprawl out our piles and make trades so we could all stock up on our favorite candy.

Every December, my best friend's dad dressed up as Santa Clause and would have a present for each of the neighborhood kids as we waited for our turn to sit on his lap. For New Year's Eve, I remember always wearing my sparkly headband or funky glasses, with a plastic glass of fine, sparkling grape juice for a toast along with the funny group photos with my family and friends.

The Fourth of July was my favorite, as all the neighborhood kids would decorate their bikes with festive glitz and glam to then participate in a bike parade with red, white, and blue popsicles to finish. Later in the afternoon was a large neighborhood cookout followed by us all going to the downtown firework display right in town. It was such a cherished tradition that I thought would never end.

I had this confidence about me that I could take on the world and be

THE BEGINNING

whoever, whatever I wanted to be. I was outgoing and liked being the center of attention. From a young age, I told everyone that I wanted to be a singer and dancer when I grew up (typical). I would play dress-up in one of the sparkly princess dresses we had in a large bin, and be a famous actress or model that all of my imaginary boyfriends would fight over. I always had a deep love for music and movement, and I was that child who could always be found dancing on my own at concerts or festivals, getting as close to the stage as possible, and making up my own moves and choreography in my head.

At our house, we enjoyed occasional 80s dance parties. When the song "Party Train" would come on, it was an immediate call to go wild and do the train around the whole downstairs. My mom still has pictures of me dancing on the furniture and being my wild self. Music was a huge part of my life and often drowned out most chances for silence. I would frequently print out song lyrics and sing them out loud with friends or in my room.

When spending time in small groups of friends, I usually suggested a game involving a singing competition, and I usually won because I took it far more seriously than the others. I loved to be in the spotlight. I loved romance and love stories, and I fantasized about having a blissful life like all the princesses or movie stars.

Like most girls, I dreamed of a fairytale future where I imagined myself as super athletic, popular, admired, and strong with the most powerful love story. I never imagined my life would look any other way than what it was then—simple and free.

I still think about those simpler times... Oh, how I loved being crazy and free to leap and spin around, jump on my bed, dance across the room in crazy forms, play kickball at recess, and move with ease. I played soccer for multiple years, and I enjoyed dribbling the ball into the goal, viewing the various maneuvers like putting together the pieces of a challenging puzzle. I was in ballet and tap dance, and on the spirit team in elementary school.

I miss the freedom my body gave me to keep up with the world around me. It was so easy to just walk anywhere I wanted and not feel stressed about how I would go places without getting tired or needing assistance. I loved having legs that worked and could get me up, down, and around quickly. It was nice being able to walk short or long distances without any obstacles, hardships, or assistance. Life was always moving, filled with activities and adventure, with new things always taking place. I felt like in everything I did, my full body was engaged and interacting. It was a gratifying feeling to end the day feeling sore and tired as if my body gave its full expenditure that day and accomplished a lot.

Being so active and fully able-bodied was satisfying because all parts of me were working and engaged in every activity. I felt as if I could conquer the world because nothing seemed out of reach. I had my whole life ahead of me and I always thought about how lucky I was to have a fun and easy

Doubtless

childhood surrounded by love. If only I knew that kind of freedom would only last for a few years before everything would change, and I would feel like a prisoner in my own body. Little did I know, I'd be the one who people stared at and who would struggle with even the smallest daily tasks.

As children, we often have a fairytale life in mind: to get the dream job, the perfect romance, the super-fit body, the impressive accomplishments, and the life of bliss. However, rarely does it work out the way we hope, as life takes a lot of sudden twists and turns and requires hard work. We often realize that we just don't measure up in the ways we expect. Society and culture have a mold that can be hard to fit into. People mistreat us, we get left out or rejected, or our circumstances don't match the desires and dreams in our hearts.

Life is filled with the unexpected, and it's often tempting to wish we could go back in time to the simple, childlike way of seeing the world where our biggest stressor can be what toy to play with next. I often miss the simpler days when I never imagined life could get hard or hurt me in any way. I was safe and surrounded by the wonder and excitement of who and what I'd be as I grew up. I always knew how blessed I was to have an amazing childhood, family, and ability to choose what path I'd take. I never imagined anything would be different or that my life would drastically change for the worst at a moment I would least expect.

2

Diagnosis

Though I seemed to be doing the same activities as all of the other kids growing up, I started to feel like something was wrong with my body. I couldn't actually ride a bike on my own until a few years after my friends. Rollerblading was harder to balance, and for some reason, my ankles couldn't fully grasp the hang of it. It didn't seem like a huge deal because I had a hundred other activities I could choose to enjoy.

But when my friends and I would rollerblade or scooter in the neighborhood, I couldn't rollerblade because my ankles wouldn't move in the same way, and scootering became more scary to me as I kept trying not to fall and felt like my coordination was delayed. I couldn't ride a bike on my own because I couldn't peddle fast enough to stay upright and moving.

There were many warning signs. I became overly cautious and afraid of different sports because physical activities became harder and I became clumsier. Swim team was something I really started to dread because I was terrified of the jumping blocks and couldn't get the diving thing down, insisting I jump off the side of the blocks, which immediately put me a few feet behind everyone else when I started my race.

My kicking wasn't very strong, though my strokes were very elegant, so I lost a lot of swim meets as I was not swimming with speed. Though I was still in dance classes and on the soccer team, I felt behind everyone and started to have a sense of dread when heading to games or recitals, as these things became overly tiring and I needed to be more careful to not trip or stumble.

Doubtless

I grew fearful and cautious when it came to physical activities and life in general because I started to hurt myself more often, and the things I loved to do slowly became more challenging. Jump rope became more work than fun because I couldn't keep up with the speed of the rope, and I ended up with a few twisted ankles. The July 4th bike parades in the neighborhood became walking alongside the other kids who rode. P.E. class still haunts me to this day as the relay races and team competitions left me in a vulnerable place with the boys yelling at me for being the slowest one who made our team lose.

"You're so slow!" "What's your problem?" "Thanks a lot!" the boys would say.

What was wrong with me? I just couldn't keep up.

Then one day my parents got the call from my P.E. teacher. She warned them that my running and movements were a bit out of whack and that I should get checked out by a doctor.

At seven years old, I was diagnosed with Charcot Marie Tooth (CMT), an inherited peripheral neuropathy. According to WebMD's definition, "A peripheral neuropathy refers to the conditions that result when nerves that carry messages to and from the brain and spinal cord from and to the rest of the body are damaged or diseased." CMT affects the motor and sensory nerves, causing muscle weakness and nerve damage to the feet and legs. It leads to poor balance, loss of control of muscle movement, and lack of coordination, to name a few symptoms. It's a progressive, incurable disease.

This diagnosis led to a new normal of doctors appointments, hospital tests, and consistent physical therapy trying to get on top of things early and also to figure it out. The biggest change was my introduction to chiropractic and having to get orthotics in my shoes to support my ankles—one was flat, and the other had a huge arch that led to my ankle rolling outward. Yet, these changes were minor at first, and my day-to-day life didn't seem drastically different, even with news of this strange unknown condition that I didn't know what to do with. The chance of one day being in a wheelchair was the main fear that began to hang over my head and was not the news I'd ever expect to hear after a physically active childhood. Thankfully, we weren't there yet.

But after playing soccer for multiple years, I became too slow to run and had to say goodbye to all sports. This seemed like the worst possible thing in the world, as it was the normal thing for everyone that age to be involved with sports and physical activities. During a sob fest one night facing the harsh reality of needing to find new hobbies, my parents tried to get me excited about playing golf. I enjoyed riding the golf cart for a couple of lessons I attempted, but that was the main excitement I had about the whole endeavor.

My parents had an amazing way of calming me down, making me feel supported through everything, and always staying calm and collected. As I was freaking out about a new diagnosis spoken over my life and what was

DIAGNOSIS

going to happen to me, my mom would ease my worries and make light of any fears. My family means everything to me, and my parents always have had a strong marriage that modeled a lot of important core values to me. I saw the importance of strong communication, love, and strength.

Before he retired, my dad was a high-level business executive who provided for our family and worked long days with commitment and excellence. I always admired his ability to give impressive speeches and presentations, to hire and fire people, and to be such a responsible individual. He walked in determination and drive, and though I didn't really understand the importance of that when I was young, I can see now that he inspired me to work for things in life and live up to a higher standard. He lived by example through pursuing excellence over laziness. Seeing my dad as a gifted speaker and confident communicator gave me a passion to do the same. For as long as I can remember, I've seen myself as a life coach, teacher, or public speaker... and I think it's how my dad rubbed off on me.

My mom is amazing, as she has always been my safe place and best friend. Since my two older sisters were four and five years older than me, they did everything together. So I did everything with my mom. She's always been fun, creative, outgoing, and laid back, but also one of the strongest people I know. She wouldn't put up with bad behavior for one second and led us all to behave and follow directions as we should. I am beyond thankful to my parents for raising me to be who I am today.

My sisters and I always talked about how lucky we were, fully aware of what a blessed life we had with our family bond being a firm foundation for each of us. Therefore despite what seemed like scary and tragic news about having a new and unpredictable nerve disorder, I had a strong family that could handle it when I wasn't sure that I could.

But as my original reaction to the news of having CMT slightly evened out, a little over a year later, I found out my dad's job was being transferred to Atlanta. Great. More bad news. I had to leave my best friends and the best neighborhood. I didn't even know where Atlanta was, except that it was south somewhere. We had found a neighborhood that was truly home, filled with amazing depth, sweet memories, and life-long friendships. My parents had their best friends nearby, as did I. How could I start over with a new kind of life and leave all I knew and learned to love behind?

I was devastated and repeatedly broke out in heavy sobs leading up to when we drove away. I acted as if I were living in a tragic soap opera scene every time I said goodbye to any of my friends or neighbors, as you know everything is so much more dramatic at nine years old. I think I was extra vulnerable to change after getting a new diagnosis around the same time. It felt like I was being handed a notice declaring "Here's your new life, filled with multiple, scary unknowns."

Yet, at the same time I remember feeling a sense of anticipation as we

Doubtless

packed up the house, and living out of boxes for a while actually became an exciting adventure. The moving truck became a secret neighborhood hangout with friends. Maybe it was good timing for something new, because it seemed like things were slightly shifting within friend dynamics, and I was growing up. Another one of my best friends was also about to move around the same time, while another one went out of town. It became evident that change was inevitable. I started to get more excited about living in a totally different part of the country because I'd never known anything else.

  The day we loaded up the truck and packed the car was tough—lots of tears. But the move was so fun. My sister's good friend made the trip with us, and we stayed in a hotel for a few nights, ate take-out and fast food for meals, and explored the new house and neighborhood. The hills and greenery around were so majestic and beautiful! My ears popped driving down the large hill of our neighborhood since in Naperville you'd only rarely see even one hill for miles at a time.

  Our new house was open and spacious, larger than our old one, but it definitely took time to get used to. It was an exciting adventure, yet it didn't feel like home. The houses around us were more spread out and isolated from each other than in my old neighborhood. Our former neighborhood, safe and flat, seemed much simpler to navigate compared to Atlanta, with its rolling hills and abundant greenery. It was like entering a new terrain of isolation with people and places so much more spread out and requiring more effort to get to. Just being in a totally new setting made me feel a new pressure to grow up and fend for myself.

  Leaving my dreamy childhood memories behind and then going into fourth grade with a new diagnosis and a new life seemed so cruel yet exhilarating at the same time. It took me years to actually feel like Atlanta was home and a place I could potentially feel comfortable in. Though starting over is fun in many ways, I soon came to find that late elementary and middle school were about to be the hardest years of my life by far. The life coach or teacher I aspired to be was tucked away for years to come and replaced with overwhelming feelings of rejection and invisibility.

3

Hidden

School days became even more difficult as I started to lose strength and mobility in my legs. I tripped in front of people frequently, and my limp and wobbly walk became more evident. I tended to take large steps because it gave me more stability as my balance lessened. It only took someone to slightly nudge me for me to fall over. I had to leave classes early to avoid being knocked down in the crowded hallways. I would sit out at camps or retreats during physical sports and games.

I became the girl who was different from everyone else, who was often on the sidelines with the adults, watching everyone have fun like I wished I could. I became the angel to a lot of my teachers because I knew they saw me struggling and not always able to keep up with other kids, therefore I often turned to them for friendship.

I was quiet and shy, and overly well-behaved... But it also led to deep insecurity, since I rarely made friends my own age. I steered on the safe side of things to avoid getting hurt and became an overly cautious person. I felt deprived of and cut off from a normal young school experience when it seemed like everything involved physical activity and ability.

Recess involved a lot of chasing each other around, jumping, kicking things, and competitions. Field days and relay races that involved the whole grade became my worst nightmare—events that made me feel sick to my stomach about engaging in. I tried to be picked last or hide on the sidelines so that I wouldn't be called on or forced to participate.

Apart from physical activities, the other common school scenario

Doubtless

seemed to be about boys and who liked who. A girl named Leila became a fast friend, and we met when she noticed my wobbly walk and tried to imitate me because she thought I was trying to be cool and "walk with swag." I told her there was something wrong with my legs and, though she felt bad, she thought it was kind of cool that I was different from others, though it wasn't something I'd ever choose. She knew all of the drama and gossip about everyone, and I learned a lot from her.

It was great having a good friend and someone who had connections to invite me to birthday parties and sleepovers. But I felt different than other kids because my funny walk was always the elephant in the room. It was such a huge deal to be even the slightest bit different in elementary and middle school, and people couldn't seem to look past my physical differences or stop staring me down at everything I attended. I started to gain a negative view of myself and my future because this disease only progresses throughout life, leading to increased mobility loss.

What did I have to look forward to? Eventually ending up in a wheelchair and life forever getting harder? Immediately being discluded from physical activities that are easy for everyone else? I doubted I'd ever be able to live a full and satisfying life with a disability. Even with a good friend, I was on the outside of the trending conversations and action.

And then came middle school. Mine was in a dark, musty, old building that felt like an institution. While my elementary school was super bright and clean, this dreary building gave me the impression that school was going to get more intense and serious. Being different or standing out in any way was so abhorrent at that age that it just made me a magnet for weird looks. I felt like I was an alien when I walked down the hallway and a group of guys would rally up laughing and say "Hey you! Why you walkin' like that, you dumb or something?" Or when a "friend" in my class referred to me as "a crippled freak."

To finish my days in the best way, I often had P.E. as my last class period. The whole class of thirty or so students would be done walking the track for the warm-up and sit on the bleachers and wait for me to finish, staring. Little did people know I came home from school most days crying, and I would cry myself to sleep almost every night.

Since 7th grade wasn't enough of a nightmare already, halfway through I had to have intensive ankle surgery. The goal was for my ankles to be able to fit into the leg braces I soon needed to wear in order to walk. My arch was so high that every time I took a step, my foot would roll out to the side, causing a blister on the outside edge of my foot. My foot looked like a claw, and having a high arch is a common symptom of CMT.

My parents and I flew out to Los Angeles to see a specialist for my condition, and it was actually a pretty fun trip beyond the surgery part. We stayed close to downtown Hollywood, ate authentic Asian food, ordered take-out, met amazing doctors, and received sweet deliveries from some of our family friends in Naperville. I received surgery to have my high-arched foot flattened, and a tendon was transferred to a weaker part of my foot. Recovery from the surgery brought excruciating pain, and I often woke up at night screaming. Flying home was horrific, as the air pressure on the plane made the ankle pain so severe, I thought I was going to die. I ended up laying across my parents' laps on my back, with my foot in the air to relieve the pressure and pain. That four-hour flight seemed to last a lifetime.

Recovery ended up taking an entire year because, due to my pre-existing condition, healing bones and gaining strength takes longer than most people. I already lacked full strength in my legs even before the surgery. So there I was, in a huge cast and a wheelchair, which I then pushed half of the time, as I needed to slowly start to bear weight on my ankles and feet again. This was the start of major physical hardship that became my new normal.

A year later came the leg braces. The doctors started to hint that braces were what I'd have to resort to if I wanted to continue walking as long as possible. Leg braces are plastic casts that stabilize flimsy ankles and foot-drop problems. My braces were hard, ugly, solid white plastic, knee-high pieces of junk with knee-high socks underneath. They brought me to hysteria when I first saw them and realized I had to wear them. It seemed like the worst news my 8th-grade-self could have ever received.

"Oh, but we have fun print options! You can have braces with flowers or stripes, or neon colors!" the doctors said. Ha, no thanks.

I chose the skin-colored ones. How could I explain these glaringly obvious, clunky objects to people? I didn't need making friends to be any harder than it already was! Who would ever want to date me? As a middle schooler, standing out was anathema, and after a year of surgery rehabilitation, I was ready to be done with standing out in such an obvious way.

For a few months, I wore jeans over the braces every day to keep them hidden. I'll always remember the day in 8th grade when I decided to show them off. It was a super hot day in the spring, and I wanted to wear a dress. I got to school early, with uncontrollable tears, trying to muster up the courage to show my face with those ugly contraptions on my legs. My mom gave me a big hug, and I quickly snuck into my favorite teacher's classroom.

He immediately said "Look at you! I'm so proud of you!"

If only my fellow classmates had responded the same. Instead of celebrating my courage, they stared me down even more than I thought they would. The humiliation faded eventually, and I got through the rest of the year, even though I felt so insecure. As a 12-year-old, this was a big step for me. But until I was fully comfortable showing off my braces, I tried my best to hide them.

I'll never forget when someone in my class had a bat mitzvah. All of the girls wore beautiful, fancy dresses like you would for a wedding or

Doubtless

homecoming dance. The special event was something I even couldn't bear the thought of showing my braces at since it was such a nice occasion. My mom tried to cheer me up by giving me the idea of wearing dress pants with a cute longer shirt. I bought black tennis shoes to match the black pants. Once I got to the party, I felt so out of place with all the girls posing for pictures in their cute dresses and heels. I got a lot of weird looks in my dress pants but tried to make the best of it. I hated that party and felt like an old lady wearing a pantsuit. It's not an outfit a middle schooler would typically choose, and I was definitely the only one wearing it.

My sisters started high school when we moved from Illinois, so they didn't have to deal with the awful Atlanta middle school experiences that I did. They were in the popular crowd and had tons of guy friends and people around all the time. They seemed to have the glamorous high school experience portrayed in the movies, with the wild parties, the tailgating for football games, the themed events, prom nights, and carefree flings and dates. While they were thriving and having tons of fun in high school, I was trying to navigate mean kids, feeling very misunderstood and unseen, and just living like a lost, hurting soul. My sisters seemed to have it all figured out, and I lived vicariously through them in many ways.

Our house was the hangout spot for their friends, with a basement for parties. My mom has always been naturally hospitable and would often cook for everyone. I always wished I could be their age and in their friend group, as they had memories that are still talked about today. I was around some, but I was always known as just the little sister. I was the quiet one. I was different. I was lonely and often felt left out, as my sisters were so close and had the same friends and did everything together. I didn't think I could ever be any more than their little sister.

I became super attached to my parents, my mom especially, because they were my source of friendship, fun, and comfort. They have always been my rock, my safe place, and the ones who saw me for me when others didn't understand. I would have sleepovers with a friend here and there, but rarely did people wait for me when walking, nor were they intentional to sit with me at school. So my family members were my friends.

My family has always been very loving and supportive, but after years and years of crying over the same things, my mom mastered the tough love and stop-feeling-sorry-for-yourself speech. I needed the toughening, but I also realized that no one could ever truly understand or have the right thing to say. So I tried to suck it up and keep my true feelings hidden.

I believed in God and prayed every night, but it was kind of a love-hate relationship. I thanked God for my family and my life but doubted most of the time that things would ever get better for me. I'd write in diaries and journals for years, long prayers to God asking for friends, for boyfriends like other girls had, for normal legs to play sports and run and dance. When anyone told me that God loved me and had big things for me, I doubted that could be true or that I actually was going to be okay. I had the same prayer for years:

> *God, I believe in You, but why is everything so hard? God, I feel like You're punishing me. I'm nice to people, I'm fun, I'm a cool person. But people won't give me a chance. They can't see past what they see on the outside. Is my whole life going to be like this? Am I going to end up alone? How bad is it going to get?*
>
> *I feel invisible and ugly. Everyone my age seems to have large groups of friends, go on dates, and get to be young and free. My two older sisters are good with hair and makeup, always have really cute clothes, always have fun things going on, and I'm like the ugly duckling in the family who seems two steps behind everyone. I have big, frizzy hair, crooked teeth, and I walk like a duck. I don't see how things will ever get better.*
>
> *I doubt when people say You are a good and loving God when life seems so unfair. I doubt that You are going to come through for me when I keep asking and You don't answer, I'm so depressed all the time. Please help me.*

At school, I felt less than everyone around me while dealing with constant stares and laughs at my funky walk, and I carried a deep disappointment in my heart. *Why can't I just be like everyone else?* I often wondered. I got by. I showed up. But there was a void and frustration with God for letting me suffer and never answering my prayers for change. I doubted that God cared about me or had good plans for my life when things seemed easier for everyone else. I doubted that I measured up or could be someone special with the physical ailments that made me immediately different.

I was shy, insecure, and had a negative outlook on the future. I was a big worrier as it was, and bitterness began to form in my heart from feeling unseen and lonely. I think I worried so much because I needed to be overly cautious to not hurt myself due to my clumsiness and physical weakness, and because I wasn't happy with my situation or who I was.

While my sisters were in their party years, I started to go to church youth groups. I was bound to find good friends there! But it came with even more hurt and rejection than I felt at school. At the church, there was a lobby where a hundred kids would gather before each service, standing with their friends in groups while I desperately looked for the one or two people I knew or one of my leaders, none of whom I was necessarily buddies with. Throughout middle and high school, I seemed to be put into small groups where all of the girls were better friends with each other, invariably running into numerous cliques.

Even going to church became an isolating experience. Along with the typical girl drama and weird friend dynamics in school, I just couldn't connect to people my age very well. So, I grew very close with my small group leader,

Doubtless

Karen, who ended up faithfully counseling me when I was at my lowest. She served as my leader for about four years and is still my good friend today. Karen helped me during my hardest years by reminding me who God is and what He has for me and my future. She got me through so many painful years of self-hatred, worry, and fear of the future, and she taught me how to hold onto hope. She always gave the best and most thoughtful gifts, involving personalized notes, decorated scripture cards, and little girly things to make me feel loved and beautiful. She was a big reason I continued to go to small groups.

Karen and I had a long chain of emails back and forth for years where I poured my heart out to her. On weekend retreats to the mountains or the occasional lake house, she would be the one to sit with me or stay up late having deep conversations when the other girls were running around having fun. I struggled to believe God was good or loved me when things just seemed hard all the time. Karen always assured me that God works all things for good and that He has big plans for my life. I tried to hold onto that but couldn't see it yet.

While on a retreat at the beach one year with a different high school small group, I met another good friend of mine, Mary Jenna, who goes by MJ. She came as a fill-in co-leader one night. As the sun set and the evening went on, the other girls in my group all wanted to take a walk on the beach. It always really sucks to have to stay back and sit by the pool, since my leg brace and walker can't easily go through the sand.

This experience inevitably led me to doubt that I'd ever be able to do all the things I wished I could since my dreams seemed unattainable with my disability. I began to doubt my abilities in life or that God would come through in providing me with different opportunities that could accommodate my disabilities.

But MJ stayed behind and talked to me for over an hour about what to do when you have to stay behind or miss out, and how God is still with you in those moments, even when we aren't able to do everything we wish we could. It was a refreshing conversation and a new perspective on limitations that really gave me hope. She understood me and had a compassion that was rare. I was so grateful for her love and support that night.

MJ had a unique strength about her that I had never seen before. She had a boldness in her words and was so confident that things would be okay. I wanted what she had. I felt like she just radiated encouragement and wasn't fazed by the things that upset me so much. She found joy right where we were in that moment by the beach, even though I couldn't walk on it. Then I didn't see her again for years after that one conversation. She was like an angel that randomly came and went when I needed encouragement the most. Meeting MJ ended up being a major turning point because it opened up the new possibility that God is faithful to His promises to us, even when we can't see it yet.

I am glad that I got involved with church at a young age because I really did get to go on neat trips, do various service projects, and grow more comfortable with sharing in group settings with others. I grew in my communication and leadership skills, in my faith in God, and as a person. I started to see that God has made promises to all of us and that He doesn't choose favorites. If He really is a good God and promises good things to His children, I wanted to believe that and pursue more of Him and what He could possibly have for me.

Back in my social life, both in church and school, I started to take more interest in participating in adult conversations and engagements because I felt more comfortable with adults and enjoyed conversations that were more meaningful and mature. I also knew I was different than others my own age and assumed that was a bad thing. I feel like I had to grow up much faster than I ever wanted to. It was a lonely life I couldn't understand or accept. It was a blessing and a curse. I enjoyed having relationships with adults, yet it was also a lonely place. So again, I automatically took it on as rejection. Rejection seemed to be what followed me everywhere I went for years, but I turned that pain over to the Lord.

4

Buried Treasure

In Atlanta, I got registered with a Muscular Dystrophy clinic that I went to about twice a year for check-ins. Clinic appointments involved a neurologist, physical and occupational therapists, a vocational rehabilitator, an orthotic doctor, and several specialists skilled in my unique condition. They would all come in and check out how I was doing, measure my strength and flexibility, and ask if I had any major needs. They would give updates about new testing or drugs available or if there was any new research going on, which there never was.

Honestly, it all seemed like a waste of time because nothing really changed much every few months, and they couldn't actually help my nerve disorder since there was (and still is) no treatment or cure. I was just frustrated when they always reminded me of that reality.

If you can't help me, what am I even doing here? Stop encouraging me to keep coming back here if you don't have any good news to tell me!

I usually left discouraged because there was never encouraging news, let alone positivity. I wanted answers and treatment, and they just looked at me with that "it is what it is" look, otherwise known as the "You have an incurable disease, what do you want me to say?" routine. I usually left feeling sorry for myself and wondering why this had to be my life and my reality. Major self-pity parties.

I often wondered how I was supposed to sit in those kinds of appointments and just not be fazed by the negative doctor reports. They are always so focused on what's wrong with you, reminding you of your problems

Doubtless

and then rarely being able to fix them unless they prescribe a new drug or suggest a new surgery. Nothing positive. They just do what they can to make sure you are comfortable in your misery. I've had a lot of doctors in my life, and sometimes it takes weeks to brush off all of the negative words that are spoken when assuring you that you have something wrong with you. I can go into doctors' appointments doing fine and leave with a new level of sadness after being reminded of what I have going on. The only perks from the MDA clinics were the access to a mobility scooter and a handicap sticker.

At the end of one of my usual appointments, a lady came in with a big, warm smile on her face, seeming excited to tell me something. I was usually anxious to leave and go home after seeing all of the doctors. She said I should go to some special camp for kids with disabilities.

Camp? It was for people with Muscular Dystrophy and happened every summer at Camp Twin Lakes. I definitely wasn't interested. A week of being surrounded by people with different types and forms of Muscular Dystrophy? That sounded terrible. I was trying to be as normal as possible, not spend a week of my summer around a bunch of sick people!

They brought up the topic of camp probably two or three times to me over the course of several years and kept pushing it as if it would be the best week of my life. My parents even said it sounded like a great idea and that I should give it a try. Doubt it, I thought. And I refused to go.

Until one year, I met Joanna. She was only a few years older than me and had CMT, the same condition as me. She was the nicest, most bubbly, and loving person I'd ever met. She also had braces on her legs and a slight limp, but her braces were more compact and stylish. She gave me a huge bear hug and gripped me so tightly that I immediately felt drawn to her joy and compassion.

She said camp was her favorite place in the whole world and was a place where she could do things that otherwise would be hard to do. We became quick friends because of her warmth and loving personality, and I finally decided I'd give this camp thing a try that summer. At least I would now know someone there who seemed normal.

Getting to camp required a two-hour drive in what seemed to be in the middle-of-nowhere Georgia during a hot July afternoon. When we arrived, we pulled into a campground with a line of cars full of parents waiting to drop off their kids. When I got out with all my stuff, I was in major shock when I walked into the gym/check-in area. It was like a busy intersection of electric wheelchairs zooming around in all directions. There was a mix of children with different forms and severities of disabilities, and it scared me. I had never witnessed such a thing. My parents seemed a bit caught off guard as well.

As we walked down a long path to my assigned cabin number along a paved trail through the woods, I felt an overwhelming sense of dread, as

BURIED TREASURE

I knew my mom was about to drop me off and leave. My counselor did not seem like my kind of person. She was quiet and serious, and she wasn't very comforting with the terrified feeling I had.

When my mom gave me a hug goodbye, I sobbed so hard. How could she leave me in this terrible place! I was so attached to my mom and hadn't done much on my own yet. She was always my safe place; she was there to protect me when times were hard and validate me when I didn't have anyone else. I felt like she was the only one who truly understood me because she was always living through things with me.

I finally sucked it up and was stuck there for the week. The girls in my cabin ended up all being super nice, and we had a large welcome activity that night in the dining hall that we got ready for. I started to see other kids who had disabilities of all forms and severities, and I realized that my situation seemed pretty minor, being one of the few who could still walk and be mostly independent.

MDA camps became one of my favorite weeks of the year because being different was normal there. It was a week to be fully accepted, seen, and celebrated for my unique differences. At camp, multiple boys had crushes on me, which never happened in the "real world." I formed life-long friendships, and everyone at camp became a big family. I got to canoe, go zip lining, shoot arrows at targets, have food fights, dress up for the big dance, and participate in the talent shows within a totally no-judgment zone. It made me really feel like I was young and free, and everything was accessible.

I started to laugh at my weaknesses and own my disability as something that I could joke about and have fun with. Especially when racing other campers on my little go-go scooter or circling around people to mess with them. I had a manual wheelchair my first year, and it wasn't as fun, as everyone else seemed to have electric scooters and chairs. I'd borrow a cabin mate's scooter when she wasn't riding it because it was so much better than having a standard wheelchair. I rarely let her use it because I was having way too much fun zig-zagging in circles and being crazy with it. It wasn't long before I ended up getting one of my own.

Cabin time involved laughing at our clumsiness and sharing our chronicles of living with disabilities while our counselors served as our support systems and caretakers that week (though we were all independent in our cabin and were friends with each other). I was placed in a cabin of girls who were all super sarcastic and fun. My counselor was as witty as I was and so camp weeks involved her nagging me, playing matchmaker with one of the boys in the cabin next door who's counselor was her boyfriend.

I remember that my camp fling, Charlie, wrote me a love note. To drop it off in our cabin mailbox, his counselor took the wheels off his wheelchair and left him stranded in his wheelchair during an intense downpour that happened right at that moment. From back inside his cabin, his counselor

Doubtless

called us and said to look outside. There was Charlie, stranded in the heavy rain, not able to move after dropping off his love note. It was sweet and hilarious, yet it also filled our hearts with pity and the need to go save him from the rain. Talk about being pursued!

Charlie was my dance date multiple times, and it felt like a prom night the couple of times he asked me to dance. Dancing at camp was just holding the arms of your partner in a wheelchair, and it was so sweet to see some people asked to dance who had never gotten that opportunity before. Many of the campers in wheelchairs would stay on the side and watch, while other counselors of the opposite sex would seek them out as desired dance partners.

Then there were the dining hall dances and chants, the cleanup party song, and the anonymous announcements from camper to camper that were read from written notes dropped into a box. We would end our meal time with a dance party and live music for everyone. I left every year with many homemade crafts, projects, and ceramic pieces I attempted to handbuild or create on the potter's wheel, and hundreds of pictures. I ended up having such an amazing week and going back every summer until I aged out at 17. I wish I would have taken the lady's advice and gone sooner.

Looking back on my summers at camp, I now realize those experiences are some of the most cherished and special memories I have. It was a week of being in a different kind of world where time seemed to stand still and personal struggles were forgotten. It was a place where everything and everyone was accepted and welcomed, and where disabilities became a celebration and something that unified us.

With the years of going to camp along with the multiple clinics, therapy sessions, and hospital visits, I have found buried treasure where I never would have expected. All of these settings have involved meeting the coolest, most unique people. It all has developed in me a deep compassion and understanding for anyone who is hurting or different.

It has given me a huge heart for those with disabilities, and I am especially drawn to people who stand out because I feel like I can truly connect and relate with them. It all started to give me a true appreciation for all kinds of people because I saw the struggles and hardships many endured and looked past their outward obstacles and into their hearts.

I have discovered that abilities come in all forms and that we are all people who want to be loved—despite our ability level or differences. Rather than viewing my disability as a setback, I started to see it as an opportunity and a key to access unique experiences I wouldn't have otherwise.

5

Heartache

Camp turned out to be a surprising gift that has come from this disability. But as I progressed through high school, I knew I was growing apart from the camp experience and had to learn how to navigate life on my own, usually being the only one with a disability in most places I went. High school was pretty average, but thankfully people were a little nicer than in middle school.

There was now a new generation of friends to hang out with at our house since my sisters and their friends started college. I had a new group of friends that fit together in such an odd and awesome way and involved a quirky guy, a math nerd, a tomboy, a party animal, and a laugher.

A lot of us had the same lunch period, and two or three knew each other from their previous middle school, as I also knew one or two from mine. We all came together as a group of friends who all equally had something to offer and who balanced each other out perfectly. During our lunch period, we sat at the table filled with people who weren't popular yet not in the gamer or anime crowd either.

Our table was full of people who were in the average middle. We were always laughing, making fun of each other, being sassy, and planning our next get-together. I loved having my crew over; my mom would cook for us, let me host holiday parties, and would pick my friends and I up from school and take everyone home. She was "Cool Mrs. Kumle."

My first year and a half of high school was nothing but fun and exciting, as I felt like I had finally found my place. My older sister and her boyfriend would sometimes come hang out with us or have us over at her

Doubtless

apartment. Our late nights evolved into memories of pulling all-nighters, playing crazy games, and just being stupid. We had a lot of good times. I became the planner and was the one always inviting and welcoming people over, and I had access to the older college kids, giving my friends a different experience. My friends had the packaged deal of hanging out with me and my sisters and their friends, which heightened my cool factor, I'm sure.

And yet, it seemed like every year of high school came with a change of friends and different levels of drama. For example, one of my good friends whom I knew from middle school and grew closer with, started to act differently. One day during a science lab, she blew up at me and later said she didn't want to be my friend anymore. The real reason was that when I thought she started to get an attitude, I stood up to her, asking her kindly to please stop giving me an attitude.

Apparently, my honesty made me a mean person she wanted nothing to do with. But it tore my friend group completely in half, making half of my friends side with her and gang up against me.

As high school went on, friend dynamics changed more and more every year. The mystery of starting high school and navigating a new lifestyle and new friend group turned into trying to find my place again. This morphed into friends that were wrapped up in smoking weed and playing truth-or-dare, hooking up with people, dabbling in cigarettes and hookah, and I started to feel like a misfit in my own friend group. I was a people-pleaser and said yes to everything because I just wanted friends around and things to do. I'd let them come over, let them invite whomever, and offered them alcohol that my sisters had easy access to. I was very go-with-the-flow, and therefore everyone walked all over me.

In the end, it backfired. The ones who I thought were my close friends got wrapped up in the popular crowd and left me for a new group of friends. Halfway through my junior year, I had to completely start over. I had a few girlfriends I started to hang out with, but after high school ended, none of us spoke again.

Though I have some fun memories from high school, I struggled. I liked having friends over at my house because it was easier and safer for me physically, but it was still difficult since I couldn't keep up or get around as easily. Fun nights or just hanging out talking often turned into me crying because I had to sit down the whole night and was never the one who anyone had a crush on (since that mattered so much in high school).

As a lot of my friends started to have flings, dates, and wild moments or get invited to parties, I was never one of the cool ones and just felt like a tag-along. I was only a part of the get-togethers that I planned because they were at my house. I realized later on that a lot of them were probably using me for my cool mom and sisters and a house to hang out at, not as much for my company.

HEARTACHE

  I was just along for the ride, not really in the middle of anything, but just there, going through the motions. I think going into high school we envision an experience like in the movies, involving a magical prom night and summer flings at the beach. For me, high school was a place I tried to fit into while feeling invisible. I ended up hanging out in the art room a lot because art was something I was actually decent at. I did go to prom in both my junior and senior years and bought the most beautiful dresses, but I went with a friend group of people who were all super close that I wasn't actually a part of. They were just very kind and said I could go with them.

  Both proms I went to I hated. I looked beautiful, went to dinner, and took pictures, but at the actual dance, I either stood around feeling out of place or sat on the side. At that point, my other friend group was pretty split up and two of my closer friends were now going to prom with the super popular girls. They all had literal ball gowns on and dates alongside them, while I was just a tag-along with a group of friends I barely knew, feeling more alone than ever.

  This friend group was very diverse and enjoyed having innocent fun with card games and anime and movie nights or dance competitions. They were the nicest and most down-to-earth group of people I got to know in high school, and I wish I had gotten closer to them much sooner. I hung out with them once every few months but was more wrapped up in my other "friends" and torn between trying to fit in with who I thought was cool rather than these nice girls, who at the time I saw as kind of nerdy.

  But they weren't trying to be anyone they weren't, and they embraced it. You could tell they were genuinely happy and comfortable in their own skin. They didn't have any desire to be "cool" to others, and that seemed like a more restful way to live during high school when everyone was trying to fit in. I was stuck in the in-between.

  In the middle of my junior year, I finally decided to take a walker to school so that I could navigate the crowded hallways without having to worry about getting knocked over if I didn't leave class early. Wow, why hadn't I tried that before?! I felt like I could safely walk without clinging to the wall. I could actually walk next to people!

  A neighbor in Naperville had an old one in her basement that she gave to me before we moved just in case I ever needed it. I thought she was crazy at the time until I actually tried using it. I didn't like how much more I stood out with it, though walking without stress or balance issues was a huge relief. I got to leave heavy books in my classes and had excuses to be late or leave early, and my teachers were always very understanding.

  I will say, I think high school is when I grew more confident in how much I stood out because I didn't have a choice. If I walked into a classroom late, all eyes were on me. And I often had a seat near the front where there was more space and where I always seemed to be more visible, which gave

Doubtless

me deeper relationships and favor with the teachers. People always knew how to locate me because my walker or scooter would be parked outside the bathroom or next to my seat, the desks would have to be moved or rearranged every time I entered the classroom, or I would squeak down the hall every time I went about my journey.

Imagine walking into a quiet library or room where there's a test going on, and you bang into the wall with your walker with loud, creaking tennis shoes and big plastic casts knocking into each other. After years of feeling embarrassed and insecure about how much attention I drew to myself, I had to just get over it and ignore the stares.

High school became a daily battle of fighting discouragement when even the littlest tasks required tremendous amounts of energy. With my flat feet and a severe foot drop, I couldn't balance on my own and experienced perpetual strain on my ankles and knees. If I didn't have my braces on, I would have to use a wheelchair or scooter when going anywhere.

Cleaning, carrying things, and getting from class to class required navigating a series of movements—a floor crawl to the chair, the chair to the walker, the walker to the wall to hold onto—before finally moving in the direction I needed to. My walker became my purse and transport system, which led to many spilled drinks and things getting knocked over. Life became one big obstacle course. *Keep going, Alyssa... Push through, Alyssa... Keep your head up, Alyssa... You're almost there...*

Giving up was not an option. Being in a constant place of defeat, negativity or sadness is not an option since that would only make me worse and wasn't going to fix anything. Through the moments of tears, jealousy of others, insecurity, and struggle, I decided to keep moving and refused to let my disability keep me from living a full life.

6

Blank Canvas

Receiving a diagnosis that I never expected came with the need to start afresh and pursue different paths. It felt, in some ways, like being given a blank canvas for life. I somewhat felt like I had to build life up from the ground from scratch. Suddenly new boundaries were put in place, new limits had come, and a new plan had to be navigated. It felt like I was being handed a new life with boundaries that I wasn't used to and didn't ask for, changing the dreams and plans I had for my life and my future.

It was heartbreaking, yet it also became an opportunity to open doors that were new to me, doors I never would have considered before getting my diagnosis. These new limits pointed me toward new avenues I could pursue to breathe new life into my heart and keep me going, giving me a different form of freedom I didn't know existed.

Now having to fully accept that physical sports and activities were a part of my past, I pursued art, music, and cooking classes to supplement my stolen extracurriculars. In middle and most of high school, I had two amazing teachers in my life.

Brandon was my music teacher. He played several instruments and possessed multiple talents. What a guy. The recitals each year were entertaining to be a part of, although they terrified me. He would get all of his students to play together in a band for the grand finale that would include some rendition of a classic song by a band like Led Zeppelin, Rolling Stones, or The Beatles. His recitals were like a big party that inspired everyone in the audience to grow in their passion for music.

Doubtless

I didn't realize how good I had it to have such an amazing teacher like Brandon, and he nailed into my head every week how if I only practiced the piano according to his instructions, I'd improve.

But I just never did. I'd go down to the basement an hour before he came each week, trying to hurry up and memorize the homework he gave me. He was smart enough to know that my rusty attempts to play the song proved that I hadn't actually looked at it since our last lesson. I began to wonder if my choice of instrument was the problem, so I decided to make a change and see if that would help.

When I decided to switch over to guitar, I thought for sure it would be my niche. The guitar was a cooler instrument, I thought, and I was determined to gain guitar skills and learn all the classic songs that everyone longs to sing along to at gatherings with friends. Well, there's a reason why guitar players take years to learn their technique and skill over hours and hours of disciplined practice…

My tiny hands didn't seem to have the ability to even reach half the distance they needed to play some of the harder chords or notes, let alone move fast enough to jump between multiple notes. I lacked the discipline to put the work in and figured the task might be too hard for me to actually figure out, though I never gave it enough time to know that for sure. After months of starting to not take this instrument very seriously either, Brandon said that he was cutting back his students to the few who would take his lessons seriously and would value his time. I left music and still totally regret that decision to this day.

Then there was Beth. She was the most amazing painter—energetic and fun, spunky and unique, just like artists often are. She would come to my house, or my mom would drive me down to her studio apartment, which was part of an awesome, artsy neighborhood in the city. She had a spiral staircase in the middle of her living room and large canvas paintings she had painted all over her walls. It was a dream to paint in an actual professional artist's studio!

Our private lessons involved experimenting with different paint techniques. We would talk in funny accents, laugh, and just relax in the creative process. When I often doubted how I could ever look at a beautiful and complex photo and paint it, she would break down the photo into colors and shapes, rather than an image of anything specific. We painted in thin, often watered-down layers that seemed easier to manage.

"Just paint what you see," I still hear her say to me. "Don't think so much! Slap it on and leave it alone."

I would try to ration my supplies by being stingy with my paint and very careful with every stroke I made. The thought of ruining a canvas seemed like such a waste. But she would sometimes make me pour out nearly a whole tube of paint in one sitting to get me over my fear of wasting art supplies and over the fear of taking chances. It was so hard to stare at a full blob of paint on my palette and not have a plan. But before I knew it, layers and layers of colors and shapes turned into a beautiful painting that I was proud of.

It was so much fun to see the first brush strokes of a painting come to life and transform into a masterpiece. To this day, I have a full bin of canvases that we messed around with, trying different colors and splatters. Some became something great and others I can now pick up and add to or paint over at any time. Beth eventually moved away, but I knew my love for art would continue because of her.

After my diagnosis, I dove deep into arts and crafts and coloring and was in and out of art classes. I thank my mom for that since she's also very creative. I think Brandon and Beth really enhanced my love for the arts and broke off fear and intimidation of art and music.

Without any physical hardships, I can't say I would have ever turned to art. But without art, I don't think life would be as exciting. Art is something that's always evolving and expressive, always changing and moving, bringing the outside world into a different dimension of deeper insight and depth. It became my biggest passion to see others express themselves creatively and press into their talents when they may feel the weight of the world on their shoulders, as I often have. Pressure to be a certain person or act a certain way is all released in the creative process when it doesn't matter how it turns out. Art has always been there for me when physical activities were not.

Through art, I began to see the world as a very colorful and joyful place. I became unable to create art any other way. The more light and joy art brings me, the more motivated I feel to share it with others and bring joy to them as well. Even neutral-toned animals I managed to make multi-colored and bright, often adding a smile to their faces.

Art became a powerful outlet where any feelings I built up would emerge in a burst of colorful, fluid expression. Art became my safe haven in the way that creating became my time to be fully me, with no agenda or rules. I found the process to be fun, comfortable, and gratifying. Painting became an activity unlike other activities in my life while living with a disability—a time without limits when every other area of my life had them. Painting began to feel like flying or dancing, which felt healing, refreshing, and even miraculous.

They say life is like a blank canvas and that we create our own masterpieces. From the moment I received my diagnosis, the canvas of my life has involved different twists and turns of colors and shapes that I couldn't have expected. I quickly realized my canvas wasn't likely to include cookie-cutter shapes or straight lines but an eclectic array of colors and shapes going in numerous directions.

Going through my earlier years with a physical disability began a dynamic, hurtful, exciting, lonely, crazy, fun adventure that I never would have expected. As a high school student navigating a disease amidst the typical challenges of adolescence, I experienced constant sharpening and

Doubtless

refining yet also a rich time, filled with deep meaning found mainly through my creative pursuits.

      Starting a new journey in art was starting to bring fresh excitement and adventure into my life, as there were so many possibilities of what I could create with the different mediums to explore. I was starting to see that God had given me the gift of creativity and that He may have been closer than I realized with the other ways He was bringing blessings into my life. Though it wasn't the life situation I had envisioned for myself, I was moving along the best I knew how and starting to embark upon a new path with a new blank canvas set before me.

7

Divine Deliverance

With the weekly music and art lessons, I believe my heart softened to new possibilities. During my last two years of high school, I took AP Art, an advanced level of art that involved juried competitions. The art room was my hangout spot, as it was for other students working on art projects during their lunch hour with cool Mr. Riggins. Mr. Riggins had a long ponytail, glasses, and a sarcastic wit about him.

He was the kind of guy who would look deeply into your eyes whenever you would talk to him. It would feel like he was staring into the depths of your soul yet with a gentleness. He always had a meek, slight smile on his face and was either creating some insane art masterpiece out of nowhere, playing cards with students, or building these odd little towns and things out of figurines or clay with his little group of gamers.

My sister's friend Rosie, who got her masters degree in art education, ended up working on art with me after school as we tried to come up with a theme for my AP art project. I ended up creating a series of drawings based on my disability and hopes for my future. The drawings told a story from getting my diagnosis, to my leg braces, to the various doctor appointments and dietary changes, the therapy sessions, and the heartbreak of it all while wishing I could dance or play sports with friends. My drawings expressed my thought life and dreams during all of those things, and the theme was about being different.

Although my project did not receive a high score compared to the other students' talent, it was an exciting time of expressing myself and

Doubtless

sharing it with others for the first time. I started to see how art can be used to tell stories and can express so much more than words can sometimes. Those AP Art years in high school brought a new level of acceptance of my disability because I found a place in art class that had meaning. I no longer felt completely lost, as I had finally found a new extracurricular I could work at. AP Art softened my heart to the journey I was on and kept my head above water when I felt other things were sinking.

As high school was coming to a close, friendships started to grow apart and lessen, and I grew in readiness to move on to something new. Things drastically began to change when I discovered God in a new way.

I found out about Passion City Church when the seniors at my church were welcomed to attend the annual Passion Conference in downtown Atlanta. It was a four-day stadium gathering of around 60,000 people ages 18 to 25 years old. It was unbelievably life-changing, to say the least. I had never been to a conference like that strictly for people gathering for Jesus. The motto was "Jesus generation—for His name and His renown."

I met the coolest people, stayed in a hotel with two nice girls from my high school small group, and got to join a family group to form new relationships with others who attended the conference. They broke the large crowds of people up into small groups of ten randomly assigned people who became your "family" for those few days during break-out sessions before and after the main sessions.

It was special having our love for Christ in common and being there together to grow in our spiritual walks. In our small groups, we prayed into our struggles, shared our stories, and encouraged each other. Passion did it all in a way that was fun and exciting. The speakers were all-powerful, had a sense of humor or shared engaging stories, and the bands that played were even better.

After that weekend event, I decided to start attending Passion City Church every Sunday. Although it was a forty-minute drive into the city and definitely out of my comfort zone as a new driver and emerging adult, I had to find this place. I began to serve as a door-holder and greeter every other week. I had never witnessed this kind of church—so bright, modern, and hip. It had an urban and trendy feel, and you felt cool the minute you walked inside.

It felt like going to a conference or concert with the high ceilings, mood lighting, and studio feel. I was met with deep kindness and many smiles in every direction, and it didn't take long to form deep friendships. Everything in the building was well-designed, clean, and over-the-top, awe-inspiring with giant art installations and wall murals.

I immediately felt excited and joyful, ready to get involved and participate in every way I could. I was placed into a family group that was filled with the most loving, caring, and faith-filled people I'd ever met. Serving on Sundays was a whole new experience, and it felt like I was a part of something way beyond myself. It felt like being part of the backstage team to the main band.

The door holder space had a little kitchen area with tea and coffee, various snacks, and an impressive spread every week for those who served. We spent time with our family groups and talked about our week and things we had going on. It was refreshing to be with older people who were always so encouraging and filled with love and positivity. It was hard not to be in a good mood there. Was this real life?

They would pray big, bold prayers out loud over each other and over situations, while really believing and knowing God was going to move in that moment as they were praying. I hadn't really prayed that way before as I would usually pray in private and just hope that maybe one day God would answer, if I was lucky. The Passion City Church members truly gave the church its name with their interactive faith and deep passion for loving God and each other.

For one of the first times in my life, apart from camp, I actually felt like I was seen and known and like I mattered. They welcomed me like an actual family member and spoke truth into my life, reminding me who God created me to be, that He is never finished in our lives, and how He uses everything for our good.

Along with my family group came many events, activities, and ways to serve at the church or in the city. I left every Sunday afternoon filled with a renewed passion for God and life that I couldn't explain. It all introduced me to the most amazing people that I continued to see and know for the next several years of being involved there.

Passion became like home. Everyone was so filled with joy that I started to see a side to church that I had never seen before. I couldn't wait for Sundays to come each week I served because the whole day was so fun. I would serve at the 5 o'clock service, so I'd have to get there at 3 p.m. for family group time over coffee and snacks, have a team meeting, get into our assigned spots that week, and wouldn't leave until 7:30 p.m. for a forty-minute drive home.

It was a lot, but I felt so alive during it all. My feet would get tired at times, but overall I was actually fueled and energized by being there. Sometimes Passion had women's nights or worship nights, and so I'd drive to the city multiple times a week to meet with different groups.

Passion has introduced me to hundreds of people through various groups. It's neat how there's such a large overlap and intersection within groups where everyone is somehow connected, like a dynamic web. Every time I was at the church, I'd run into people from different walks of life, reconnect with long-lost friends, family members of friends, or someone who knew someone that I knew from somewhere else. With it being such a huge and well-known place, something exciting always seemed to happen when I was at a Passion gathering.

Doubtless

One week while I was in worship at a service, I looked over to someone waving to me. It was MJ! I never thought I'd see her again after that random night by the beach. She was with her friend, Kenneth, and they invited me to a gathering at their friend Beckie and Danny's house every Friday night. I was excited to get more involved with another faith-filled community! They were an awesome married couple who hosted weekly gatherings at their house. They would stream a sermon through the internet, play worship music, invite people to come and go whenever they chose, and serve snacks in the kitchen. I saw why MJ came off as so bold and filled with confidence and faith when I met her a couple of years previously, as her friends were all like that.

On my first night there, the preacher on the TV spoke about taking authority over the things that bring us down, standing firm in faith, and knowing who you are in Christ. He preached that, through Jesus, we could be free from sickness and disease, guilt and shame, insecurity, depression, rejection, and all the other negative emotions I was living with.

I bawled my eyes out on my first night there, as it was an overwhelming amount of powerful new information all at once. MJ, Kenneth, Beckie, and Danny laid hands on me and walked me through a prayer of coming out of agreement with these things and surrendering them to the Lord, asking Him to cleanse me from all of the heavy burdens that were weighing me down.

Praying like that together multiple times and being walked through replacing lies I have believed with the truth of God's Word brought layers of freedom to me that I had never experienced before. Each time energized my body and refreshed my spirit. I felt a tangible difference every time I went to their meetings, and I began to experience how real the power of Jesus truly is! I'd stay at their house until midnight sometimes, talking with them about all kinds of things. I learned so much more about God and met a core group of people that grew close to my heart, and I still consider them to be spiritual mentors and family today.

This house church was more than just going to a large and super loud church service with all the lights and the in-crowd. It was intimately doing life with people, having real and vulnerable conversations, and sharing our stories and struggles. They helped me wrestle with the hurts and fears in my heart. I started to grow in my prayer life by declaring truth over circumstances, over various areas of my life, and over myself. Anything not of God, such as fear, worry, sadness, or stress, we commanded to go. I learned the ultimate power of spiritual warfare.

With Passion and this new spiritual family, I started to see past typical religion and view Jesus as exciting—someone who answers prayers and heals people. I saw how God is actually directly involved in every aspect of our lives and is so present in each moment. He wants to partner with us and sends angels on assignment to fight battles with us.

I learned that the spiritual world is extremely alive and active, but we have victory through Christ in all things. I learned to pray for His will to be done on Earth as it is in Heaven and live in the awareness that Christ died for our freedom and our healing. Everyone around me was living with so much joy and freedom, and I learned that God still does miracles and moves in powerful ways. He has abundant life available here and now.

Through Becky and Danny's house church, I started to be exposed to the deeper things of God, and I met people who had prophetic dreams and visions, prayed in tongues, and would have intense encounters with God's love. I met friends of strong faith and went to many conferences, worship nights, and ministry events. People around me started to speak healing over me and encourage me that God has more for me.

I saw supernatural healings and answered prayers in other people's lives as people simply declared Scriptures over situations. I started to learn how to pray in boldness and with strong faith that something would happen every time I did. I witnessed that God's will is healing, freedom, joy, peace, provision, breakthrough, and living an abundant life regardless of our circumstances. So why was I not fully living this way?

What do we do when we are in a trial that is out of our control, and there's nothing we can do about it? How can God be good when He allows us to experience pain and doesn't always take it away right when we ask Him to? I started to dig deeper into who God really is when we are hurting and in circumstances we don't understand.

Although I had experienced powerful breakthrough in my life, I still felt like I wasn't living in the fullness of what God had for me. I still felt broken over my physical condition. My heart felt like it had been broken over the years, yet my new experiences with God were stirring a deep hunger and openness to go deeper in my relationship with Him. As I was starting to apply to colleges and figure out my next steps, He began to take me on a new and exciting journey of discovering who He is and who I am as I wrapped up my rollercoaster high school years.

8

Uphill Climb

At last, college had to finally be my time to shine! I was so ready for a change. Since it was supposedly going to be the 'best four years' of my life as culture implies, I was expectant. I had just started this new journey with God, so I was excited for what was to come as I stepped into a whole new season of being on my own. I was definitely no straight-A student and didn't get into very many colleges due to my average high school GPA, but the one that I did get into was the University of West Georgia. Even though it was my only option, I was pretty excited!

I expected the dorms to be like the movies where everyone's doors are open and there are frequent pizza parties and people throwing footballs down the hallways. I was so ready to be in an environment with a clean slate, totally starting over and becoming the person I wanted to be.

Well, after one year there, I was as lonely as ever. To my surprise, the dorm I was in was so quiet and dead that I ended up having to knock on people's doors from my single room to introduce myself. Yet, it seemed everyone already had their friends and were not looking for more. How did a bunch of new freshmen seem to have it all figured out already?

I had an ADA (Americans with Disabilities Act) room with shower bars, which were only offered as single rooms. It was okay with me not having to deal with having a stranger as a roommate, but at the time, it seemed like everyone had become good friends with theirs. I often felt like I was missing out.

My classes were all fairly close by, and the dining hall had good food.

Doubtless

The library had a nice Starbucks, so I made my rounds. Then Rush Week came, and I decided I would give it a try, as Greek life is supposed to be super fun and a great way to get involved. One of my sisters was in a sorority for a while at the University of South Carolina and seemed to have fun. I figured I'd always have parties to go to and trips with girlfriends to go on! But Rush ended up requiring a lot of work. I was the only girl in a scooter rushing, and it seemed like all eyes were peering at me as heads turned back to see me stuck in the back of the line to get into each house.

As I looked around and assessed the street of houses we would be going in and out of to meet and greet our potential new sisters, I saw no ramps to get inside. A sense of dread came over me as I realized they had to make special accommodations to get me in the houses with multiple girls coming to walk me in and out. I got the impression they all scattered in surprise when they saw my name on the list and had to make new arrangements. I got multiple comments on how brave I was because they had never seen someone with a disability going through Rush before. How was I brave for wanting to fit into a group like everyone else? Doesn't everyone want that?

Those remarks made me feel even more out of place until a day later when I got cut over a phone call. "Oh but we really liked you!" a girl assured me. After a moment of tears and feeling like a failure, it wasn't long before I realized it all felt very forced. How could they cut girls after a five-minute conversation about what their major is and where they're from? I was okay with their decision, realizing that there was so much more to me than they ever saw. But the whole process was draining and left me emotionally fragile. I'll never know how different college would have been had I actually gotten into a sorority.

Thankfully, I made a few friends at a ministry that met for weekly dinners. These people were down-to-earth and welcoming, so I befriended some of them, and my classmates were fairly friendly. The couple of girls I got along with most were roommates and were also both dating other people, so this left me at a disadvantage of being more of their acquaintance. Another two girlfriends I made quickly turned boy crazy and then drama-filled, moving on quickly. I got good grades and made the best of that school, but my mom was literally driving an hour and a half every weekend to bring me home since my dorm life was severely isolating and the town had pretty much nothing going on.

After a few months, I decided to take a big chance and transfer to the University of Georgia in Athens, Georgia which was a desire that came to me suddenly when I went to see my leg brace doctor who lived in that exciting college town. Going to such a large school seemed out of my league and overwhelming, and I wasn't sure it would even be a possibility for me. The only way I got in was through transferring. I lived at home for a semester and took classes at a community college before starting mid-year of my sophomore year, which wasn't ideal as I felt late in the game. I researched student clubs and events, found all of the hangout areas and food spots, and I always went to as many events as I could to meet people.

The campus was so huge that meeting people was much more difficult than I thought it would be. But I met some nice people at the student center who I always seemed to run into and would study by or chat with between classes for a few minutes. The dining halls were overwhelming because being a mid-year transfer student involved sitting by myself for meals, desperately looking around for a possible welcome from anyone open to making a new friend or who was also feeling lost. Transferring to a large university in the middle of a school year felt like walking into a party filled with people who are all best friends and realizing you don't know anyone there.

I lived in an apartment-style dorm for upperclassmen in UGA's East Campus Village (ECV), which sounded like the nicest option for student living, though was far away from central campus and was even harder to navigate without normal mobility or a car. In the ECV part of campus, I was at least by the gym and one of the better dining halls, yet I felt like college life festivities were always happening across town. I was far from the clump of freshman dorms right in the heart of UGA's historic North Campus, where most university activities seemed to occur and people seemed to congregate.

I was assigned my first roommate, who was super sweet and had a great sense of humor. We had our times catching up after school days and having our laughs, yet overall, I didn't like being in my dorm. I found myself in a funk on the weekends when once again, I had nothing to do and nowhere to go. I'd text the rare couple of people I knew, searching desperately for rides and plans. Many times, courtesy of the insane hills and inaccessibility of that huge campus, my only hope for getting anywhere was the embarrassing disability service van.

While all the students were walking by, hopping on and off the buses or their bikes, I was being picked up by a minivan that had a ramp to wheel me inside and an obnoxious high-pitched beeping noise to reverse. Talk about grabbing hundreds of people's attention. I had to be on a structured schedule to let them know when to pick me up and take me places, and, God forbid, if I changed my plans or told them I'd call when I was ready, I'd usually have to wait twenty minutes outside for the van to come.

I really wanted to break free from my scooter and just walk to my class that didn't even look that far away for an able-bodied person. But it was the only way to get places. I would tell people just to go ahead, and I'd meet them there eventually if the van was able to go to that certain location.

I wished more than anything I could easily move about like everyone when I was there. I loved seeing students riding their bikes and motor scooters, hopping on and off the buses, and quickly going to and from classes and meeting friends. For me, I'd often find a nice bench between buildings and

Doubtless

watch the world move around me, only doing the small things I was able to.

Though weekends were hard, the handivan took me to most places that were close by. While being dependent on the van for my transporation was a bummer, I tried to become friends with my van drivers. There was only one older man who had been driving the campus buses for over fifteen years. He was my favorite. We talked about life and sports and food but also about how he couldn't wait to retire.

The UGA transit system was all run by students, and he mentioned how he was the only one who still cared about his job and the people he drove around. I knew exactly what he meant because most of my van drivers were either late, would text and drive, speed, blare rap music, or not even strap me in properly. I could tell a lot of them just needed a job but cared little about passengers with disabilities and attending to their needs.

I never knew who was going to pick me up in the van each time. I always hoped it was someone who was cool and at least a decent driver. It was a relief when I finally got my own car for my last year, and I didn't need to stress out about finding rides to get everywhere.

It definitely wasn't ideal to have a disability at a huge and hilly college campus that was a small city in itself. It was very spread out and difficult for me to traverse, which made it feel lonely. Looking at the campus map while at first learning where things were was like randomly putting your finger on the place you needed to be yet not having any idea how to get there or how long it would take while relying on a student-run van service being your transport source. Whenever my classes were scheduled in the beautiful historic North Campus, right across downtown Athens, my excitement was always short-lived, as they would inevitably move my classes to a far-away part of campus that was newer and more accessible for scooters or wheelchairs.

I started going to a church on campus in one of the older historic campus buildings, where I met some nice friends who went to the same dining hall as me. Unfortunately, the ramp entrance led me around the opposite side of the building, which took much more walking for me, and into a closet door that was locked half the time. Once inside and navigating the storage through that tiny closet, the whole space was on a downward slope, like a theater. My walker could only make it to the front row, where nobody sat. The bathrooms were all the way in the back of the building down a steep staircase.

Thankfully, I could use the little one next to the stage, but not without the whole audience staring at me every time I did. And students usually wanted to get dinner or Starbucks before or after service, but that was about a block away from the building, and I couldn't walk that far without being exhausted. Let's just say I felt pretty uncomfortable going to church.

I also started to go to a campus ministry that had a lot of student events and activities to get involved in. I had had luck meeting great people in ministry settings before, but trying things out, going and doing, took being very intentional and always taking a chance and showing up to things alone, not sure who'd be there and how accessible the place would be.

Being at such a gigantic school felt surreal. What was I doing here? Was I actually at the largest university in the state? It seemed like a dream. Yet, it was lonely and hard to navigate. I called my mom every day, always in awe of living the college dream yet not quite feeling a part of it. Physically there but socially missing out on something.

I lived with the constant feeling that many things were going on around me but I wasn't aware of them, nor invited. I knew there was something for everyone at this school, but you just had to find it. You had to figure it out on your own and navigate this huge, ever-flowing, dynamic ocean of students in a super fast-paced environment, and it was lonely and kind of scary.

It was a deep desire fulfilled for me to be at a school like this that so many people dream of going to their whole lives, and every day I'd pinch myself feeling like I would wake up and not have actually made it this far. Yet, I felt alone and kind of sad. Sometimes, I would go to a student hang-out spot at a campus ministry building, ride into the chapel on my scooter, park, and sob as others around me were resting or playing music.

I'll never forget my first game day in Athens. I woke up around 10:30 a.m., and people had already set up tents and started grilling out. I heard voices and music from afar, so I decided to try and scooter up the huge hill onto the more central parts of campus.

My tiny little mobility go-go scooter clearly wasn't made for half of the terrain I attempted to take it on as it started to shake and make strange noises as I desperately pray for it not to die on me. There were people everywhere in red and black, tents set up on every street corner, and wild tailgate parties all around. I called my mom describing how fun it was to be seeing all this going on yet also wishing my family had come or that I had a tailgate to go to.

I scootered around assessing all the partying going on, people who had clearly set up early that morning and gotten their prime spot. I had missed the memo. I had no idea this is what football gamedays were like—the grilling smells and loud music, the cheering and laughing of big friend groups. I longed to be invited to someone's little pow-wow. I invited myself to a few I scooted by, introducing myself and hoping they'd be excited to invite me to their cookout or yard game.

But as I made my rounds, I felt so isolated from the festivities taking place all over the town. I ended up just defeatedly heading to the dining hall as I made tentative plans in my head for my family to come to the next game and tailgate with me. Eating in the dining hall during game day immediately made me feel like an outcast.

Over my college years, I did attend a few games, but being in the handicap section made me feel awful as I gazed on the opposite side of the stadium to watch the big sea of fans in the student section watching the game

Doubtless

with groups of friends. I was right behind one of the end goals, which, don't get me wrong, was very cool, being so close to the field green and the players, yet half of the game was totally out of my view since football games don't take place on one end of the field the entire time. It was easy to lose focus and interest in that section, and being surrounded by wheelchairs just made me feel like the crowd behind me was staring down my neck.

I was allowed to invite one friend to sit with me, which I did for a couple of the games, but I felt bad pulling anyone away from the student section with all its hype and energy. Football games became something I dreaded and would rather watch on TV, as not many of my friends even enjoyed football. I realized the whole college football experience is overrated. Yet, I also secretly wish I had more fun memories involving football tailgates and games. My parents and sisters came twice to tailgate, and it was just us and a friend of mine. At least we tried. How did people get invited to all of the awesome tailgates with a ton of food and friends? Why was I not being invited to anything?

UGA is a great school and was an exciting place to be, even though it was easy to feel like a tiny fish in a big sea. I got rides as much as I could, and I showed up to lots of different events and activities. I thankfully lived in an apartment downtown with a good friend my senior year when I had a car. Yet, it was the year she got engaged and wasn't around much. So, once again, I had to learn to do a lot on my own. At least with a car, I was able to drive between a couple of coffee shops or restaurants to fill my time, but it was a solo life.

After wrestling with the decision of what to study, I decided on a smaller major called Human Development and Family Science, along with a certificate in Disability Studies. My coursework involved the study of people—communication styles, family life, and how all the differing factors around us affect who we become. I came to really enjoy my teachers and classes.

With Disability Studies, I was in my element because I was living with one and didn't need to be taught how to treat people with disabilities. A lot of my classes were about bringing awareness to students on the importance of accessibility, inclusion, and understanding. How cool that there was a whole department focusing on the area of disability and inclusion!

One of the professors at the Institute on Human Development and Disability was in a wheelchair and had Cerebral Palsy. She communicated with a device and had an assistant to teach. She was always joyful and shared stories of how she often has a hard time going about her day when others often don't realize how capable she is. People would assume, if she didn't have a caretaker with her, that she needed help or was lost and struggling. A cop was called on her a few times, as people who saw her running errands or grocery shopping thought she shouldn't be doing those activities unattended.

She was witty, and though she had a difficult time communicating clearly, her mind was perfectly sharp and healthy. I ended up running into her everywhere, it seemed, and we had a connection because I related to her and joked around with her a lot. I felt like I deeply understood her and was able to connect with her even when a lot of others didn't really know what to say or do. I knew that disability awareness was my niche.

Through the Disability Resource Center on campus, which gave me help with books, transport, and whatnot, came the invitation to join the Disability Speakers Bureau. This was a group of students who spoke on panels and in classrooms to students about topics related to various disabilities.

The Disability Speakers Bureau was created to give students with disabilities an opportunity to speak up, using their hardships as a strength to make a change. Being a voice in this way was a neat and unique opportunity, and I felt like I was able to use my disability to make a difference.

I was surprised to discover how many common issues for people with disabilities don't even cross most people's minds. Students asked questions about accessibility, which reminded me of the extra obstacles in my path that are not obstacles for others and how people take things like walking for granted. The Bureau also provided the opportunity to see others with different forms of disabilities conquering college life and witnessing how we all learn in creative ways at different paces. Being reminded of such truth gave me a new level of confidence in being able to earn a degree and get through college, even if it took extra help or a longer time than some.

There were many options for different learning styles and resources for those who had difficulties in classes. You could leave classes early, get extended time on tests or assignments, or get notetakers. One student, who was deaf and used hearing aids, brought his recording device to class and sat up front. A girl I met who had epilepsy, wore headphones to block out distracting sounds and focus more efficiently. Another girlfriend I knew from MDA camp was accompanied around campus in her power chair by students who served as her caretakers during the day.

Sometimes we would pass each other while getting on and off the disability van, along with my professor with Cerebral Palsy who also used the vans. It became a community in a way, and it reminded us that we weren't alone. These resources became a gift and made going to UGA possible.

I finally found my place within a minority group that many didn't wish to be a part of, yet it felt like a secret army of people who had superpowers and special privileges. Through daily hardships also came a knowledge and understanding that I was taken care of and offered support whenever I needed it. At last, on my huge and overwhelming campus, I found a little family of people that made the university feel a little more like home.

9

A New Diagnosis

Navigating college was a wild mixture of ups and downs, and it definitely pushed me physically. My scooter received its fair share of wear and tear and battery exhaustion getting up and down the hills, riding the long ramps in and out of dining halls and from buildings to classes, as well as the steep disability van ramp. But it became more than just increased reliance on my scooter—it was also becoming more demanding on my body as I struggled to navigate it all.

As the years progressed, I started to develop symptoms that seemed more severe than just CMT. It was more than just my legs and feet. My eyesight seemed blurry, even with my glasses on. Sometimes it seemed to take a lot more concentration to fully focus on something with clarity. My digestion system became more sluggish with differing kinds of cramping or pressure with worsening constipation, and, worst of all, a dysfunctioning bladder. I felt like it was just because I drank a lot of water, but it became abnormal how often and with what urgency I had to use the restroom. Talk about inconvenience.

I'd often have to go to the restroom two or three times during a fifty-minute class, with no ability to wait or hold it. This led to many issues during meetings, road trips, bus rides, flights, or being outside with friends and not being close to a specific bathroom at all times. I could see the bathroom in view but sometimes wouldn't be able to get there in time. I would feel the urge to get somewhere as fast as possible, but when my legs tried to move quickly, I often tripped or lunged. It wasn't a pretty sight. Or at events with a

Doubtless

long bathroom line, I'd be in big trouble. It was pretty embarrassing to say the least.

Another worsening symptom seemed to be my slurred speech. I felt like I had a crackly voice, and it caused me insecurity when I spoke. Even now, I think I sound strange—a mix between high pitched and low, cracking in and out, and producing an abnormal amount of saliva on which I often choke on with my words and have to stop and swallow. If I'm in a group of people or a loud place, I feel like no one can hear me or that I'm easily drowned out by others talking over me. All these symptoms began to progressively worsen, along with my already weakening legs, and I didn't even know how to explain what was wrong.

I asked my mom if we could see some new doctors because there had to be someone who could explain to me what was going on. Surprisingly, I never have been one to get sick much or really need to go to the doctor often. For me it was always MDA clinics, which didn't change much when you have an incurable and progressive disease. Physical therapy was my only option.

Where were we even supposed to start to look for a doctor to assess these strange but seemingly minor issues that were accumulating and worsening? I had gotten used to wobbling around with my weak feet and leg braces, and I was getting around ok, but what were all these other things? We then began a new adventure.

We ended up going to Emory in Atlanta, one of the best hospitals in the nation. It was an extravagant hospital—newly renovated, modern and bright, and we felt hopeful about seeing new specialists beyond the MDA clinics. I participated in a variety of tests and saw a number of doctors, all who were very professional, super friendly, and overall said I was strong and healthy.

I had appointments with a urologist, a speech pathologist, a pulmonologist, and a neurologist. My bladder was healthy, my breathing was pretty strong, and my speech tube had no blockages. The speech pathologist gave me vocal exercises to strengthen my voice. I was happy to hear good news about my health, but I still had no answers.

Our Emory visits became enjoyable because we switched between the two campuses for appointments, and it gave my mom and me an excuse to get coffee and a treat on our way there in the mornings and try new restaurants in the city for lunch. Our "big" appointment finally came with the head neurologist. I hoped he had news and results after looking at my blood work.

"Call it what you want," he said. "It's obviously a progressive nerve disease. I don't know how else to diagnose it."

My parents and I just gave him blank stares. He almost seemed bored and unsympathetic in telling us his findings. I wanted to keep prodding him to tell us more than what was clearly obvious. It felt like a wasted appointment.

A NEW DIAGNOSIS

He suggested maybe going to Johns Hopkins to further assess me since he didn't know exactly what to tell us. Ok, next.

My Emory appointments at least brought some peace of mind now knowing nothing more serious was going on. But what was causing these symptoms? I knew I wasn't crazy.

So next was Johns Hopkins Hospital in Baltimore, an even more well-known hospital. Johns Hopkins is like the Mayo Clinic and often diagnoses rare diseases that less-specialized hospitals cannot. And now my parents and I had an excuse to have a little vacation and explore Boston and visit Washington, D.C. We had some nice dinners, and we took an amazing evening trolley tour around all of the Washington D.C. monuments. And wow, was the hospital impressive. Everyone was extremely professional and accomplished. Everything was so fancy. I felt like we had finally made it to the right place.

We saw three neurologists in one day. One thought I had MS, which seemed like good news because I could potentially treat and manage it! Nope, she ruled that out, too. They required intensive blood work that involved nearly seventeen vials of blood.

"My goodness," I wondered. "Why in the world would they need so much blood from one person?!"

They did a genetic workup panel looking for CMT specifically and also looked further down the line for anything different that showed up in my genes. My mom's cell phone rang a few weeks later from one of the doctors; they found something more conclusive in my blood work. They discovered I didn't have Charcot Marie Tooth as I had thought for the past thirteen years of my life, but I have a condition called Giant Axonal Neuropathy (GAN).

GAN is an extremely rare neurological disease with around fifty known cases world-wide. He also told us about a clinical trial going on for GAN and about a girl named Hannah who started Hannah's Hope Fund, a nonprofit with a mission to find treatments to slow the progression of the disease. We didn't really know what to think until we did more research but were also perplexed as to why no one had discovered this diagnosis sooner.

We went on to discover that, according to the National Organization for Rare Disorders, GAN is a "progressive nerve death that severely affects both the peripheral and central nervous system, often causing low muscle tone, muscle weakness, decreased reflexes, impaired muscle coordination, seizures, and intellectual disability. Cranial nerves may also be affected, leading to facial weakness, abnormal eyesight, and poor vision, along with skeletal abnormalities such as scoliosis, and mental changes/dementia." It is a rapidly progressive disease, usually starting in early childhood, leading to dependence on a wheel chair by the second decade of life and death in the second or third decade.

Wait, what? How could that be my diagnosis? It didn't seem real or accurate. I did not match a lot of those descriptions. But was I about to? Was

Doubtless

I dying?

I now had an extremely rare and severe terminal disease diagnosis. GAN basically attacks every part of the body and has no cure. I wasn't too upset when I first read about it because I was already over twenty and was still living life while hardly matching that terrifying disease description, but we had so many questions. Of course, looking up anything on the internet can be intense, as a slight headache may actually mean stage four brain cancer, according to WebMD, but still it sounded really awful.

We looked up Hannah's Hope Fund and learned about the research going on for the disease and the gene therapy clinical trial happening at the National Institutes of Health in Bethesda, Maryland. My mom made some calls, and we booked our next trip in our search for answers. I enrolled in the ongoing clinical trial. It entailed about five days of testing at the NIH toward their research for this disease.

Visiting NIH was a pretty intense experience. We needed badges and personalized IDs, daily security checks like at an airport, and we had to park in a specific spot and then take a shuttle to the right building. It was quite the operation.

It wasn't just a hospital but a top-notch institution that comprised 27 separate institutes. It felt like an honor to be there, surrounded by professional and impressive people in business suits and top-quality scrubs and medical gear. Everyone walking around was on a determined mission. I came to find that the NIH is a government-funded medical and research facility from which major developments and discoveries have emerged. They provide funding to multiple research facilities around the world and is one of the top-ranked health institutions in the world.

We were in the gene therapy building. What was this week about to look like? I received a schedule for the week with about three tests per day. I had a brain and spine MRI, breathing and speech test, urinary test, nerve conduction, lab work, ophthalmologist appointment, physical therapy, gait lab... It seemed exhausting and like an unfair amount of testing for one person in such a short time. I don't fear hospitals or tests, probably because I'm so used to being pricked and prodded, but there were times I cried at the intensity of that place and the days ahead of me, wishing we could just go home.

"I'm fine. I don't need this." I thought.

One day on our lunch break from tests, we went to the hospital cafeteria. I saw a girl in a wheelchair in the food line accompanied by her mom. She had wild curly hair, even more so than mine, and looked eight or nine years old, with extremely skinny limbs and leg braces similar to mine. Our eyes met.

It was Hannah! She was the girl whose mom started the GAN foundation to raise money for research for a cure. I didn't know who she

A NEW DIAGNOSIS

was at first sight until my mom told me she matched the picture we saw on the website. Her mom quit her job and has given her whole life to this cause with the mission to save her daughter's life, as well as other patients with the disease. She happened to be at the NIH the same week as I was. We ended up having lunch with her and her mom, and it felt like a big deal to be meeting this icon for the disorder we shared.

They mentioned a birthday party that was going on at the Children's Inn that afternoon, and how it would be an awesome opportunity to meet some of the other GAN kids. What others? How many others were here at the NIH? It was cool to think I'd be meeting others I could relate to and become friends with, and it was comforting to know I wasn't alone with this new diagnosis, but were the others more like me or like Hannah?

The Children's Inn was pretty cool, like a hotel with rooms and a common area with a kitchen and couches, where all the people coming to the NIH could stay with other kids and families rather than being alone. If someone's child was sick or had to be at the hospital for weeks at a time, it was a place that felt more homey than a standard hotel. I entered a common area where they were having a gathering and a cake for the birthday party. I was in shock at the group of kids all in wheelchairs, much younger than me, and all seemed to have many more physical hardships or disfigurations.

"Was this what GAN looks like?" I wondered. "Was this what was going to happen to me soon?"

I felt like they looked at me like some kind of superstar because I was going back and forth between walking behind my wheelchair and sitting in it. I met those who were there, gave hugs, and shared friendly engagements. By the end of the trip, they began to look up to me like a big sister. After growing closer with all of the children, my heart began to break the more I realized how physically and mentally fragile they truly were, so much more so than I was. I also engaged with the five or six adults staying at the Inn that week, yet I had a lot to process. You could tell my parents were also in a weird state of mind due to the sudden shock of it all and how real and scary their situations had just become.

GAN was a harsh diagnosis. This could be what my future held. These poor kids were fighting for their lives, Hannah especially. She had a difficult time speaking, eating, and moving her face and body and needed assistance with using her hands. Another kid had a very deformed spine and body, and another one was blind. I felt guilty for still being able to use my hands, see, and move about pretty well... and it wasn't something I chose. I wanted to do something to help these kids who were going through so much, hoping with urgent anticipation every day for a cure and for a slowing of their disease progression, while mine has progressed very subtly over the years.

My parents and I came to learn that I have a minor form of this disease and am one of the oldest people with it and also one of the strongest physically. I praise God every single day for this and the fact that He has sustained me and kept me going all these years… I know how severe this disease can get, and I'm determined to stay strong and take care of myself the best I can.

We learned that GAN is caused by a shortage of a functional gene that makes a specific protein for nerves to work properly. I am missing a gene and have a mutation on my second gene. Others with GAN, like Hannah, are no longer making any protein and, therefore, have less to work with for their muscles and nerves that are still functioning. At the time, there were eleven kids enrolled in the gene therapy clinical trial who had gotten the gene injection. Hannah was the first one.

Those who receive the injection need to go every six months to the NIH for retesting and tracking what improvements have been made, if any. A lot of research and funding still needs to be done. I am on the waitlist for the injection, but they prioritize the kids who are more severely ill and still have some active muscles and nerves to work with. They are also still in the very early stages of this clinical trial, and there's a lot of experimentation involved in the process.

All along my new journey in navigating GAN, I've been resistant to having any interest at all in this injection and clinical trial because I don't want to deal with it. I've always believed God would heal me on His own because I know that He can. I would rather that be the case than having to make constant visits to the NIH for more testing, research studies, potential side effects, or negative results that are possible outcomes.

I made a second visit to the NIH in August 2018, two years after my first trip for their research study. My family really had to pressure me to go back because I was clearly stronger than other GAN kids and didn't feel like I needed to test and assess every single part of my body to see if I was getting worse and at what rate.

Obviously, since GAN is progressive, the disease never improves. Did they want me to do all these tests and hear negative reports from doctors about how bad it's getting? No, thank you! I never wanted to be in that situation again or ever go back to the NIH for another exhausting week of being their guinea pig.

"But do it for their research; they could use your help and information to get closer to a cure," my family said.

And so, kicking and screaming, I went.

Why did we see so many doctors who had no idea how to diagnose or help me? I sometimes felt isolated in this strange world of weird symptoms and hardships that met me daily, with no one able to relate, let alone help. Now when I feel like I'm ever getting weaker or struggling physically, I know exactly why and understand I cannot complain because I have seen how much worse off I could be. GAN is a terrible disease, and there's no treatment or cure, making it difficult to accept and destroying all hope for improvement. So I have my moments of feeling dejected, but I have to keep moving forward the best that I can since it's all I know to do.

The new diagnosis created doubt-filled mindsets within me that tried to dominate, along with the temptation to give up. I had a new challenge at hand—a legitimate explanation for various symptoms, along with the knowledge that there was nothing to help it. Not even doctors were familiar with the rare disorder, making me feel even more alone as I faced it.

At the same time, I gained a new level of determination to fight this horrible disease. I knew I wasn't near death, as I was still super active and doing pretty much everything a healthy person could do. I had made it to college, driven a car with hand controls, traveled, and gotten involved with normal life activities. I tried to look at the prognosis with a grain of salt.

I joined a Facebook group for parents of children with GAN with lots of updates on what their children were going through and what resources and information were available. Common issues discussed include sleep apnea, seizures, feeding tube problems, temperature extremes, difficult hospital visits–you name it. The children fight for survival every day, and the parents' only support system is in this virtual group. Many times, updates included children who had passed away. It was (and still is) very difficult to look at and be a part of this extreme and harsh reality. Meanwhile, the number of individuals with this diagnosis continues to rise around the world.

GAN is not the diagnosis you would ever want to have, and it all became more real after I met Hannah and some of the other children. I realized that the condition comes with a variety of hardships and symptoms that are progressive, even though, in my case, it's been slow. A new level of struggle presented itself as I realized this would be a lifelong journey and fight, not just to stay strong, but to survive.

10

Outcast

Seeking to get involved with a Christian ministry to meet fellow followers of Jesus, I explored several different organizations on campus. I finally settled on a prominent UGA campus ministry, where I served for the next four years. It is the largest campus ministry of its affiliation in the entire country, where hundreds of students attend every week. The organization put on weekly church services, student activities, and outreaches. It was an exciting place where something was always going on.

During the week, students would sit outside with their mentors, relax in the chapel or play music, sit on the couches, play foosball in the main office space, or throw a frisbee in the parking lot. My time there involved many small groups and one-on-one mentorship sessions, staff activities and games, lunches and coffee dates, holiday gift exchanges, and worship and prayer nights.

It was a pretty sweet time of freedom, and I got to do life with a lot of awesome people. It was a safe place to take chances and practice praying for others, sharing what we thought God was speaking, and encouraging each other. The ministry focused on teaching foundational truths found in Scripture, basic knowledge of who God is, and how to cope with common life challenges, which are never easy to master.

After college, I became an intern on staff, where I led my own small groups and mentored six girls every week in their spiritual walk. I led two mission trips, served on the prayer and hospitality teams, and participated in Encounter, the ministry area that taught students how to hear God's voice

Doubtless

and pray for healing over others.

Services were held every Wednesday night in the student center ballroom where they set up a stage and chairs and had music and a message. Walking into my first service as a student was overwhelming, as there were almost one thousand chairs to choose from in this huge room. The worship set was always so powerful, and students would sprawl out on the floor, in the aisles, along the walls, and in the back of the room to dance, worship, sit, and soak—whatever the vibe was. It was always an energetic, concert-type atmosphere. The sounds, the lights—it felt like I was at home because it was like a mini version of Passion City.

The lead pastor would give a sermon and lead us into ministry time when interns would be up at the stage available to pray for students during the worship sets. Wednesday nights were great because you saw hundreds of students you recognized each week, all in the same place. Yet, it took some time to find my niche where I could finally find a friend to sit with each time. It was easy to get lost in the crowded and loud environment, and it was too easy to slip in and out and not feel seen. The best thing to do was to get involved with leadership and join one of the ministry areas where you really got the chance to get to know people, which I did.

During my senior year, I got the opportunity to be a leader on one of the freshman mission trips to Jamaica. I was always disappointed that I missed my freshman year at UGA since many said that was one of their most memorable times and was also the only year you can go to Jamaica with the organization. But the lead pastor said he'd love for me to go as a leader! He looked after me a lot—probably because he could tell I was struggling.

Jamaica was tough for me, being one of the eldest students and not really being a part of the freshman friend groups. I didn't really have friends on the trip, but I loved being there. It was an awesome week working at a school and doing local service projects on a beautiful island, eating authentic Jamaican meals, and having sweet times of worship and small group bonding within our open-air hotel lobby. Only a couple of nights in, while in a time of ministry with worship and prayer, I had a moment filled with faith. I went up to one of the interns and asked for prayer for healing in my legs.

"I am so tired of living this way, and I believe God will heal me!" I told him with hopeful anticipation.

He was moved to tears, as he had always believed my healing would happen at our ministry for so many people to witness. He got down on his knees and started crying out to God, held my legs, and prayed over them. He encouraged me to take my braces off as a step of faith and believe God would restore my arches completely. As we were both crying and praying, students started to come up one by one—a couple of girls in my small group, then a couple more, then before I knew it, I opened my eyes, and all eighty or so people on our team were surrounding me, praying, crying, begging God to heal me.

God moved so powerfully in that moment, especially because a chain reaction that took place that no one planned. The pastor shared how he was so moved by the community bonding that took place within our team that night and said he was extremely proud of me and the faith that I had to go after God in the way I had. He encouraged me to keep believing in God for healing and that he had rarely seen a bunch of freshmen going after God in that way. It felt like we were all connected and were like one big family. We were all believing God for a miracle, filled with faith for the supernatural.

Even though nothing happened to my feet or legs that night, which is always hard to understand, later that night and into the next day, I received a lot of encouraging notes from people. Notes about how strong I am, how I taught them what faith and trusting God looks like, and how they witnessed what true community can be through me being on the trip with them. A few notes mentioned how going on a mission trip with my physical limitations was inspiring.

Multiple notes made me cry because they were all direct answers to my prayers going into that week: *God, why do I feel so out of place? Show me why you opened this door to go to Jamaica and what you have for me here. Show me what my purpose is on this trip.*

I'd gone as a response to the pastor's generous invitation, not really feeling seen or known by anyone. That night changed everything. I realized I wasn't on that trip for myself but for others.

The last day was a free day, so we went to Dunn's River Falls and Park near Ocho Rios; a hectic, touristy spot that seemed like a theme park. It is a well-known attraction in Jamaica that has a beach at the end and a steady waterfall flowing for a mile down twists and turns of rocks. The students started at the beach at the base and climbed up the waterfall along the slight incline of rocks and flowing water.

I knew I couldn't do that, so they led me to a shady overlook to sit and watch. One of the interns and another student hung out and watched the group as they made their way up the waterfall. It was the most magical area. Sitting on that bench felt like being in a rainforest, and honestly seemed like the better option than the long and slippery trip climbing those wet, large rocks that were easy to slip on.

As some students from our group approached us, they convinced me to get in the water down a couple of steps by my spot, and climb some of the waterfall. I wanted to do it more than anyone knew, but it seemed daunting and more work than it was worth. Well, they all pushed me to take my shoes off, hold their arms, and walk through the flowing water. As I started to get in, more and more members of our team were approaching, and there was suddenly a chain of arms linked together to walk me in a huge circle around the flowing pool. It was like the whole team suddenly appeared at that moment

Doubtless

to help me be a part of the waterfall climbing experience!

The cool flowing water in this shallow area was refreshing and life-giving, but the rocks were slippery and slimy, with different dips in the water almost knocking me over. My feet weren't stable enough to keep me up, but their arms were my lifeline. I didn't go far after I walked in a circle around that rock, but they were all cheering me on and encouraging me to keep going as long as I wanted. I came to find out that the pastor teared up when he witnessed this collaboration to include me. Every time I felt afraid of falling in the water, everyone surrounded me with encouragement and support.

Heading back to the buses, two of the leaders I had been sitting with pushed me while I sat on my walker, one holding my legs and one dragging me down the long sidewalk. There's a bold print warning on my walker that says "Not Made For Transport," yet it has been my wheelchair multiple times with some help. It was an amazing experience getting to see the waterfall and even go in it, and I ended up having a really sweet time!

Jamaica is still ingrained in my memory as a time when God used me as a leader when I didn't even feel like one. I got to be a small group leader for a few girls that week, and they all encouraged me that my going on the trip despite all the obstacles and unknowns really impacted them. I'm so thankful I got the opportunity to go on the freshman trip as a senior! The week confirmed the fact that I wanted to be an intern for the ministry and be on staff, helping with trips and putting things together, pouring into students, and staying surrounded by like-minded people. I knew that's what life was really about.

I interned for two years on staff post-college. Working for the ministry and setting up the weekly events and services was exciting since I was now on the leadership end of the ministry. As an intern, I was able to do so much more than just attend weekly services or small groups, and I became a part of making the ministry what it is today. My experience as an intern was great as a whole, but I disliked the favoritism and cliques I encountered.

I went in with the expectation of meeting new best friends, as I saw that happen for so many others who were older than me. Jamaica gave me a glimpse of what interning could be like, after getting that opportunity to be a part of younger students' lives. Unfortunately, the internship became a super lonely and painful couple of years. Being a part of a ministry, you would assume it would be super-inclusive and welcoming, as 'belonging' was basically their motto. Yet, I experienced the total opposite.

I felt like within college social settings and specifically within the ministry I was in, there was always the drive to be trendy. A lot of the ministry staff dressed one way: dark skinny jeans and Converse shoes or boots, tucked-in soft t-shirts, blue jean jackets or oversized vintage sweaters, beanies, big, dark-framed glasses. It was the place for hipsters, and they were all friends with each other.

They dressed the same, behaved the same, and talked the same. If you didn't fit that mold, you didn't fit in the cool crowd. The popular crew was well-known, and everyone seemed to worship and look up to them. Being cool seemed effortless for them, with their super "chill" personas and confident outlook, as if they had really made it.

Looking back, I realize I was more affected by these kinds of group dynamics and resulting cliques than I realized because I was never able to be myself around them. They were friendly but difficult to reach and connect with. For reasons I couldn't understand at the time, an inner wall would come up within me every time I went to my internship and was in the ministry building. Why couldn't I easily engage with others or feel comfortable? I guess because I was different from most people there, which didn't seem cool. And I would constantly jump to comparison, rejection, and condemnation.

I thought getting involved with this ministry was going to be like all of the other churches I had been a part of before, like Passion, where the community was welcoming, loving, and supportive, as you'd expect people at church to be. But at my campus ministry, it sort of felt like there was a high school hierarchy of popularity where even the ministry directors showed favor to the most attractive and admired people most of the time. If you were not in their inner circle, no one made time for you.

A Christian ministry is supposed to be all-inclusive and a place for everyone; this ministry was filled with cliques, favoritism, and people competing to fit in. There was no diversity, but instead rigid groups of friends who stuck together, and I wasn't in any one of those groups. People got caught up in the excitement of a mission trip, the spiritual gifts they walked in, and how good certain people were at praying or speaking, yet they never seemed that interested in actually living out the gospel and loving their neighbors as themselves on a daily basis. Inclusivity wasn't valued, but elitist conformity was. Many loved people within their popular friend groups but never took the time to reach out to the people who felt left out or different, the people hurting or lost, and anyone who looked or acted a lot differently.

I felt unseen, misunderstood, and so left out, and, therefore, struggled with comparison and wondered what the heck was wrong with me for not having the time of my life like so many others. I remember thinking, *Wow, is rejection STILL my reality, even here?*

I was so nice to everyone—I'd sit with new people, I'd ask people for coffee or lunch, I'd wait around to see what everyone was doing after work ended but would still end up going home alone while later finding out many went out to dinner together and didn't think to invite me. Here came the rejection I had felt back in high school and middle school all over again.

Even with these difficult dynamics, the internship definitely had its exciting moments. Being an intern for the most popular ministry on campus felt like working for a large, trendy company that everyone wanted to work

Doubtless

for. Interns were looked up to by students, and we felt like we were part of something important. Interns set up and took down the Wednesday night services, planned and executed campus events, and made the ministry building what it was in the ways we cleaned it and held staff meetings inside. Wednesday nights were the climax of the week for our staff and took a lot of preparation and set up. I'm still in awe of how they manage to put together such a large and impactful service every single week.

A big van unloaded speakers and musical instruments, a collapsible platform and stage, tables and lamps for visitors, and an information table. Students got food or Starbucks from the cafeteria below for dinner before it all began and came and went at different times with their friends. The entire operation often required five to six hours with all that went into it. The band would practice their set for the night and often play long after the actual service ended as students hung out and talked in the hallway outside the main room. Then after tearing it all down, a group would go out to eat afterward, sometimes until after midnight. It was all neat and exciting, but it was definitely a lot of work.

But during those nights, I never felt like I had a group of friends to enjoy the experience with. I just felt like a student attendee, not an intern who was a part of putting it all together. Every Wednesday night, the other interns seemed to have the best times, and I could tell these nights were the highlights of their weeks. Yet, I just felt alone.

The required meetings and staff activities often felt like a lot of wasted time because "fun" was one of the ministry's core values, and meetings often involved silly trivia games or ball toss competitions. Everyone seemed to be so interested and engaged, laughing and taking videos, yet they never seemed as invested when we actually talked about things that mattered, like Scripture and God.

I personally don't care for silly games and would rather be in a meeting that involves something of importance. I like that fun was a core value, but these various activities to keep us entertained were not fun to me. Instead, I was often in a mental funk with all the free time I had and the sitting around that I did after my morning meetings and in between mentoring sessions. And with not having a lot of friends, free time was more like going to a coffee shop, journaling, and planning for my future while feeling stuck in a season of isolation.

There were mixed messages from the pastors or directors on staff. They always assured us what a great season it was of freedom and opportunity to work on ourselves, grow in the Lord, and gain skills and talents that we might never get again. They would talk about how working in full-time campus ministry is a rare and special gift, unlike any other season of your life. They shared how this experience should be enjoyed and not wasted because this ministry was an amazing place, and no place would ever be the same. These points just made me feel like I was missing something or not getting it.

Then, during the next staff meeting, the talk would be about how the campus ministry could be a bubble and to make sure to be intentional about getting outside friends too. Well, what if you were like me and didn't have many friends within the ministry? I felt like I only had outside friends and wasn't a part of the ministry bubble where most of the staff lived and thrived. I tried to be, but it just never came naturally.

If this season of working in ministry was so special and rare, why was I having such a hard time? The staff implied that life after working in college ministry would not be as good and would be a whole lot harder. And yet, I didn't feel like I belonged there. Did I miss my chance if I couldn't even belong in a campus ministry in a sweet college town where life is simple, safe, and very special?

With all the free time and lack of structure or routine, feeling unnoticed by people, and the longing for my goals and aspirations as a hopeful young professional to take off since I had finished college, I felt stuck. Yet, I knew God had called me to intern, especially after the Jamaica trip, and I had hopes for it to be super exciting. When else would I get the opportunity to be an intern on staff at a college ministry and be involved with the campus and student events? What better way to really get to know myself and figure out what I want in life before getting a career?

But with the social hardships I faced, I felt like something was wrong with me once again. People were friendly, but something strange came over me that made me tense up and not be myself when I tried to engage and be a part of conversations or groups. I couldn't stop feeling the same strong wall come up and cause me to choke on my words or just stay quiet. Or when I did try to be myself, it just came out as an awkward comment or wasn't heard by anyone.

To this day, I cannot explain what it was that caused this wall between me and the people there, and it was so frustrating to not be able to be myself in that place. Being in full-time ministry seemed like something that would be life-giving and done with ease.

Yet, it was exhausting with the constant painful social dynamics, the non-stop hyper-spiritual conversations, and everyone around me being in their own process and their own growth journey but never really sharing real life. In addition, being a highly empathetic "feeler" in tune with others' emotions each moment and experiencing so many swirling around me each moment, I found myself reaching a point of burnout.

With all of this, along with having to go the longer, accessible way to get in and out of the ministry buildings, it was hard to keep up. An easy two or three steps up and down to the immediate next-door building took an obnoxiously large amount of energy for me, and I had to use the two long ramps going opposite directions from each other. What required five steps

Doubtless

for most took about four minutes for me to go between two side-by-side buildings for meetings or students hanging out.

My disability definitely affected other aspects of my internship experience as well, when I found out I had to take a second trip to the NIH during the first week of the second year of training.

Seriously? While the staff is training and getting excited and ready for the new and upcoming school year, I have to be in a hospital for a week of annoying tests?

Crying on our way to the NIH in the parking lot, I begged my mom for that to be the last time there. During a break between hospital tests, feeling depressed and anxious for the long week to end, I had a fellow ministry intern suddenly text me with a voice recording. It was good timing because I was sitting in the lobby with my mom waiting an hour or so for my next appointment, feeling sorry for myself for dealing with such a long and boring week when I wished I could be in Athens. *What could it be?* I wondered.

I heard a bunch of voices from a crowded room... Then I heard some prayers being spoken... and then the lead pastor of the ministry said my name. I suddenly realized I was listening to a recording of the 7:30 a.m. Tuesday prayer meeting, where interns and students come to pray and worship. And they were all praying for me. I heard the sound of probably over a hundred voices all praying for my strength during that hard week, healing over my body, wisdom for the doctors, and peace through it all.

I was so touched by the love that was being sent my way from afar and felt honored that people were praying for me and thinking of me in a place I felt like I didn't belong. In that moment God was showing me that I was making an impact at my ministry. Even though I didn't feel like I fit in, I was loved and acknowledged. Maybe, as I realized in Jamaica, my being there wasn't about me but about where God wanted me to be during that season.

Looking back, during my two-year internship, I often felt like an outcast. Feelings of rejection can give us a skewed perspective of ourselves and the world around us. When we feel rejected, we can develop a negative view of God and life because we may feel like we do not belong. It can turn into a downward spiral of comparison and loneliness.

This was my campus ministry experience, and I so wish that I could redo it sometimes. If I were more secure in who I was and what God had for me, I believe I would have enjoyed my time there a lot more because I wouldn't have felt as much pressure to fit the ministry mold. Feeling like I didn't fit in created a wall of insecurity that prevented me from connecting with others.

The intense striving to be comfortable around people there kept me in a box of oppression and self-condemnation. While in a fun environment with a lot of activities going on and friend groups hanging out, I was also stuck in the overwhelming feelings of constantly being left out and unseen, unsure how to break out and be myself.

11

Breaking Point

From Passion to on-campus ministry events, I received prayer for healing and strength often. Many people encouraged me to have faith that God would heal me, and I did. I gained my passion for prayer the year I lived at home before transferring to UGA, and I knew my niche was within these kinds of church groups.

During those years I got a glimpse of what living in more freedom and wholeness could look like, but after finishing college, I began to feel like I had gotten far away from this spiritual progress. I had gone from an older group of people pouring into me and praying and encouraging me often and feeling refreshed and energized, to a place of feeling drained and at my wits end. I learned God's will for healing and how He still heals people when our lives are in alignment.

What changed? Wasn't I still following Him and pursuing His will for my life? I believe now that I was bringing unhealthy striving to bear on myself to prove to God that I was doing enough for Him to heal me. I believed I must be doing something wrong if God was not healing me according to my faith and His promise in the Word. I thought I needed to be perfectly disciplined in all areas of my life. I tried to make changes to prove to Him that my faith was strong.

If only I had the perfect diet and worked out at least six days a week, God would heal me. If only I had perfect faith at all times, and never doubted or got sad or messed up, God would have more compassion and would heal me. I saw multiple naturopaths in high school, trying to completely detox

Doubtless

and heal through diet and cleansing. Don't get me wrong, we should all eat healthy and holistically, but it became something I failed at often because I am human and love food like anyone else. When friends were eating chicken fingers and fries at lunch, I was bringing salad and homemade vegetable juice with floating green chunks in it, which became difficult to get down. At one point, I was on an 80% raw vegan diet that a doctor placed me on. I honestly had never felt better in my life, yet it wasn't sustainable, let alone enjoyable in any way.

So every time I ate gluten, dairy, sugar in excess, or any food that was semi-unhealthy, I'd beat myself up for it. If I didn't go to the gym for a day or more, I would tell myself, *Well, no wonder I'm not getting better, it's my fault. If only I were more disciplined with my therapy and stretching.*

This vicious cycle turned into years of striving, with multiple diets, doctors, and therapies. I am affected physically if I don't stretch or work out daily, yet I never seem to get stronger when I do.

"You have a progressive nerve disease, so your goal is maintenance, not gaining strength," doctors always said.

I actually can't improve; I can only slow down the rate of deterioration. Great. It's like I'm always fighting an uphill battle and never winning. It's exhausting. It feels like all of the hard work I do is for nothing sometimes since my body is going to grow weaker anyway. I found myself feeling like I had tried it all—every kind of diet, therapy, and exercise under the sun—and only felt burnt out. I was on a never-ending path and always found myself feeling exhausted and discouraged.

I needed a miracle because nothing I did personally seemed to help. I had also attended countless ministry events, healing and worship nights, Christian conferences, and altar calls.

"God's healing people tonight, just receive it! Have faith! Your time is now! God wants you well. Miracles are happening in this room tonight!" the words from the powerful preacher or guest speaker would assure the crowd.

I've seen people healed of hurting limbs, cancer, poor eyesight, arthritis pain—you name it, during powerful gatherings like that. I know what God is capable of and have witnessed many miracles with my own eyes. I'm so happy for those people. But does no one realize I've had my disease my whole life? Many people ask for healing of a problem they have had for a few months and get healed right away. Everyone celebrates a miraculous healing. Yet, it's hard to not get frustrated because of how often I've asked and believed for it without anything happening. I'm immune to it, it seems.

So many times, I've had a large group of people surround me, laying their hands on me, and praying for my healing with nothing happening. So many times, I've gotten prayer from a pastor directly, so sure that was the moment and the time for my miracle, and nothing. So many times, I was filled with courage and would stand in front of a whole crowd of people, and nothing ever happened, except for me being super vulnerable and often crying in front of a bunch of strangers. So many times, other people right next to me will burst with joy and excitement when they realize their physical ailments have improved, and I'm left disappointed and heartbroken, feeling rejected and unseen by God Himself.

This has happened hundreds of times. I've seen and I believe in the power of prayer for healing, but it doesn't happen to me. I got to the point where I didn't even want to put myself in those situations with that pressure. Then some people would say I don't have enough faith. I'm tired of the emotional roller coaster of trying to figure it out or strive for it. I remember crying out to God in prayer to express my pain and frustration.

God, don't You see me trying? Constantly going, doing, fighting, believing, and hoping? I'm always left behind. I'm always still hurting and struggling no matter what I do. I don't know how much more I can take of this sickness and disease! This isn't who I am! I've tried everything and still feel like I'm physically declining. What do You want me to do? Please stop this.

I'll never forget one of the Christian conference events I went to with some friends. It was a free gospel crusade event in Atlanta around the same time college had begun. Something happened in my body that I cannot explain to this day. As the preacher, Reinhard Bonnke, was in the middle of a sermon, I started to feel tingly and numb in my ankles. I could feel as though my arches were being formed within my tennis shoes. I kept brushing it off, but it felt like my arches were completely full and formed and grown in an instant. I told my friend, Emily, to hurry out in the hall with me to check something.

Wondering what was going on, a few of our friends followed. When I told them I thought my arches had just formed in my feet, they said, "Hurry, take off your shoes and see!"

I took off my braces and socks and everything, only to find they were still flat and the same shape. What was that feeling then?! But they encouraged me to walk around barefoot, which I can only do if in my carpeted bedroom while holding onto a safe wall. I thought they were crazy. But my friend Kenneth held my arm, and we started walking.

Before I knew it, we were halfway around the large outside loop of the sports arena! He said it seemed like I was running and hardly holding onto him. I then put my braces and shoes back on that my friends were carrying behind us and tried walking again. I went almost another half of the loop without any support at all, walking fully on my own out of my scooter. I felt like God was healing me in phases!

That's when they opened up the stage for people to share their testimonies if they had experienced healing. Though mine didn't seem complete, I wanted to go testify about what God had done and was doing in my legs. So barefoot again, I walked down the steps leading to the stage, but, as soon as I got there, the stage closed for more people. Bad timing. But I was

Doubtless

now right in front of the stage where a band called Jesus Culture played some of my favorite songs and my friends and I danced passionately. Afterwards, my friend, Kenneth, gave me a piggy back ride up the stairs and back into my scooter to put my braces and shoes back on.

I have no idea what happened till this day. It was like a mini miracle in my body that came and went. My friend MJ told me that oftentimes God gives us a glimpse of things to come, so I'm going to choose to believe that God was reminding me of what He is capable of. However, it was another moment where I felt like my big act of faith only led to disappointment yet again. I began to grow so tired of having to make my own path.

Why can't things just be easy for once? I often found myself wondering.

Daily life was so challenging to face with a disability. Yet, it seemed like those around me with normal mobility and great health weren't even happy half the time. I wanted to shake people and say, "Want to trade?!"

The exhaustion and never feeling like I could move around easily led me to feel like I wasn't doing enough, even when I was doing so much. If God loved me as much as people said, why wouldn't He heal me? I believed He could, so why wouldn't He do it?

"He doesn't like to see you suffer," people would say. Or "He's in your suffering right with you." "God wants you well even more than you want it!"

Yeah, okay. So what's the problem here? What's the disconnect? Am I doing something wrong?

I didn't know what else to do except to keep showing up like I already was, though I was feeling drained and doubtful of what God had in store for me.

During this time of so much hurt, confusion, and overwhelm related to fighting for my physical healing, I was also dealing with nonstop FOMO (fear of missing out). I think FOMO is one of the biggest issues for many people in their younger years, especially with the constant social media reminders of how many friends everyone else has. Even worse, is that even when I was invited to things, it didn't mean I could or should have always gone due to physical reasons, creating a whole different form of FOMO.

Yet, I always pushed through and went out of my way to attend things, find new places or events, and live a fulfilling life. It was tiring. I felt like I was always searching for more, attending every event I found, driving distances to go to parties and gatherings, showing up to places, and having no idea what or who would be there. I became a go-getter, and probably in an unhealthy way.

FOMO controlled my life after having to miss out on things from an early age. Even though, as an adult, actually missing out on things wasn't as clear cut as it was when I was younger and literally had to sit on the sidelines, that familiar feeling remained strong in numerous situations and social settings. Observing people hanging out in groups or sharing fun things they had done brought up the paranoia that I didn't have the same good things going on or available because of my disability. Things had always seemed harder for me, so I assumed they always would be. I felt like even though I was doing the best I could and staying active, I was a step behind everyone. Because of this belief, I was living from a place of rejection and letting my false perception of others and myself define me as a person.

A heavy sense of disappointment accompanied my FOMO. Even when surrounded by people or having a good time, the lenses of disappointment clouded my heart and dictated the way I saw my future.

Why were things always harder for me? Why didn't I ever have that many friends? Why did I have to have an incurable disease that puts harsh limits on my lifestyle? Why was I not seen as beautiful or worth pursuing like other girls around me? Why was my youth wasting away as my physical abilities were?

All I could do was cry and have my breakdown moments with nothing that could take these realities away, and no one who truly understood. There was a period of a couple of weeks when I hit such a low point that things that could normally cheer me up only left me in a bad mood. I was frustrated and defeated, didn't want to talk to anyone or be in social settings. Going to my campus ministry internship every day was annoying me, and I was anxious to leave and pushed everyone away, which was no problem when I didn't feel seen there anyway.

Meeting with my discipler was agonizing as she assessed how I was doing and how my week was, trying to take care of my emotional health with godly guidance and wisdom. It all sounded like "Christianese" as she talked about how God loves me, and how to find balance in my day to take care of my spiritual health. Blah, blah, blah. I felt like she was trying to put a bandaid on my gaping wound. I didn't want to hear all the same things—I wanted to jump out of my skin and be someone different.

I was numb to any encouragement or friendliness. I didn't want to hash out my day with my roommates and stayed more to myself. I didn't know how to talk to my mom about it because I have an incurable progressive disease that there is no cure for, and there was nothing she could do to change that. I felt that complaining about it would be more of an inconvenience to everyone at this point.

I remember throwing things against my wall and sobbing, not even wanting to talk to God except to beg Him to make my life easier for once.

When is it going to be MY time for once? Will I ever actually have a fulfilling and fun lifestyle when a crippling disease is in place and stealing true freedom from me?

When the moments of self-pity passed, I had no choice but to keep going forward, even though I was discouraged.

Doubtless

It was nearing the fall season and the ministry was hosting a retreat for second-year interns at one of the director's friend's lake house. Though I wasn't close with the other interns, I felt it should be a fun time of games and meal sharing at a fancy lakehouse. Lake houses are always hit or miss for me because the geographical features can present difficult challenges.

This house specifically presented one of those challenges, as the lake and dock were far down a hill with rough terrain through the woods to get there. Meaning, half of the time, the group was down by the water or hanging out on the dock, being carefree out in the beautiful weather and enjoying nature, while I was up on the porch alone. No one thought to help me down to the dock.

I found myself stuck in the house with the two adult leaders who were hanging out and preparing dinner, looking down at all the interns on the dock, laughing, swimming, and having fun. What was I supposed to do? I just sat there, wishing time would go faster and we could jump into dinner time when everyone would be back in the house again.

I ended up having a conversation with one of the directors, and she asked me about my family, myself, and my disability. I explained how my family is amazing but being the youngest, I had to make my own path apart from my older sisters. I told her about my new diagnosis and about the sadness it brought my parents, as well as the hardships it brought to my daily routine, especially being on a college campus. I shared my familiar feelings of being left out and misunderstood, especially by the people in the ministry. It didn't seem like many interns had empathy or compassion for anyone who wasn't just like them, which was my reality many times in the past.

She encouraged me to share with the staff the next week about myself and what I had going on physically since not many people actually knew my story. I told her I'd be happy to share, but I didn't think the ministry staff members would be interested. It was refreshing that she was interested, and definitely an unplanned conversation with someone I only knew from afar.

Come Thursday, the day of our weekly staff meetings, after announcements, they made time for the "Alyssa Segment." They had a chair for me in the front of the room, and the students had no idea what was planned. Instead of our usual staff meeting, teaching, or fun activity, they called me up front to share. To help me feel more comfortable, we agreed to a Q and A segment on the topic of disability.

Well, after the director encouraged me to open the conversation with my testimony, it quickly turned into me opening up to over eighty interns, staff members, and some students—while they all stared at me. I shared the details of my GAN diagnosis, how encouraged I was when they prayed and fought for me at the Tuesday morning prayer meeting when I was at the NIH, and how God has really sustained me over the years. I talked about how I'm thankful that even though things are hard, I still have life and many things going for me.

But I totally lost my composure and broke down into uncontrollable sobs as I opened up about the hardships of being different, of asking God for healing and not ever seeing it, of feeling invisible, and how I felt like I was trapped in a body that wasn't mine and wished I could break free. I went into the morning with hopes of it being a bold, inspiring public speech kind of moment, yet it ended up with me word-vomiting the hurt that was in my heart, and how I constantly see healing happen for others and always end up disappointed.

Some people in front were crying along with me, never having heard my thoughts and my heartbreak so openly before. I said I would never stop fighting, never stop believing, for I know God is good, but I didn't understand why He lets me suffer all the time. I had planned to give an empowering message of endurance, yet I clearly hit my breaking point. All the deep, pent-up sadness and turmoil boiled over and out that morning, despite my best intentions.

The morning ended with all eighty or so people surrounding me, laying hands on me, praying, and speaking words of encouragement and affirmation. It was sweet, and I felt loved and supported by everyone, but I felt like it was a moment of pity. People encouraged me for days to come, even through some handwritten notes, telling me my strength and vulnerability was admirable.

I left the moment embarrassed after handing my heart on a platter to a large crowd of people, people I didn't fit in with and barely had relationships with. I felt completely exposed and wanted to take it back. Being vulnerable and breaking down in front of that many people was truly uncomfortable. I wanted to justify my blabbering sobs and squeals by saying, "I really am fine, I'm okay, don't worry. I'm stronger than I currently appear to be." But it was too late to take it back. That's not the way you want to be remembered.

I shared my insecurity about the whole thing with the director, who encouraged me to continue opening up about my feelings with my discipler in the weeks to come, and they both said my words were perfectly conveyed and deeply touched people.

Maybe God wanted me to share about how I was hurting socially and emotionally within that ministry. Maybe it was good for people to know what was really going on in my heart even though I always appeared joyful and self-controlled. Maybe it was a time to invite people into where I was at in a powerful way, letting them carry my heavy weight and surround me with encouragement and love. Maybe it was good that these people I interned with knew how I felt and how I was hurt by the social dynamics there.

Even though I was ready to be done with my internship, maybe God made space for that moment for a reason: to remind me that this disability

Doubtless

can challenge others to think differently and encourage us all to live with more vulnerability as well. The unplanned, raw sharing of my experience that seemed to explode into a room of eighty people was out in the open. I was uneasy about the experience for days to come. I had to let it go, own it, and keep moving forward yet again.

Through my breaking point came a release of confidence and a new freedom from caring what people thought about me. That in itself brought a halt to the swirl of rejection that I lived in for those two years. The hurt that was built up in me was slightly diminished, and I finally stopped striving to be anyone I wasn't. It was liberating, and I was ready to launch into life with my newfound freedom of self-acceptance.

12

Sustaining Grace

After my big breakdown in front of everyone during the staff meeting, I surprisingly started to feel slightly empowered. Though no one wants to be a blubbering mess in front of a crowd, it brought a release to an extent. Rather than staying embarrassed by sharing my hurts, I stopped feeling ashamed of what was true and what I was experiencing. I decided to suck it up and keep showing up with positivity, even though I hadn't found my true sense of belonging yet.

I was doing life, even though I was overwhelmed by all the new emotions that college and ministry had brought me. What could (and should) have been a season of thriving in my youth at a sought-after university had become a time of feeling heavy pressure to escape the torment of insecurity and rejection I couldn't seem to shake off, no matter how hard I tried. Yet, opening up to the staff in the way that I did led many people to open up to me about their personal struggles, which allowed me to connect with them on a deeper level.

God clearly used the embarrassing "Alyssa Segment" for a purpose beyond what I could see in that moment. For weeks to come, I got to pray over some people for strength or for healing. Another intern asked me to pray for her aunt who had cancer, and asked me for advice on how to stay strong with all the hardships she had going on around her. That was such a neat moment of connecting with and encouraging her since we had barely talked before. In the following months, she kept me updated that her aunt was on a path to a healthy recovery and doing better each day!

Doubtless

Suddenly my perspective started to shift. I started to wake up to the reality that when I thought my struggles were keeping me back in life and withholding good things from me, these trials were actually propelling me forward into a new awareness of God's divine leading and plan—a plan that was filled with His overflowing grace and abundant joy. I was becoming more aware of His presence in the times I was hurting because I'd get this overwhelming, supernatural strength to push the heaviness aside, keep going, and hold my head up high.

Though I wasn't over the fact that I didn't exactly click with people in the ministry, which was discouraging at the time, I started to see God's grace being strongly extended to me in other ways that alleviated the negative feelings I was experiencing. I prayed for people more, and I walked some people through things they were struggling with.

My intern friend also was feeling left out within the ministry. She was quiet and shy, and she also struggled to find her place within the cliques. I understood her, I saw her, and I loved her. She always told me she thought I was going to be a public speaker, as my bold declarations over her and the way I spoke truth into her life and identity broke her out of her insecurity. I was more of a tough love-giver, while she was very tender and sensitive.

As the two years of our internship progressed, I saw her develop her voice and her confidence. I was only a tiny part of her life, but I'm so honored for the few times I got to support her and relate to her when not many others could. Many times it just takes being reminded of the strength we carry within us. It's all about our mindsets.

She and I ended up being on the same mission trip team to Los Angeles during my second and last year of interning. On the Jamaica trip, I went as a student, but for the L.A. trip, I got to help lead as an intern. We worked with the Dream Center, which is a place that serves as a resource center focused on providing support to those affected by homelessness, hunger, and lack of education through residential and community outreach programs. Many of the men there were also in recovery from addiction

On that trip, God reminded me how He was using my disability in ways that I didn't realize. We handed food out on the streets in some local neighborhoods a couple of times and participated in food drives, while some individuals from the Dream Center program would help us give back to the community. We would set up a truck of food and supplies and bagged items to hand out in an assembly line. I'd usually be at the end of the lines with my walker, where I could take sitting breaks.

Often, because of where I was placed, somewhat separated from the flow of the large group, I got to have conversations with a few of the men from the Dream Center or the community. One had been in recovery from a hard life of drugs and alcohol and, thus, had many health issues and problems with his brain. After hearing his story of finding Jesus and the process of getting his life together, and finding healing in his body, brain chemistry, and mindset, I got to pray over him multiple times.

Before that even happened, we connected quickly because when he first saw me, he told me that I encouraged him by coming all the way across the country with my physical ailments. Something about my disability drew him to me, and then I got to bless him with prayer and encouragement!

The same thing happened with another man involved with the Dream Center who was helping us with food distribution; he had had a really hard life of drugs, alcohol, jail, family issues—you name it. Again, being at the end of the line gave me direct access to converse with him and hear his story while our team was serving. He was a big guy with lots of tattoos and piercings, very tough and physically fit. You could tell he had been through a lot in life, and I also sensed that he didn't openly share his heart with people too often.

But as he opened up to me, he shared his whole life story with me. I think it's really what he needed at that moment. These interactions happened when the rest of my team was busy assembling food into bags and hustling in lines, while I was building relationships with the people we were serving, sharing our struggles, and relating to how hard times strengthen us and bring us to new places of discovery.

I'll never forget the van driver, Juan, who worked with the Dream Center. He was from Mexico and filled with lots of joy and love. Juan helped me get in and out of the van multiple times, calling me "pretty girl" and "sweetheart." Juan loved Jesus, as he told me about his wall of pictures of people and nations he prayed over every day. He asked for me to send him a photo of our ministry and the name of the state we lived in to add to his prayer wall so he could pray for us too. He also prayed multiple times for my healing and encouraged me to never lose faith. At one of our food distribution sites, he gathered the whole team and some people in the neighborhood who were receiving food, to lay hands on me and pray for me. Juan was such a sweet surprise!

The LA team of students and interns I was with was the majority of "cool" and "popular" people from the ministry I was a part of. Great. Again, I didn't vibe with these kinds of people. Yet, my wallflower intern friend came, along with a few others who were in the in-between crowd. During the week, we had three vans to get places, and there were three interns leading the trip. So, one leader per van.

Well, my van (though I wasn't the driver, just one of the leaders), was the misfit group, including my friend and a few others on the quieter and more timid side. We quickly became like family. We had fun conversations on our drives, stopped for ice cream, got good parking spots with my handicap pass, and they took care of me by dropping me off and picking me up wherever we went. They got my walker in and out of the car, always waited for me, and were true friends. My friend, while driving, shared his struggles with his faith,

Doubtless

and told me how encouraged he was watching me keep strong faith and go on mission trips with all that I had to deal with. I got to pray for him during our van rides and encourage him about where he was at in life.

These friends pushed me in a wheelchair through the airport and security lines, helped with my walker on the side, and we had VIP access due to my disability. My intern friend and I got to talk with the people working at the airports who pushed my wheelchair to and from the gate. One lady barely spoke English, and I was kind of impatient with her at first, not very friendly, and annoyed that I had to go the accessible, long way through the airport apart from the rest of my team with this foreign lady whom I wasn't in the mood to talk to at the time. But as we engaged in small talk with her, she started to open up to us and shared the struggles she was having being away from her kids in another country.

My friend and I prayed over her before boarding our flight, and she cried, giving us multiple hugs—so touched and thankful. She ended up moving us to the front section of the plane, right behind first class, while the rest of our team was in the back. My friend and I had the best of times as the girl sitting in the middle seat between us was moved, and we were constantly given free snacks throughout the flight, with a lot of extra room between us to put our stuff and spread out.

I experienced multiple encounters that week in LA that only happened because my disability had given me direct access to people's hearts and lives. And most, if not all of the people I met and interacted with, commented on my disability being a strength, modeling to them how to keep going even when it's hard, and faith in God when our circumstances challenge us.

The week was filled with God-encounters and divine appointments with people that I doubt I would have otherwise seen or met. I was being shown how God was using my weakness as a strength and that I had reached a new level of influence I had often overlooked. God reminded me that He had given me so much grace to walk out my life with a physical disability because He was using it to open doors to neat and rare encounters.

I was reminded that our struggles are often for more than just ourselves, but are for others too. I was continuing to gain opportunities to help other people through my personal story. It all opened my eyes to see the fact that I didn't need to strive to be someone I wasn't but rather rest in where I was and what God wanted to do in the midst of my struggles.

A few months later, while talking to an older friend from my church on a weekend retreat, he brought to my attention that I was stuck on what he called "the ministry treadmill." I was constantly going to events that were positive, yet I felt worn out and drained. He had found for himself that not until we get alone with God, are quiet, and seek Him for ourselves will we fully have peace and clear direction in life. He had been in that kind of season where he had to rediscover himself and gain clarity from all the noise of life, and going to a few weekend getaways by himself had brought major breakthroughs in his life. He broke it down by reminding me that we cannot depend on other people or events to fully sustain us, and we need to seek God for ourselves.

As I was nearing the end of my time in Athens and about to move back home with my parents, he was excited for me to have this new place of rest that he was sure I'd soon discover. I felt relieved after that conversation with him because, while it seemed so simple, it was profound and made so much sense. I was tired of striving to fit in and be a part of everything.

But how could I be okay with not fitting into the mold of people or things I thought I should? I was living under the pressure of trying to fit into the college lifestyle and in the student ministry, while God clearly wanted to set me apart. I obviously wasn't meant to fit in because so much more was happening around me, and I was on a different path.

Breaking down in front of the staff earlier in the year opened up opportunities for me to minister to others and then meet with the awesome people I met in LA. I think I needed to surrender my desire to change myself and instead be more content with who I was and how this disability was becoming an opportunity in many ways. Just like in LA, I didn't go searching for the amazing encounters and people I interacted with; rather they just came onto my path by me being myself where I was.

God stirred a desire in my heart to seek Him alone more often and pursue an intimate relationship with Him for myself. He led me into a season of seeking Him in a new and different way: by embracing my authentic self and not feeling any obligation to go and do but rather to just be. Taking a step back and surrendering my former ways of striving to become someone I wasn't helped me build confidence in myself and embrace the unique path I was on. I needed to learn to rest and be more in tune with what God was speaking to me personally without trying to get those answers from others.

Working in campus ministry taught me how important it is to have healthy boundaries and know when to say no in order to refuel. Constantly attending spiritual events and seeking to grow in my spiritual walk through other people and church-related gatherings was leaving me worn out and tired. Full-time ministry created a hyper-spiritualized environment, with deep and reflective conversations. I felt like I was always having to pour out advice and support for others but also having too much time to reflect on my own thoughts and feelings.

Both of these aspects of life and spirituality are important of course, yet it can turn into an unhealthy religion of do's and don'ts, guilt for not doing enough, or shame for not being on top of things all the time. I needed a break to have fun again and not always be in this kind of environment. I felt pressure in these settings to be in 'ministry mode' and prove to God I deserved healing because I had faith and was a good Christian, and then would leave disappointed and discouraged. It became a vicious cycle.

Doubtless

Learning to choose our best yes to things while also knowing when to say no brings much more balance to our lives. That way we can give ourselves fully to what we choose to do. It's a disservice to ourselves and others when we don't give our best selves and are spread too thin. We need to realize the importance of rest, which for sure hasn't come naturally to me. Just because my work obligations involved going to church-related events didn't mean I was seeking God for myself.

The main way to gain clarity and direction, to feel connected to God and in tune with yourself, is through personal intimacy and relationship with Him. Constantly going and doing can really wear us out. I was always living in the fear of missing out, trying to do everything and be friends with everyone, and it was exhausting me. Participating in all these religious activities and events didn't always leave me feeling satisfied, refreshed, or content with who I was, or not wishing my situation could be better.

If anything, the more ministry events I went to, the more tired and discouraged I became. We can strive to stay on a "religious good" treadmill where we do all the "right" things, but it often wears us out rather than fills us up, leaving us unchanged. I've learned that the only way to truly know God is by just spending time with Him one-on-one, reading His Word, and resting in His love. We can get caught up in the popular new worship bands, the famous speakers, the bright lights, and the moments that give us spiritual highs, but we often leave feeling empty or no different than when we came in.

I was about to finish my ministry internship and move back home, and my friend said it was the perfect timing because I was about to enter into a season of not being surrounded by hundreds of people each day on campus and in Athens. I'd have to ignite my own flame, he told me, which is where breakthrough and self-discovery would come. I started to accept who I was and the fact that I didn't have to be invited to everything going on to truly be accepted or loved. God is the one who decides who we are, and we get our worth from Him alone, not from others.

While I was in a place of striving for good health and staying on top of things, keeping up with ministry duties, and trying to find my place and my people, I realized that I was trying to earn things from God. I was chasing after things believing my relationship with Him was dependent on my works and how disciplined I was in the decisions I made. God made it clear that I needed to rest to receive what He had for me. God's grace was never something I could easily receive because I have always had high standards for myself and have easily blamed myself for my struggles. But my high standards have never been attainable, which has led to striving and guilt in my life.

What did it look like to receive God's grace? What is grace?

Ephesians 2:8-9 says, "For it is by grace you have been saved, through faith—and this is not from yourselves, it is the gift of God—not by works so that no one can boast."

The revelation hit me that we do not have to strive to earn things from God because He freely gives to us out of His abundant love. He was showing me His freely-given favor through the sweet blessings that were surrounding me that I wasn't acknowledging. He was showing me that He loves us because of who He is, not because of who we are or what we have or haven't done. I think that really is the essence of the gospel: Jesus died on the cross for our salvation, and it is His sacrifice—not our good works— that saves us.

Everything we do in life flows from that understanding of grace. We don't *earn* anything from God; we simply *receive*. Every good and perfect blessing in our lives is a freely given gift from Him. With this new revelation, I realized I just needed to rest and learn to be content with who I was and where I was in life and let go of the pressure to constantly be on the go or have it all together. Turning to busyness and other people to sustain me caused me to lose touch with myself and what God was saying to me personally. It was time to get off the ministry treadmill.

I knew things were changing for me when at a ministry service one night when I'd usually be trying to be overly engaged and socially active as students were coming in and mingling in friend groups, I found a new joy by simply sitting down alone on the side of the room. I was in a place of total peace of not feeling a need to be anywhere but there, alone with God.

I had a great night during the worship service because I was just fully present rather than feeling a need to "fit in." I realized I had started to grow up and be more independent because it became easier for me to be content with just being still at various places I went. With my roommates, I would usually hang out in the kitchen for hours talking every day after school.

But as I became more comfortable spending time in solitude, I would stay in my room more often, starting to paint again, read, or just chill on my bed. I felt like something huge had been broken off of me. It was so nice to not feel any pressure to stay social like my extravert self constantly needed to. I didn't recognize myself, yet after my friend's comment about needing to slow down, I transitioned into that desire with ease.

It was after finding peace in rest and solitude with God that I started to experience breakthrough in my confidence and relationship with Him. Things started to fall into place as I took a step back. Showing up for my internship every day looked different because I was just there, being present and not trying to keep up with others moving about. I started to notice people coming to me more often when I just hung out and was nothing but myself. I started to read God's Word more. The hunger and desire for it increased because I wasn't looking at it as a religious obligation on a to-do list but rather as something I genuinely enjoyed and wanted to study. Going forward, I started to have a different lens on where I was and find more joy in stillness, surrendering the need to be a part of anything or be someone I wasn't.

13

Kingdom Family

Apart from my ministry internship, I started to get more involved with a local church in town called The Awakening, which met at a local gym. That gym environment was surprisingly amazing, as they set up a small stage with speakers for a music set, chairs, and carpets to lay out on the floor, and bam, a musical set and production took place. Many young couples who did life together and had known each other for years came along with the small waves of college students who came and went for a season. The church hosted a lot of community events, including dinners, homeless outreaches downtown, and handing things out on street corners to bless people walking by—it was so fun!

This little church became my family, and though it was a mix of generations, we all were friends and on the same page. One of the married couples hosted a young adults group at their house for about two years, where we enjoyed worship music, small group discussions, card games, and fires at their vintage and artsy home in a whimsical neighborhood not far from downtown. It was such a powerful thing to have them and multiple other married couples pouring into us college students.

Another lady had an open invite at her house most Sundays after church, where she would cook a variety of things and we would sit around her table, maybe play games, and come and go at any time. Her name was Ms. Deborah, and she always had neat stories to tell about her job in DFCS, her Latina background, and her experience with missions. Ms. Deborah was like a mother to so many people and gave life advice and wisdom to anyone who

Doubtless

needed it while loving people through her gift of hospitality.

She and her kids were also connected with a local family who also had weekly bible studies at their house—Fernando and his wife, Laura, and their daughter, Sofia. Every Tuesday evening, they would put chairs in a circle in their living room, offer pizza and snacks, and welcome anyone and everyone for fellowship, prayer, and celebration. Fernando and his family are from Bolivia, and their home was often filled with people representing various nations. I'd always meet new people, many of whom spoke Spanish, and listen to Fernando and his wife, Laura, read scripture in Spanish and then translate it into English (or vice versa).

Each week held a different surprise, usually someone sharing a testimony, needing prayer, or having a group discussion about life and God. It was the most diverse Bible Study I had ever been to and was so much more exciting than any typical small group gathering I had witnessed. Though there was vast diversity represented in their living room, we all shared the commonality of our love for Jesus. That alone took away any barriers that blocked us all from loving each other and feeling like family, even though I didn't know who was going to show up each time.

My main connectors to Ms. Deborah and Fernando, along with The Awakening, were my roommates. They were definitely a huge part of my time in Athens and changed everything about how I looked at myself and the season I was in while bringing exactly what I needed to my life in surprising and unusual ways.

During the two years of interning with my campus ministry, I lived in a cute little neighborhood off campus called Pineview, also known as the "Christian ghetto" since it happened to be filled with a lot of Christians, many of whom worked for the same campus ministry I did. It was one of those student housing complexes that everyone knew about because a ton of people lived there and it was very cheap—a college student's dream. There were always a bunch of cars parked along the street and people having friends over at their houses. I had three roommates I met during my time in college who were down-to-earth, very inclusive, and not involved in any cliques. I was the only white person in the house, which I thought was awesome because we were such a diverse group.

I began to realize that all these deep, diverse (culturally, racially, ethnically, and generationally) friendships were pointing to a common theme in my life with Passion, Refuge Ranch, and The Awakening. Unfortunately, it took me a long time to understand the rare gifts these groups were because they were not the typical friend groups that others around me had. God was showing me extended grace through these various groups of people to get me through many years of struggling to find myself and where I belonged.

Though I was resisting the fact that I didn't fit in at the campus ministry I was involved in, these roommates and friends were overflowing with acceptance and love, which challenged me to accept the fact that God perhaps had a different path for me than the popular crowd I so desperately wanted to be a part of. Life became an interesting mix of being at the ministry building all day, every day, and feeling bad about not finding my place there, to then coming home and feeling totally understood and appreciated by these roommates of mine.

Yet, at the same time, I struggled to fully accept that these were my good friends because they didn't look or act like anyone else I had ever known. Our conversations were deep, real, and transparent. Our roommate time involved sitting around the kitchen table over tea and sharing our hearts, pains, and dreams or discussing things we were learning at that time. They were all strong believers, and we would talk for hours about topics in scripture, testimonies we had heard, and issues we were wrestling with.

They were also all extremely mature, and there was never emotional drama, only honest confrontations. Disagreements on different issues would look like discussions about how we can better ourselves and help each other in certain areas. Our conversations often looked like healthy counseling sessions.

These friendships challenged me to be bold, speak the truth in love, and speak up about things that were on my heart, even when they were hard to say. These friends cheered me on no matter where I was, what was going on, and how I was feeling. If one of us had something we did that was bothersome to the others, we would share it honestly with them and then resolve it and move on. These were the healthiest friendships I had ever had, and it was extremely healing to my heart after all the years of feeling misunderstood or invisible.

Our time together involved a lot of tears, resolving conflicts or disagreements about things in the house, or laughing and being silly. We fit together so well because we were comfortable with each other, would make fun of each other, support each other, and were completely honest with each other. We had an open-door kind of house where our friends would come and go. Most of the time we would play board games and cards, get food from one of our favorite local restaurants and bring it back to the living room, and just hang out on the couch talking. We would sometimes just sit and process life, not always having anything to say but just being, praying, and reflecting. These were my people, and our house was filled with love and laughter.

We had a couple of guy friends who were neighbors down the street and who would come over a few times a week. This morphed into holiday gatherings and birthday parties at the house, and it became the main gathering spot. I give my mom credit for that because she decorated and furnished most of the living room and kitchen area. Her gift of hospitality is one I tried to foster in that Pineview house, and I planned to make dinner for my roommates at least once a week.

Doubtless

They were with me through the tears I shed when they asked me how working in ministry was going, about the guy I had feelings for there, and about my heart when I was really struggling the most.

And yet, even with all this going on, I still often felt and thought I couldn't find my people and didn't have many friends. Why was I not counting them as my people? Probably because they weren't your typical friend group. They didn't fit any mold but were just truly themselves. They appreciated their alone time just chilling or sitting and talking. They were open to hanging out with anyone and doing activities without any agenda. It honestly was just what I needed, yet while I was living with them I was still trying to follow after something more "exciting" and "cool," like the multiple groups of friends I saw within the ministry, who were always going out for coffee, shopping, and getting their nails done.

Within the ministry, there were groups and cliques, and conformity was embraced. It was easy to feel left out or like a misfit, especially if you stood out in any way, weren't caught up with what was trending on Facebook or Instagram, or didn't participate in group discussions about pop culture.

I found I just couldn't relate to these groups or be myself since they were always talking about trending celebrities, movies, or the newest popular app. I never had knowledge or interests in these areas or even knew what was going on half the time when it came to pop culture. It made me believe I wasn't interesting or intelligent.

On the other hand, my roommates and I talked about things of the Lord, spiritual encounters or dreams we received from Him, memories, and what was on our hearts and minds. We were such a racially diverse group of friends, each of us looking so different and from a different background. My friends weren't known by a lot of people but were faithful to the few good friends they had.

They did not seek more people to know or things to do, to be seen or known or noticed on social media. They didn't dress in any specific way and were not a part of any cliques. They were fully content with who they were.

But, for some strange reason, I was still seeking more. I considered them my roommates more than my friends since I was still striving to be more seen and known by the popular ministry crowd. What was I chasing exactly? The more time went on and the more I continued to struggle within the ministry, the more I realized that my roommates were truly the friends that God had for me. This was a group I was fully comfortable with and was fully myself with, and I knew that our house dynamic wasn't normal but very rare and extremely special.

The people who came in and out of our Athens house were of different races and ethnicities, different cultures and backgrounds, and the diversity of people I got to know and do life with was so much more exciting than any friendships I had had in the past or at the campus ministry. None of us looked or acted the same, and we fully celebrated each other.

Times hanging out often involved all of us sitting and being; one would be drawing, one sleeping, one telling a story, one just stopping by to eat and then leaving, and then another coming over for prayer. We were like a group of misfits because none of us were in the "in-crowd." When life was kind of quiet on weekends and I felt like many things were going on around me that I wasn't invited to, I had to find happiness by just being where I was, even if it was quiet and not filled with exciting adventures all the time. My roommates were good at just chilling. During that time in my Pineview house, I started to learn how to just be and to let life be what it was without fighting to make it look a certain way like I thought it should.

My introverted friends call joyfully missing out on things and knowing when to say no "JOMO." Though I want to do everything that comes up around me, I often spread myself too thin. I've always liked to stay out and busy, but busyness can keep us distracted, preoccupied, and stressed rather than being at peace in the present moment. I had spent most of my life overwhelmed with numerous thoughts, dreams, and desires, which led to discouragement.

God has continuously reminded me that we are all on a different path and all have different life situations. He gives us what we need and what is best for us, in His timing and His way. Living with these specific roommates helped me to stop comparing myself and trying to go to everything all the time.

In time, I saw how special this group was and how God had a different plan for me than what I was trying to be or fit into in campus ministry. The sweet friendships I formed during my time in Athens are lifelong and so unique. Though we are geographically spread out now doing very different yet meaningful things, we still get together over group Zoom calls and share a tight bond.

I remember the first summer that I was planning on staying in Athens and not going home. I had a house now with roommates who were all going to be staying. What was I missing at home? I was used to hanging out with my mom, doing errands, going to lunch, to the neighborhood pool, to Passion City. It seemed like at home near the big city of Atlanta, there was always something going on, while Athens was a small town with your usual favorite coffee shops or restaurants, and everything was within a ten-minute drive.

The college town was known to be quiet and dead over the summer. I had heard numerous people say that Athens in the summer is the most amazing place because most students leave. What was so amazing about it? It seemed like it was going to be painfully boring! I'm not a TV watcher, there wasn't even a pool in our neighborhood—I already felt the funk starting to kick in. But the roommates and I started discussing things we wanted to do that summer, and how nice it was to not have school or ministry activities going on. It ended up being the best summer of my life.

Doubtless

With no major plans or agenda, we made many special memories. We enjoyed trips to Chick-Fil-A for milkshakes, went to the pool in another complex that didn't check if you lived there or not, hosted game nights at our house and backyard bonfires, and attended a lot of community events at our church. We sat outside, went to the botanical gardens nearby, and had movie nights with brownies in the oven while our neighbors came over and stayed late. We made many memories in our house and went for drives through the quiet town. It was simple living. That summer was sweet and such a breath of fresh air. It was just us roomies and some of our other friends around, and every day was spontaneous and laid back.

While I felt like such an outcast in student ministry, as I did many times in life, I wasn't an outcast with these friends. I was fully me. I believe God gave me much grace at the campus ministry to hurt and be refined, to grow in myself through a time of not feeling seen or included. He then provided these friendships that were so much more meaningful and were exactly what I needed to get through the hurt and self-discovery. He reminded me that we are not meant to always fit in but to be unique, which is where the real treasure lies.

I'm so grateful I didn't fit the campus ministry mold because I see now what a short season of life that was and how it didn't really matter if I had fit in perfectly there or not. God had different friends and different experiences for me. I see how He used being in full-time ministry to show me the importance of finding rest in yourself and in Him, and not relying on spiritual events and gatherings to fully sustain you. Rather, it's essential to find quietness and be still, away from the constant momentum and noise that can leave us feeling worn out and like we can't give any more of ourselves.

I was running on empty trying to give and give to others and realized that we cannot say yes to every single thing. We need to find balance in our lives and take time to take care of ourselves so that we can fully be the best version of ourselves when we do end up attending events. Yes, most ministry activities were required for interns, yet in between these I had to learn to be alone and enjoy times of resting to refuel. Resting hasn't ever come easy or been natural for me, yet I see its importance and how it helps me find direction and clarity in life. I began to learn to choose my best yes and to say "no" when I needed to.

Though I knew my time in Athens had come to an end, the artsy college town became dear to my heart and played a significant role in my spiritual growth. It's where I saw many aspects of who God is, made many amazing friendships, and found joy in the mundane aspects of life, which was what I needed in that season: to discover more of who God created me to be and His purpose for me.

These specific friends taught me how to joyfully say no to busyness and prioritize rest. God showed me He had a different, very specific group of friends for me, and they were just what I needed during that season even though I was resisting it and it didn't look like I thought it should. I've learned to not have specific expectations of what I think life should be like and to just be expectant for God to work things out. He always does. He brings neat surprises and blessings. He may not give us what we think we want, but He always gives us what we truly need. His ways are higher than our own.

I've realized that even in moments when I feel like I'm missing out, He has us each right where we are in every moment for a reason and already knows what's ahead of us. Trusting that He has the best for us is crucial because we don't have to feel pressure to be at everything going on around us. We can find a healthy balance between who we see and when, how many things we take on at once, and when to rest when we need to.

As I have learned to joyfully say no to things, I have come to feel the most peace. I feel more confident in knowing that what I decide to do is what God's leading me to. If I don't mind missing it, I know it's probably not important enough for me to attend. That's how kind God is; He gives us peace in our decisions, gives us discomfort when something may not feel right, or the freedom of choice to decide while working out any decision we make for our good and His purposes (Rom. 8:28). Therefore, we can't go wrong because no matter what we do, He is with us, guiding us and providing for us in every step we take. How comforting it is to know He uses every decision we make and brings us what we need when we need it when we trust Him!

Looking back, I realize what God was doing during my time in Athens. I had to learn how to be in a season of making my own path, without belonging to a certain mold, having expectations of what life should look like, or ideas about what kind of friends I should have. God brought new roommates into my life who were different from the mainstream Christians I knew and worked with at the campus ministry. Most groups of friends looked and talked the same, but my groups of friends were all so diverse. They were the perfect fit for me, but they came in a completely different package than I could have expected.

I realized I wasn't an outcast but was finally in a like-minded group of people who encouraged me to be radical, creative, and fully myself while my campus ministry embraced conformity. Through this, God was also encouraging me to embrace my disability and my differences and be fully myself. These friends saw it as a treasure, and they were never in a rush but moved slowly, taking their time, and helping me along the way.

They encouraged me to get into art again, to write when I said it was a new thing I was pursuing and saw giftings in me that I didn't see myself. They were always good at being still and being content with not being seen or known by anyone. They were at peace when they had no agenda but to just hang out. As I started to accept and embrace these friends, I began to accept myself and where I was in life more fully.

14

Selah

Moving back home with my parents felt so exciting as I had only been in and out for the last four years. Now I was a college graduate, and the possibilities were endless. Who was I going to be? What career would I have? I started serving at Passion City again, going to networking events and career quest meetings, seeing a job coach, and exploring potential opportunities to pursue. I was starting over with a clean slate, and I had a new motivation to make something of myself, get an actual paying job, and volunteer with things that would better myself and tie into my future.

I sent emails, went on many coffee dates, and explored many new opportunities. I met some great people and found some neat nonprofits and creative businesses nearby, but the answer was always the same.

"I wish we had the funds to hire people, but we are mostly volunteer-based right now," or, "We don't have any openings because our foundation is very small, but we will keep your information on hand just in case."

The responses were never promising. I knew what I was interested in—working with nonprofits or in ministry, working with people with special needs and disabilities, or working in some kind of creative setting that involved art. My gifts and talents fit a small and specific niche. I didn't know how else to find a job or what to search for. I knew I loved helping others and making an impact, so I struggled with the idea of getting a nine-to-five office job. I avoid technology like the plague and don't have skills with numbers, science, administrative tasks, sales, business—any of the traditional career experience needed to get a stable full-time job. And, to make things even

Doubtless

more challenging, I can't have a job that requires me to be very active on my feet.

My new job had to be specific. I am also picky because I am a creative. I have a passion for people, for helping others, and for making a difference. I'm very unhappy in places that are high-stress and fast-paced.

My dream job is to have a creative art studio with a coffee shop and gallery attached where there is live music and art and people counseling or mentoring others while somehow supporting international missions and helping individuals with special needs. I went on the quest to find this specific job that involved all that I love in one. I knew it sounded far-fetched, but I tried to find something close to it because I had seen a brief glimpse a few years before and knew it was possible.

One summer in college, I discovered such a place that combined all my unique passions and interests, which I hadn't been sure even existed. I needed an internship for my degree, which could have been anything. I ended up thinking of a friend I had on Facebook, who had a creative arts ministry. It sounded right up my alley, so I reached out. She invited me to come up for a visit.

The day I showed up, I was in awe. She had a house and barn on acres of land in Ball Ground, Georgia, about forty-five minutes north of my house. It was a winding drive and was out in the woods, in a quiet area not surrounded by much. When I arrived, I was greeted at the door and walked into a peaceful living room area with subtle worship music playing, various cozy sitting areas, and Christian decor. I immediately felt overwhelming peace in this homey environment.

Attached to her home was the barn that had been transformed into an art studio. Each stall had a different medium to create with and an area to work in. There was a painting area with easels and chairs set up, a woodworking area with tools and wooden projects that had been finished and hung up, a beading station with sprawled-out jewelry projects in progress, a stained glass area, a clay working space, and a sewing area with a ton of available fabrics, including leather to sew purses. Had I died and gone to heaven?

The lady who lived at the house, Patricia, and I became quick friends. It all seemed so easy and like a gift handed to me. The internship was going to involve creating art, coming up with projects for different ministries and people who came to visit, and assisting her with taking art and music therapy to nursing homes and a special needs school in town. That summer, I ended up being around right when a young woman was staying in the house who was in recovery from addiction and hoping to find healing through art and God. Patricia mentors individuals, hosts spiritual retreats for women, and brings the arts to people in need.

Throughout my time there, I got to paint with a few people coming for community service, as well as a couple of young adults who had autism. I got to walk them through painting simple compositions we came up with and realized I had something special to offer to these people. I saw the power of art in so many ways. People came in from various places with brokenness, sickness, depression, or anxiety, and I saw how art made them open up and feel real peace and joy in the process.

One of the young adults who had autism came to the art barn every single week, and I found out his painting sessions were the highlight of his week. He was nonverbal, but he came alive and laughed and smiled as he painted. A few of the elderly people in the nursing homes lived hunched over, lonely, or unhappy, and when we went for a time of group painting and singing along with a guitar, they would suddenly be sitting up straight, more engaged and energetic than when we first showed up.

I'll never forget the young guy who came for community service. Patricia had us sort beads together. Sounds silly, and I was sure this wasn't his ideal project to be working on. Yet, in time, during a time of quiet and leaving him alone, I came to find he was crying during his bead sorting. Patricia said healing was taking place as he engaged in this color-sorting activity. I didn't get the chance to hear his whole story, but I knew it involved a hard family life and some kind of accident he was in. Who knew sorting mixed and colorful beads could soften the young man's heart in a unique way? What a special opportunity it was to be in this environment!

The young lady in recovery who was staying in the house and I became closer, and I saw her gain various life skills, engage in many hands-on projects, and get her life back together. She, Patricia, and I would go to lunch or dinner, have coffee and paint, or have a bonfire out back. This woman was a mother who was escaping a toxic lifestyle of addiction and relational issues with her significant other, who had her daughter at the time.

She needed time to get her life back on track and heal. I loved encouraging her and affirming her about who she was and in the areas she felt insecure. She did a variety of projects that summer including building things with wood, learning to sew, and scheduling visits to nursing homes and meetings. As she got the chance to serve and help others in need, she matured. It was awesome seeing her progress as an individual and get her life back on track.

She is now back with her daughter and doing well, and I loved that I got to spend some time with her and witness how Patricia's ministry was helping her and others in such powerful ways. Patricia started to pray for me and prophetically speak into my life. She was convinced God had this kind of life and ministry for me, and that He was showing me a glimpse of the beautiful future He had in store. She encouraged me that I was gifted in working with individuals with disabilities, leading group art classes, and pouring love into people going through hard times, as I felt in my element.

Doubtless

I formed neat relationships with many different kinds of people that summer, and it was not only healing for others but for my heart as well. The power of art and music is not like anything else, and it opens people up deeply. Patricia was convinced that I needed to keep pursuing art and ministry, as it was my niche and what I am called to.

I came to hear Patricia's story of sickness and healing through art and spending time with God. She had problems with her legs, leading to muscle pain, fatigue, and inability to walk. Through painting, proper nutrition, and seeking God and His direction, listening to His voice often, her body and life started to heal and transform. She rested and painted, and it changed her life. She encouraged me to do the same—to not push art aside as I had been for years, but to see it as a gift He has given me and something I'm called to.

She said she saw that I was on the verge of major blessings in my life and challenged me to keep pushing into creativity and to believe God would open the right doors. She even encouraged me to write a letter to God, asking Him for all that I see and hope for in a home, art studio, and ministry someday with specific details, believing it will come to pass. I still visit Patricia at her art barn every so often, and I am always reminded of the power and healing of the arts and how they bring people rest, direction, and clarity to their lives. We are all creative beings because God Himself is creative. I wanted to take this experience with me and allow it to transform every day of my life. I will forever hold it close to my heart.

Thinking back to Patricia's, I still couldn't believe I had found a place that involved everything I loved. It was a dream come true and is still significant to my heart. The experience and connection gave me a fresh drive when searching for what could be next for me. I ended up discovering a nonprofit school in downtown Alpharetta, Georgia called Lionheart for students with special needs.

I loved everyone I met there, yet they were also not hiring. However, I soon became a fill-in job coach for a few months where I took an individual to their job site, coached them in life and job skills, and helped them when they needed advice or assistance. It turned into a paid job for a short time until they didn't need my help anymore. Working at Lionheart was another unique opportunity that would help affirm my calling and passion for helping others with disabilities.

Around the same time, I discovered BrewAble, a little coffee shop within the Alpharetta Community Center, which hosted many meetings, sports, and recreational activities, as well as employed individuals with intellectual and developmental disabilities. I wanted to be a part of it somehow, and I came to find that they were looking to sell art in the lobby area where their coffee stand was set up featuring art created by individuals with disabilities. They started hanging some of my paintings on their wall to sell on my behalf, and people in the community started taking notice of my style.

    I painted mostly bright, whimsical animals with vivid colors and cute expressions. I came to discover that some frequent BrewAble customers had become collectors of my art and had hung up multiple paintings of mine on their walls at home. Though it wasn't a large or consistent income, it was something. The coffee shop accepted any art that I gave them with joy and excitement, and they even invited me to set up a little art booth at a few events that they had in the community. This was neat because I had reason to create a variety of things and present them to the public for purchase.

    These events connected me with even more awesome people as I was able to share with BrewAble regulars that I was the face behind the art adorning the walls of the shop. Lionheart and BrewAble happen to be right next to each other, and I loved seeing the overlap of people within the disability community and their friends and family. I saw a lot of service dogs at both places and individuals with different forms of disabilities. This led me to start volunteering at Canine Assistants. Through another coffee meet-up with a man who had a nonprofit for supplying individuals in need with wheelchairs, I continued to grow my network within the local disability community.

    From my new connections, I found out about Synergies Work and Pianos for Peace. Synergies Work is a nonprofit organization that empowers individuals with disabilities by helping them build sustainable businesses through entrepreneurship, art, and networking events. Through it, I had the opportunity to be in an art exhibition at World of Coca-Cola and paint a large mural with a group of people for an auction.

    The lady who started Synergies Work introduced me to the man who started Pianos for Peace! Pianos for Peace is a nonprofit in Atlanta that takes donated, painted pianos and places them in schools, nursing homes, hospitals, and other places in the community to spread awareness of the arts through music and education, bringing unity and peace to people around.

    My mom and I embarked on the adventure of painting a piano, which took us about two months. A few times a week, we would drive down to this storage facility in the city and hike up to the third floor. The piano was located down a very dark and narrow hallway, so every time we painted we would set up multiple lamps and flashlights and just go wild. Take into account that my mom and I are perfectionists, and if we are going to do an art project, we are going to do it right. The piano ended up with big daisies, multi-colored polka dots, squiggles, and glitter.

    We had the best time as they played old seventies music on the radio above, and we would go out to lunch somewhere after. Painting a piano was definitely a long process, but I knew it was a special opportunity! It is currently placed in an office building in downtown Atlanta.

    In addition to all of my exciting projects, outings, and budding new relationships, being at home was also great. My mom cooked dinner every

Doubtless

night and would bring me my coffee in the mornings as I sat on the back deck and journaled. I felt like I was able to breathe again and refocus. It was a season of new things. I found an awesome Passion City group that enjoyed group dinners and fun outings together. I started to paint again, and I was mostly on my own. Resting and being myself brought more healing to my heart and mind.

The moment I stopped striving to find God and figure out all these things in life is when I heard His voice more clearly. When you're faithful with what's in front of you and where you are, He gives you more. He shows you how He is moving in the specific season you're in, as much as you may be fighting it. He wants us to show up and give our all in every season and situation, even when it's hard and we may not see where we are going. He is trustworthy, and He always has a higher purpose for each season of our lives.

As I started to fully accept who I am and where I was at in life, I found more joy and peace. He started to heal my heart, and I regained my desire to press in for physical healing again. Though I was also job searching and feeling pressure to get a "real job," doors were not opening. But God was breathing on my art and ability to be an advocate for others struggling with disabilities like myself. BrewAble, Lionheart, and Synergies Work connected me to people who were moved by my art and my ability to encourage those with and without disabilities to press into their talents with confidence no matter what it looked like and no matter what the obstacles were.

I started to see that God had me on a different path, yet again, but I still wrestled with accepting it. I was chasing after your non-typical career path, which I knew would be difficult to find on my own unless God opened the specific door as He did with Patricia. I loved everything about it and felt like I really had found my passion, but I felt like it wasn't enough. I had literally prayed for God to open the right doors and lead me to where I should be. I shared with Him that my main passions were creativity and disability advocacy. But whenever I stepped into the open doors He provided involving both of those passions, I still couldn't fully rest and enjoy them because I almost felt guilty for not having a "real" job.

Even as I was active during this time to find ways to fully engage my talents and passions, I was feeling the pressure to get a more consistent job and make money, as well as use the degree that I had worked toward to better myself and grow in job experience. My dad was a very impressive businessman in sales for thirty-eight years, so he kept encouraging me to go for interviews, send my resume out, get my elevator speech down, and communicate what my strengths are. My two-year internship at the campus ministry wasn't a paid position, yet it gave me an opportunity to mentor students, lead groups, develop stronger communication skills, and grow in my faith. But when it came to "real job" skills, I felt insecure. I had not gained many hands-on life skills. I liked to communicate and be with people. Could that be my job?

I started to feel bad about my lack of skills and compared myself with others in their early twenties who were farther along in their careers. I started to be surrounded by people in their twenties and thirties who had a variety of job titles in different companies, and when they'd ask, "What do you?" I would give them a lengthy list of my various activities and interests while failing to provide them with a definitive answer.

"I dabble," I'd add.

I felt like I was staying busy and actively pursuing my passions, yet I lacked consistency and routine. Finally, my dad and I had the job talk again after a few months once I felt hopelessly stuck. He implied that he had been cutting me slack but that I could not be picky anymore. I needed to fill the gap in my resume.

Here's the thing about the culture we live in—a lot of people tie their worth and their confidence to what their job title is and how much money they make. But, as I was looking to see what jobs were out there, I kept being drawn to pursue art and advocacy more seriously. I felt more fulfilled doing what I loved, though I didn't have much money coming in or consistency in my routine. Yet, other doors were not opening. And honestly, I didn't find interest in most available jobs I saw posted online.

So, yes, I wrestled with pressure and comparison and self-criticism, but I started to grow in confidence that maybe my dreams of being an artist and advocate could be real if I fully gave myself to it and treated it more than a hobby that I did on the side. I knew art and disability advocacy was what I wanted and loved the most, but I kept feeling bad for not working a nine-to-five office job. I began to wonder if my career dreams would ever come true.

You just need to work harder and not be so picky. You aren't going to find your dream job right out of college. Just get a job, Alyssa. Stop being so selective and over-complicating it. You can learn anything, but you're not trying hard enough. Art is your hobby, not your career. You're doing more thinking than doing. You're falling more behind everyone in the job market the more you overthink it.

What was wrong with me? I couldn't describe it. I felt like I was doing a lot. I had sent emails to so many different nonprofits and organizations, churches, schools, creative agencies, and a variety of healthcare offices, and I was proactive about reaching out. I knew a lot of amazing people, but I was envious of them having jobs I wished I could have and felt frozen in place, not making progress.

All of a sudden, in the midst of my turmoil, a word I received from the Lord a few years before became heavy on my heart: to write a book. I had the desire and idea, and I felt it was something God was calling me to do, yet I had not actively worked toward it for a couple of years because the thought overwhelmed me.

I had never written a book before. I didn't know how, and I wondered

Doubtless

who would even care to read it. I'm just another average person. There are millions of books in the world by talented and well-known writers, and I wasn't one of them. So I pushed the thought away. But here was the idea coming up again, eating at me to write. I had initially received the thought while living in Athens and even started a Word document. I felt the introduction had potential, but then I stopped.

Now here I was, a year later, trying again. I'd type some thoughts here and there, but I just couldn't stay consistent. Sure it would be an awesome thing to accomplish one day... but it wasn't my priority.

So, in the meantime, I went for interviews and painted for BrewAble. It wasn't much, but I was finding joy and rest in my new routine. It felt so good to have art in my life again. It was like a fresh start as I was painting simple, bright, and whimsical animals, flowers, and other fun compositions. Although they seemed like childish paintings, my art was blessing people and was being bought at a quick pace. I set up a booth of different paintings at several coffee events, and they sold very well, leading to some calls and commission work.

No, I didn't have a real job, but in the meantime it was giving me momentum to stay in the fields of art and disability advocacy, sharing my story of living with a disability, helping others with disabilities or special needs, and expressing my life through creativity. Having a reason to paint again was like a breath of fresh air. I was surrounded by things I loved: art, family, and being at Passion City again. Life was good. Home was a sweet blessing.

I also wanted to invest more time in my family. The holidays, my favorite time of year, were approaching. My sister, Jaime, would be coming home for Thanksgiving, and it had been forever since we had talked or seen each other, or that our whole family had been together. Jaime and I hadn't been as close, since we were both in different life seasons and places, but reconnecting seemed so timely. Thanksgiving and Christmas were always sweet and simple times of mom cooking, football on, and puzzles on the table. We would always attend a holiday show at the Fox Theater as a family, take lots of group pictures, and enjoy nice dinners.

This upcoming year seemed filled with aspirations and goals that I hadn't felt motivated by for a long time. I felt that I was truly about to enter a new season of exciting opportunities, with a new career path and a place of independence. 2020 was approaching, and along with it an expectancy of 20/20 vision. 2020: a year of perfect vision and goodness, a year of alignment and straight paths.

I have always been big on New Year's resolutions, goal setting, and starting afresh each year. With 2020 about to begin, I felt anticipation that I never had before. I was telling everyone and truly believing it was going to be the best year of my life. I give myself a word for every year and set a theme for myself depending on what I'm hoping to accomplish. My theme for 2020 was "just do it," since I felt like I was going to be doing a lot of new and powerful things in the next few months.

Therefore, the holidays and time with family seemed different than the years before because, for the first time in my life, I was finally in a place of confidence in pursuing my purpose and resting in who God created me to be. I was bursting with ideas for paintings and looking forward to trying things out. Time with my sisters hanging out in the kitchen looked different because, in a way, I was no longer just the younger sister, but a young woman who felt more confident in where I was going.

Since Jaime could only come home for Thanksgiving because of work, Christmas was quieter and simplified, but so sweet as my parents, my older sister, Lauren, and I laughed and worked on a puzzle, enjoyed a nice dinner, and were all just present in the moments we shared together. My small family had a cozy holiday month of watching many movies and simply enjoying our time together. The tree was lit, the holiday candles scented the air, and my home felt like a peaceful winter oasis.

That Christmas was a carefree time of creativity and resting, fuzzy socks and soft blankets, and no agenda. We didn't have much going on or planned that year, yet we had a wonderful time watching old classics, drinking glasses of wine, and baking in the kitchen.

A few weeks later I went to the Jesus Image conference in Orlando with friends over New Year's Eve and stayed in an Airbnb with a large group, which was a blast. The midnight countdown involved a huge dance party in a crowd of thousands, and the conference was a powerful few days of speakers and worship bands. The positivity people spoke with over the new decade about to start left everyone with high hopes and good vibes.

I was bursting with excitement for what was ahead and fully believing for a year of perfect vision. Life was really good, and I couldn't wait to see what 2020 had in store!

15

Unexpected

2020 was off to a good start as I loved being home and was in the process of discovering what could be next for me. This 20/20 vision year would be my year of getting my life on track, I was so sure! Finally, I felt at a place of rest since I had gained more confidence in where God had me and what He had for me. I always felt super close to my family and knew the importance of spending time with loved ones, bringing me total contentment with being home during this time in my life.

While in college, I looked forward to going home on the weekends to spend time with my parents because I really do enjoy time with them and think they are super fun. We laugh, we joke around, we go to dinner or to see live music.

My sisters and I had grown more distant over the years due to us being at very different stages of life and my living in Athens. Lauren was in an apartment nearby, and Jaime was living in Asheville. What do I say about Jaime? Well, she was tough. A bit of a rebel, very individualistic, and liked her alone time. She was intelligent, spunky, hilarious, and beautiful, and she completed our family. I was excited to hopefully all be together again soon after the holidays.

Over the years, we had shared many memories of family vacations, concerts, parties at our house, camping trips—all kinds of fun adventures. God has always blessed us, and the most important thing to me is my family. Losing them had always been my biggest fear in life, so much so that I'd cry at the thought of it since I was little.

Doubtless

I spent countless hours praying and journaling about it, pursuing strong faith in how God has blessed me over the years, and praying He would protect my family. I never imagined I would ever face the sudden loss of someone close to me. I never thought death and tragedy would be a part of my story... until it was.

I had spent the evening at a worship and prayer night, feeling encouraged and empowered, only to come home and walk into the kitchen, where I found my parents standing. They were crying, speechless. My heart started racing and sank, and I was hit by a feeling of dread. They said to come inside due to some bad news.

I wondered, *Did grandma fall?*

"Jaime was walking to the store and got hit by a truck. She is dead," my mom shared with me, hardly able to muster up the words. My heart seemed to stop.

My stomach dropped... *What? Just like that?*

I found out that a few hours previously, around 7:30 p.m., my other sister, Lauren, received a call from Jaime's boyfriend, who was hysterical. A cop had come to his door with news that Jaime had been hit and run over crossing a busy road while headed back to their house. He was told not to tell anyone because they were trying to get an officer to come to my house and tell my parents directly.

My poor parents, hearing the news from my sister Lauren, desperately tried for over three hours to get in touch with an officer on the crime scene to tell them what was going on. One finally gave confirmation that the pedestrian who had been hit was in fact my sister, Jaime. No one ever came to our house to share the news. And during that whole time, I was having a fun night with friends, having no idea what I was about to come home to.

I had been praying for Jaime for years. For her to know the Lord in a deeper way, for freedom from the anxiety she had been plagued with for most of her adult years, and for her to find herself and her purpose. And now this?

Family memories from trips, parties, girls' nights out, and so much more flooded my mind. It was mid-January of the year 2020, and I was filled with vision and expectation for the new year and all that was to come. I'd never dealt with major grief before, and I had no idea how to navigate it. This deep gut pain kept resurfacing—the thought of my life forever being altered, having to live out a "new normal" that we would have to find as a family, and the void in our hearts of Jaime being gone from the family forever, at least on this side of heaven.

It is sobering to think that life truly is this unpredictable. I have always faced fear over time moving too quickly, the fragility of life, and the inevitable reality of loss and death. In that moment, I suddenly had to face my greatest fears—all at once. Only a few weeks before, I got a new pair of leg braces that I was adjusting to and retraining myself to walk in, which caused constant pain, therapy, and chiropractor appointments, and having to slow down. I was already feeling worn out and discouraged, so it felt like the worst possible time for this tragedy to occur.

I can't catch a break. God, can You stop taking me through trials of some sort? Can You just give me some good years of freedom from pain and hardship for once? I start to get closer to finally enjoying my life, and then a major tragedy happens to set me back yet again. How will I ever get over this loss? I'm too young for this! Jaime was too young to die!

Only a few days after her death, I was already seeing life differently. Moses prayed to the Lord, asking Him to "Teach us to number our days, that we may gain a heart of wisdom"(Psalm 90:12). Life is short, like a vapor. But I guess you don't really think about that until someone close to you is suddenly gone without warning.

She was only going to be turning thirty, and I still don't understand why her life ended so suddenly and tragically. I never got to see my prayers answered for her.

How are we going to move forward and still live full lives when vacations, birthdays, and holidays will never be the same again? I wondered.

Then on the rare days when I felt like I was finally recovering, I hurt for my parents and how they must have felt facing the loss of their daughter. They had raised her, had hopeful plans for her, and had invested so much into her life, and it was all ripped away in a second. I hurt deeply for them and wished I could fix it.

I have always been one to take the burdens of my family onto my shoulders because I care so deeply for the people I love. Grief is an uncomfortable thing because we all have our own processes, timing, and way of grieving. And there is no right or wrong way—you just need to let it happen, feel what you feel, and know that it's okay. That's what people kept telling me. I was unsure what the months to come would look like dealing with this tragedy, and it was only January...

The following weeks were a blur. I was numb and in shock, and I began to live with a deep gut-wrenching pain that words couldn't describe. Each of my family members was severely hurting and not sure what to do or think. I would get out just to breathe. I'd sit outside, in my car, go to the coffee shop, and just stare. I didn't want to be home with this intense heaviness and dark cloud I felt over my family now.

The day after the accident, my parents and sister drove to Asheville to pack up Jaime's personal belongings from the little house she had been living in. They also saw her body for the last time. Her ashes were shipped in a box in the mail within a few days of the accident, and it was traumatic to see them come as just another piece of mail. Seeing the box sitting on the kitchen counter made me feel sick.

We had to cancel all of her accounts, and it was strange to just close

Doubtless

and nullify things as if they had never existed, like her car payment, her school loan, and any debt in general that she had accumulated. All wiped clean and removed. It all was moving so fast and was too much to take in. It's freaky how the lives we build for ourselves and the accomplishments we work toward can suddenly disappear as if they (and we) were never here.

After a couple of months, people had moved on with their lives. Life and death were suddenly put into perspective for me as harsh realities beyond our control. I was abruptly awakened to the brevity of life and the importance of prioritizing what matters because time is not promised nor on our side.

My dad, being the amazing communicator and hard worker that he is, immediately took on the job of preparing Jaime's memorial. He knew right away what he was going to do. He got all the pictures out, forming picture boards filled with years and years of photos of Jaime with family and friends. So many special moments and memories. I have no idea how he did that so soon after it happened, as any pictures were devastating to even glance at for me. He prepared the most amazing speech and PowerPoint presentation, and he made it through without shedding a tear, articulating it so well. I was and am so beyond proud to have him as a dad. His motive was to celebrate and honor her life, and that's exactly what it was—an amazing tribute to who she was.

The service was a beautiful remembrance, and everyone was in awe of the worship songs, the thoughts from the pastor, and my dad's tribute. A lot of good friends came in from Naperville, Jaime's high school crew that was always at the house, and a ton of my Passion friends. The turnout of people was special and filled with love and support. I realized how blessed we are to have a life full of love, and love was poured out abundantly for those first few months in unexpected ways and places.

It still doesn't seem real, as I keep expecting Jaime to walk through the garage door and complete our family time over the holidays and such. Instead, life became extremely quiet. Losing her became an entirely new frontier for our family, and it was confusing and scary to navigate with the knowledge that our lives would never be the same again. I could not believe this was my family's new normal. I hate that death can knock on your door when you feel like you finally have your feet on solid ground, creating a rocky, unsteady path, ready to trip you up once again.

After Jaime died, I started to reach out to people right away, receive prayer, and go to church. Most people need time after a fresh loss, but I knew being around people of faith was what I needed. I remember going to meet MJ at Starbucks and just sitting there crying, not sure what to say or do. When I told my parents I was going to meet a friend for coffee, I think they were surprised that I even wanted to go out in public at all. I didn't really, but I was at a loss for direction.

I showed up at Passion City to serve a few days later, and people were in shock and wondered what I was doing there. It definitely wasn't easy, as I was pretty much sobbing the entire time, especially as people kept coming up to hug me. The door-holders at Passion all surrounded me and prayed, as I broke down in uncontrollable sobs.

There were multiple moments like this that were painful to go through but each helped me get through my grief. Each time I showed up and opened up, I experienced new levels of healing and emotional release. The Lord started to connect me with others who had stories of loss, and it seemed people were coming out of the woodwork! I hate it when loss and tragedy are the unifying factors that bring people together, yet it's a powerful reminder you're never alone in your hurt.

I came to hear many stories of grief and loss and saw how people were still moving forward and still living. It assured me that I'd get through this and be okay, even as I wondered how we would ever make it. They said it would always be a painful scar, but that the raw and gut-wrenching pain would lessen. People really lifted me up when I didn't know how to even appear to be ok.

Two months after Jaime passed, the whole world shut down due to the Coronavirus pandemic. The year was already off to a dreary start for me and my family, and it just kept getting worse, due to the compounded trauma. Covid-19 had people quarantined or out of work and also brought a slowdown and quietness to the world. It was an unknown and scary time, and we would go to the park every day as our only option of places to go while trying to navigate an unprecedented situation.

It seemed like the whole world went into a panic within a few days, with people suddenly stocking up on things due to new stay-at-home orders. Apparently, this flu-like virus was highly contagious and deadly. Now social distancing and mask-wearing measures were being enforced, and being around groups of people was frowned upon or even illegal in some places. Since no one knew how to handle this unprecedented pandemic, extreme measures were taken, and the news was consumed with it.

Businesses and stores were either closed or rearranged to keep people distanced from each other. Any place that had a food bar or serve-yourself component was blocked or taken away. A healthy, human need for social interaction was suddenly regarded as a crime. And it was during the time in my life when I needed people the most.

Then, only a couple of weeks later, one of my best friends, Lauren, lost her mother unexpectedly to a heart attack and stroke while also in the middle of facing challenging health troubles.

What was happening? As I had cried to my friends after losing Jaime and felt like no one truly was able to help or understand, she could suddenly now relate. I was now able to understand her grief as we both struggled to survive the hardest seasons of our lives, holding each other up, and trying

Doubtless

to navigate this strange world of loss simultaneously occurring during an unprecedented pandemic.

If I have seen God remain faithful throughout my entire life and write a better story out of my brokenness than what I thought could be possible, He will get me through this grief too.

That's the only thing that got me through—the knowledge that God has always been faithful and will be again. There were so many questions, hurts, thoughts, and emotions, yet I knew the truth that God is good, though I was not able to see it yet in this specific tragedy. I knew that eternity in heaven is better than life on earth, even though I could grasp what heaven is like, God gave me peace that Jamie was now healed, whole, and free. I know God didn't cause her death because God is not a mean God, but He is sovereign and allows things to happen for reasons we won't always understand.

Loss is painful and tragic. The Lord immediately began to use it to shake me. I decided to allow this tragedy to propel me into living a life that matters. I decided to run my race of life for Jaime and for others who lost their lives early. Life is fragile. It's filled with pain and brokenness. But the hope of God is everlasting. We can have hope and peace and joy in the middle of the storm, and the Lord walks us through it, sharpening us and refining us so that we come out stronger on the other side.

No pain has been wasted with my disability, and I know it will not be wasted from my sister's death either. Losing Jaime delivered me from fear that I had always lived with—fear of loss and fear of death. I'm not so afraid anymore. If my biggest fear came true, and I'm still living and doing okay, then I feel like I can do anything…

God, in this trial, I have to choose to trust You. That Your ways are higher and that You'll get me through this, too, even though it's the worst pain I've ever experienced. Use this part of my story to encourage others and bring healing to others who are walking through a loss. Show me how You turn brokenness into beauty. Breathe new life in my family again, Lord.

16

Trust Triumphs

When tragedy strikes, life can feel like a hard slap in the face, and it's a strange and sobering thing. I don't know how the loss of my sister plays into my story yet, and I hate that my life has now been forever altered. I never expected this, and I don't know what to do with it. Struggling with my ever-increasing physical pain and limitations, feeling stressed and worn out, and now facing this deep grief and heartbreak with hundreds of questions and thoughts for life and God, I was spiritually hurting too. What a roller coaster...

Help me, Lord. I'm numb. I'm exhausted. I can't do anything to change any of this. Life is beating me to the ground, and all I'm trying to do is keep moving...keep getting out, keep meeting with people, keep sitting at coffee shops, and keep showing up. That's all I can do.

During that time of grieving, I often wondered, Will I make it through this? I know it fades in time, but will I ever be actually free from this deep heartbreak? How will things really be okay when there will always be a void in the family and in my heart? How will I ever be free from this trauma that keeps replaying in my head from that terrible night?

And yet, through the grieving, I saw abundant love poured out from so many unexpected places. It made me realize how loved and cared for I am. My family and I were surrounded by cards, flowers, homemade gifts, deliveries, and meals. The day my parents drove to Asheville to get Jaime's things and see her body, new friends showed up at my house to spend time with me, pray for me, bring me food, and just be there during my cries. A ripple effect of blessing came from people I barely knew or had lost touch

Doubtless

with, and I saw how Jaime's life impacted so many people and how our family has been seen and known by so many over the years. It showed me tangibly that, even in our hardest moments, we are never alone. God sent people and brought comfort in our time of greatest need and support. I began to grow in trusting Him to get us through our biggest fears and in a situation I never imagined I'd be in.

Losing family has always been my biggest fear, and after losing Jaime, and still being able to keep going, I feel like fear has been broken off of me. When you face your biggest fear, and get through it, other things seem so small. I started to see other things I was worried about as nothing. Death shakes you in that way. I think when people get to a place where death isn't a fear, nothing else can shake them.

We can trust the fact that God gets us through things we cannot do on our own. He brings little blessings when we need them the most. I started to hear other people's stories of hurt and loss, and, though relating to loss wasn't anything I chose, it brought a whole new dimension of growth to me that I didn't expect.

I began to see life differently—as a gift to be cherished and appreciated since no one knows what tomorrow holds. We are only promised the moment we are in. It's a hard thing to think about, and is scary to comprehend, but is a bittersweet reality. Our time here is short, and nothing in this life is stable. All that is given to us is a gift from above, and God gives and takes away. We build our lives, work hard, get the degree, build a family, accumulate stuff, and go through so many things, and we can lose it all in a split second. What are we focused on or getting so worried about?

God clarified to me how the only things in this life that truly matter are how we love people and our relationships with Him. We can get so caught up in earthly things that truly do not matter and will not last. Life on this planet goes by in just a blink of an eye. This world is just a temporary home that we are passing through to get to our forever home in eternity. Losing Jaime made me press into God more because I didn't know what else to do. He was my only comfort and hope. I had to keep going, and I wanted to be able to find healing in this and overcome it instead of letting it break me down and destroy me.

Losing Jaime forever shifted my perspective on life. I have been awakened to how thankful I am for those around me while they are here and for living a life that matters. I have awakened to the fragility of life and the importance of living with momentum and productivity, using my days wisely to the best of my ability. Rather than waiting to do something, I rather act on things quickly. Losing my sister has propelled me forward to do what I can with the time I have been given. I hate that it can take losing someone to become more awakened to this way of living, but it's proof that God uses painful things to grow us.

What brings me comfort is knowing Jaime is safe and living her best life in her new glorified body. She is free from any hurts or pains and is waiting for us to join her in heaven. The first week after the tragedy, I asked for peace, for comfort, for a sign that she was with me somehow. I wanted to make sense of it all. And in a hot salt bath with a candle and worship music going, trying to find relief from tense, sore muscles and stress, I saw Jaime in my mind so clearly.

She was holding her soulmate of a dog, Jack, in her lap who had died a few months before she did. She was a shining bright light, with a huge beaming smile, reaching her hand down to me. I lifted my hand while worshiping, and felt my fingers tingle. Tears of joy ran down my face, and I felt like I was holding not only the hand of Jesus but Jaime's as well. I think it's true that heaven is closer than we think. It's just a door away, leading into the next room.

God has also been faithful to bring me and my family comfort through various dreams that have been given. The first came through an old friend in Illinois. Her husband had passed away the year before, and she had a dream of her husband, Rick, my dad's best friend in Naperville, and Jaime riding bikes in a field of sunflowers, laughing and having fun. My dad had a dream a few weeks later of our old house in Naperville, and he saw a car suddenly pull up in the driveway.

Out came Jaime as a small child, wearing her favorite polka dot pajamas, with a big smile on her face going up to hug my dad. He woke up feeling so good, wishing he could stay in that embrace and that moment forever. For my dad to see her as a little girl reminded me that God sees us all as children and that Scripture says in heaven we will all be young and our happiest, healthiest selves. I have to believe Jaime is currently her carefree, childlike self.

About a month or so later, my mom had a powerful dream as well. She saw a room where Lauren and Jaime were laughing and rolling around on the floor, goofing off like they often did, and my mom tried so hard to get them to pause for her to take a picture. Suddenly, the scene changed. Jesus, Himself stood in front of her, and told her "Everything is going to be okay." Then she woke up. These dreams were extremely comforting to me because they showed me that Jaime is safe with the Lord and that things are going to be okay.

A few months later, our family friend, Rosie, who is Lauren and Jaime's age, had a dream where she saw Jaime walking down a road. As Rosie was calling her name and trying to get her attention, Jaime stopped, turned around, and smiled at her. These dreams are significant and powerful, and I know that a major way that God speaks to people is through dreams. Though I haven't had many I remember or that makes sense, I remember the ones that my loved ones have had and believe that God has used them to really show His

Doubtless

comfort and faithfulness to us.

Jaime loved the snow, and a random burst of snow flurries graced the greater-Atlanta area the day after her memorial service, which is a rare occurrence here in the South. My dad even mentioned her love for snow in his speech, and the thick white blanket covering the whole world that next morning was a sweet little God-wink. My phone blew up with messages from friends who had come to the service saying, "Look! It's Jaime!"

A couple of days after her service, we received a letter in the mail. It was from one of Jaime's high school English teachers, whom she always said was her favorite teacher. It was a note sharing his condolences, along with a paper Jaime had written that he had held onto for years because of the writing quality. Jaime was very intelligent and a strong reader and writer. He felt led to send it to us. He had given Jaime an assignment to write about a meaningful life experience.

Jaime had written about a dream she had had of a snowy day, and how snow brought her to a different world of bliss, calming her and bringing her peace that she couldn't describe. In the dream, she also saw our grandfather, and how it was so special for it to snow because it reminded her of him. And now, shortly after the intense and rare Georgia snow burst following her service, the common theme of snow was clear. God was really speaking, and Jaime felt so present.

Since then, we have noticed so many other signs from God reminding us of Jaime, including red cardinals. My mom and sister started to see them fly across their path or sit outside our window almost every day. They say there is spiritual significance with red cardinals and a lost loved one. Whether that be a myth or whatnot, I like to believe it is God assuring us that Jaime is okay and that she is visiting us every day. We also started to notice the type of car she had owned, a little silver Honda Fit, often when we were out and about. I also started to see yellow butterflies nearly daily, no matter where I was.

Around that time, my good friend, Melissa, asked if I could paint a book cover of a vision she had had of her standing in a field of wallflowers, gazing at the sky, with a yellow butterfly in the sky. She told me that yellow butterflies were significant to her, reminding her of God's blessings.

For me to see butterflies was a rare phenomenon, but after painting her cover art and losing Jaime, I now see them fluttering all around me, often in the most random places. Other things happened that reminded us of Jaime: we would notice her dog's name written on signs, or her favorite things show up like Taylor Swift (who was her favorite) playing often. Heaven is closer than we realize, and I believe our loved ones are too. God is near to the brokenhearted, and I really felt that during this time.

I'll always remember Jaime saying to me that my disability was helping her in more ways than I could ever understand. While I always saw it as the worst thing about me, she saw it as the best gift to her and everyone around us. She was in a rough period for a few years, and, during a talk with my dad one night about a month before she passed, she mentioned how seeing me struggle with so much yet still have a lot of joy got her through her hardest days.

Jaime and I had drifted apart for a few years due to our different life stages. While I was in college and working in ministry in Athens, Georgia, she was living in Asheville, North Carolina, and was dealing with intense anxiety. I prayed for her for years to find a good group of friends and for her to grow in her faith and find stronger peace and joy, and I really believed she was getting closer to that until she was gone so unexpectedly.

She won't get to be a part of my life anymore in a physical capacity, but I am realizing she actually is very present, still. Though I cannot see her, I feel her. I never got to see the fruit of my prayers for her on this side of heaven, yet maybe through all of the things God was showing me, my prayers were answered for her in heaven now that she is living in glory, rather than dealing with the daily hardships of this earthly life...

I look back at years and years of family memories and clearly see that Jaime was always one of my biggest cheerleaders. She would dress me up, do my hair and makeup, and make me feel so special. She saw my disability as something that truly made me unique and stand out and said she always talked to her friends about me. She mentioned over the years how she really admired my commitment to church and God, and how strong it had made me. If I was getting down on myself about my looks or about my fears of not being liked by anyone, she would encourage me that things have always had their way of working out for me and that they would again.

Jaime was my best friend during the years when I felt especially hidden or unseen in the process of growing up as a young woman. I could reach out to her about girl things, from boys to style to common emotions that came up with friend issues or whatnot. It was always a mix of real talk and sarcasm or making plans for our next sleepover at her apartment.

Jaime got me, and she often felt like an older version of me. She would listen and give her witty, often blunt two cents that would crack me up and bring light to any situation. She would tell it like it was. I loved Jaime because her toughness was refreshing and straightforward, cutting to the chase and almost on the verge of brutal—in the best way. I've never known anyone like her.

She was bold and refreshing, hilarious and fun. I have a hard time finding words to describe Jaime. She was truly herself. She was majestic and looked like a supermodel with stunning beauty, makeup, and an upscale sense of style. Thinking of her reminds me of how much I miss having her around and having her as a part of my family.

Around the same time, I joined a new church, Restoration Church, based in Alpharetta, Georgia. I was suddenly surrounded by prayer warriors who were faith-filled, joyful, and mostly much older than me. It gave me life, got me out of myself, and helped my heart heal. During my second or third week there, a lady lost her husband. The reaction was for everyone to celebrate his life and celebrate the fact that he was now with the Lord, living in glory.

Celebrating his life rather than mourning his loss was a refreshing reaction and reminded me that "to die is gain" (Phil. 1:21). The lady was surrounded with love and support, and I felt like I was too, even though people hardly knew me yet. A timely message it was, and a reminder of the hope of eternity just when I needed it.

That same week at church, a friend of mine, Jan, and I ran into each other. She had been my group leader/team captain while serving at Passion City Church. She and I had always had a special connection, and she was like a spiritual mother who was always looking out for me. Seeing her now at this church showed me that she was going to be in my life for a much longer time. We started to get together over coffee once a week, reading the Word and talking about life. She has become my mentor and my accountability partner. It's been such a meaningful connection, and God brought us back together when I needed it most.

While still grieving the loss of my sister, God showed me that He is bigger than our pain and is present in our suffering. He showed me that He is worth trusting and gives us what we need in our hardest moments. His timing in who He connects us with is very strategic, and I have learned to always be aware of who is around me.

As these things were playing out, I felt a renewed desire to write my book. The desire was much stronger than I had ever felt before, and this time I knew I had to do it.

Now? How could I do it now? I am dealing with a whole new level of change and hurt in my life!

But this time I felt as if God was yelling at me to do it, and I knew how clear He was being about it. It was actually the perfect time to work on a large project because I had a lot of time on my hands quarantined at home. But with an unpredictable pandemic, the media chaos and political strife that surrounded the election, as well as the personal loss and changing social conditions around me, my mind and thoughts were all over the place, making focus seem impossible. I doubted I could take on such a project. God's timing is never what we expect, especially when He tells us to do something.

Sitting outside of a coffee shop with Lauren, my friend who had lost her mom two months after I lost Jaime, both of us feeling stuck and beaten down, I told her I knew God was telling me to seriously pursue writing my book again. It was the only thing that was clear at that time of grief and a global pandemic.

"But how will I find an editor and publisher? How does that even work? Am I crazy to try and pursue this?" I spoke my thoughts aloud.

Surprisingly, she gave me a grin, as if I had forgotten she was right in front of me.

"Hello, Alyssa! I edit books. I can be your editor!"

Wait, what? I just saw her as my friend, not a professional editor. She is only two years older than me, went to school with me, was in the same friend group, and I wasn't aware of the writing and editing experience she had, which was extensive, in addition to her bachelor's degree in journalism. But I put my trust in her, and she sent over a contract agreement for me to sign. Though I had no idea what I was doing, I chose to trust her. We came up with weekly assignments, and I was committed to following through this time, even in the middle of intense heaviness and discouragement.

So I went to a coffee shop every day just to get out and showed up with my journal and laptop the best I knew how, even while having no idea what was to come. Showing up to write took focus and discipline and fighting through many emotions that changed daily. I doubted I could do it, yet I wanted to follow what God was inspiring me to do, despite my fragile state. And, just like that, my book-writing adventure officially began.

As I started to get more involved in writing this book, I continued to doubt I could bring it to completion. How does one write a book without any previous experience? I had to decide to invest my time and energy fully in the writing process. I suddenly felt a new urgency to give myself to it rather than putting it on the sidelines for another two years. I knew for a fact that God was calling me to work on this book and create art instead of pursuing a job, and that seemed like a scary step (although I hadn't had many doors open for jobs in the past anyway).

I had to remind myself daily that He would provide for me and take care of it all whenever I started to feel insecure about where I was at. I even set up a GoFundMe to try and raise some money for publishing costs, not really sure if anyone would want to support a personal book project.

Give me the words to say, Lord. May this book be Your words and not my own. Use me as a vessel to bring encouragement to others. Help me have full confidence in my voice and my story and not doubt myself or my abilities. Show me that I'm doing the right thing, Lord.

Later in the evening after praying that, I received a Facebook message from one of the moms of the kids who have GAN. She said she wanted to cover the rest of the GoFundMe fundraising goal for my book and sent me a check for $1,500! She said she was excited and was looking forward to reading my perspective on life with a disability, specifically the same one as her son. She encouraged me to do it for those who cannot. I was in awe of her generous gesture and the immediate confirmation from the Lord that I was doing this for a greater purpose than myself.

At that moment, I think my mom also saw the importance of this

Doubtless

book and said, "You definitely have to do this now."

I raised over $2,000 on GoFundMe and other social media outlets as people shared the vision and heart for the book. People continued to ask how they could help. The generous support I received served as a sweet reminder of how God provides for us when we are obedient to His calling and faithful with what's in front of us!

During the next year, even in the midst of grief and still facing repercussions from the pandemic, God was so good to me in ways I cannot fully explain. I made many meaningful friendships during that time and had extremely special days at my couple of go-to coffee shops. As I became a regular, I befriended the baristas and connected with different people who gave me writing tips, art advice, and emotional support.

One of the other regulars who I often saw at the coffee shop kept sneakily picking up my tab, and I later found out that he was a retired NFL player, now using his time to bless and love others. We are now friends after some neat conversations over coffee and his constant willingness to help me. He even set up a perpetual tab for me at the coffee shop, and I have not paid for a single check ever since!

During the craziest months, along came new open doors and a new impetus to my greatest dreams. I started to finally gain momentum in my life as God breathed more life into my future and my calling. In intense grieving was also this new peace that I had found that surpassed my understanding, and I knew God was near. I felt His presence strongly in the months that followed, and my daily coffee shop attendance brought healing to my soul and birthed new ideas for my writing and future ministry endeavors. I finally committed to going to the coffee shop almost daily to work, even when I didn't have any words to express. I had to trust it would all come together, eventually.

My friend, Lauren, was such a Godsend in offering to be my editor. There was something special about us both being in a similar place of brokenness and loss. It felt as though we were both more in tune with God's leading and guidance as we felt we had hit our lowest points and were even more reliant on Him to get us through such a painful time. We were more sensitive to hearing His voice and were receiving divinely inspired ideas for writing.

A large part of Lauren's editing process is praying with and for the writer, prophesying over them, and encouraging and supporting them. When we talked on the phone and bounced ideas off of each other, we invited the Holy Spirit into the process, and He gave us many solutions when we were stuck. When she or I felt like we hit a wall, we would pray and wait until we got direction on what to write about. In time, the title and chapter names, and the development, framework, and structure of the book came together.

Then God would confirm we were on the right track by whatever was going on at the time in our lives or hearts, showing me that ideas or memories that were coming to us were what He wanted me to write about. The doubt related to my calling to write this book and pursue art and disability advocacy full time was beginning to flee as faith and hope filled my heart once again.

During that time, I knew there must have been a whole new grace to write because I now had even more to say, and I found myself journaling more as an emotional outlet. My journal pages consisted of written prayers, goals, and dreams, hurts, scribbles, and sketches. It was the only thing I could get myself to do during that time that didn't take effort or thought. I didn't know how I'd ever structure anything together that made sense beyond my personal journal, but as I opened the Word document I had started two years previously in Athens, the words started pouring out of me quickly.

I no longer experienced writer's block, nor a wall up in my mind, blocking me from my thoughts and ideas. There wasn't all the insecurity about what kind of writer I would be or how I'd ever be able to write a book. I honestly didn't care about all the details involved, as words were just flowing from my fingertips, in bits and pieces, like random patchwork scraps sewn together like a quilt.

Memories from growing up, old friends, family get-togethers, mean kids in school, the numerous doctors and hospital visits, the camp experiences—my whole life was coming together like a slideshow or a movie in my mind. Reflecting, remembering, and analyzing moments of my life were so therapeutic and healing, and this new year of hardship and tragedy was propelling me to write in a way I never had before.

When the world seemed to be pushing me down, keeping me drowning and suffocating in intense emotions of all kinds, it was as if words were being extracted from me like squeezing juice from a lemon. I was seeing past the hurts of being left out, being different, and feeling invisible for so many years in a different light. I was suddenly seeing my whole life as preparation for writing this book.

Things that I had never understood suddenly seemed to make sense as I wrote, and this inspiring sensation brought healing to my broken heart. The writing process began to purge me of the confusion about why certain situations in my life had played out the way they had and encouraged me as I wrote about event after event where I experienced doubt and fear that God delivered me from every single time.

Though I didn't know how all my words would come together into a story that made sense, the words were finally flowing and weren't stopping. I never envisioned loss to be what would awaken me to stop doubting what I felt God was calling me to do. Tragedy was motivating me to live with purpose and use my voice in a whole new way. Escalated pain had pushed me into what I was feeling could be a new calling, and I was choosing to put doubt and fear aside and trust God to get me through this book-writing process as He had

Doubtless

with countless other challenges I have faced throughout my life. Trust triumphed.

PART 2

As I sat down to write my book, I realized that the Lord had given me many keys, lessons, and reflections on life that could be encouraging to both able-bodied and disabled people, as well as those struggling mentally and emotionally. As words flowed out of me, I was able to see tangibly what He had taught me over the years of struggle that I had faced. I had gained a lot of wisdom that could potentially encourage those who are struggling physically, socially, or emotionally.

As someone living with a chronic condition, my desire grew to provide insight to able-bodied people about what life is like living with a physical disability. My heart to demonstrate God's power and faithfulness to help His children overcome doubt and fears related to their unique struggles was being fueled. If He could get me through countless things that seemed impossible, then I want to motivate others to believe He could do it for them as well.

The most common question for many remains, "Is God good if He allows bad things to happen to good people?" I hope to share my life journey as an example that, yes, He makes beauty out of brokenness and brings purpose out of pain.

Throughout my journey, doubt has been the largest blockage to true freedom. Whatever situations or opportunities were before me also came with doubt about myself and my abilities, and doubt about God's character and promises. But as I reflect on my last 26 years of life, I can wholeheartedly say, without a doubt in my mind, that God is better than I could have ever imagined and is a much better storyteller than I could have ever dreamed.

As my story continues, I hope to share some of the key lessons I've learned and the reflections I've gained throughout my journey, and I hope to bring various perspectives that have helped me keep going even when it's been hard. As we face various trials, putting our hope and trust in God's timing and plan is important, as He is always working when it doesn't seem like it. Instead of being filled with doubt, we can be at peace knowing that He is the one granting our hearts' desires and making our paths straight.

17

Wild Heart

Writing a book was never something I saw myself doing. I thought I'd be a full-time missionary, always on the go, doing something new and adventurous. But to sit down and write, how boring! How would that make an impact on the world? I never wanted a typical life but a life of impact, something rewarding and exciting.

I've always had a hard time focusing on one thing or being in one place for a long period of time. I'm a dreamer, always flitting back and forth between a multitude of thoughts, ideas, and desires, and it can be overwhelming and hard to focus. I'm bursting with a thirst for adventure and creativity. Maybe it's the artist in me, or maybe it's ADHD.

Ever since I was a little girl, along with my love for singing and dancing, I've had a burning desire to see the world. I still dream of the times growing up when my body was fully mobile and able to sprawl out in any direction and bend and move in any way or in multiple ways, all in an instant. It felt so natural to spin in a circle, hop up and down, jump over things, or move side-to-side, and feel the effects of gravity at play with various movements. My body did what I wanted it to do, and it was easy. I felt like I could take on the world and do anything without limits.

As a young child, I loved exploring and interacting with the world around me. I was always in my head, making up stories or making dead things come to life. There was always something to discover in my backyard or on the playground somewhere, at my best friend's house, or in the creek behind her house. I'd gather piles of sticks or rocks, leaves to kick or jump in, or

Doubtless

would sit and ponder life and who I would become.

I've always struggled with the thought of having an ordinary life or having a repetitive daily routine. I want adventure. I want new things and new places. I want to see beautiful views, feel the stimulation of all of my senses, and experience different aspects of nature and geography. I've always taken an avid interest in other parts of the world and other cultures. I have an insatiable interest in international things: people, foods, various art forms, and traditions. I want to actively participate in any and all things related to learning about other parts of the world.

Growing up, one of my best friends across the street, Maria, was from Colombia and didn't even speak English yet. She was four years old, and I was her first American friend. With her black hair and deep olive skin, she says she always remembers how watching me walk up to say hello and introduce myself with my bright, orange hair and pale white, freckly skin made her laugh hysterically because we were from such completely different backgrounds.

Her house felt like being in another country, with the bright, South American colors, the exotic smells from her nanny cooking authentic dishes in the kitchen, and her family's Colombian nick-nacks on display throughout the home. They had cactus plants, picture frames, colorful rugs, and cozy decor. During the holidays, they always adorned the home with the most festive decorations and celebrated with large gatherings and parties. The Nativity scene in their house involved multiple figurines and a beautiful display spread out on their table.

I always loved the way they celebrated family and life, and it was super exciting to see into their world. Having them as our good family friends gave me a taste of a different culture and part of the world for the first time, and I loved it. I believe that having them in my life has played a large role in my love for different cultures, considering I've had that fascination for as long as I can remember.

Years of being involved in church also opened the door to introducing me to diverse people in different situations through the various service projects I participated in. We made fleece blankets for kids with cancer, went to nursing homes to play piano and sing, put together boxes for Operation Christmas Child, went to homeless shelters in the city, put together goodie bags for single mothers, and wrote letters for soldiers, just to name a few. Through these experiences, I gained a deep interest in and love for different people groups and populations.

In mid-high school, I went on my first mission trip to Costa Rica. It wasn't exactly roughing it, as we stayed in a super nice hotel with amazing Costa Rican meals and a large bus that dropped us right where we needed to be each day. However, many parts of the city had pockets of harsh conditions, and the school we were working at that week was run down and felt dark and depressing. It was filled with children who were desperately in need of love because of bad home or family situations. We spent time playing with the kids, hugging them, holding them, and helping them feel safe. We also helped with improvements around the building like painting classrooms and helping to clean and organize.

That week reminded me of how blessed I am to have a loving family, be surrounded by nice things, and be provided for in the way I am. Even though loving on these kids seemed minor and easy, I saw many shy and timid children suddenly turn into outgoing, loving, sweet, and joyful balls of energy who didn't want us to ever leave. Loving those kids so deeply for a week when they rarely had that kind of love being shown to them made them come alive and connect to us deeply without them even understanding English. The language barrier, though awkward for a short moment, wasn't even an issue. The playing, embracing, and love that we shared were far more powerful than any words we could have expressed.

During our times off from working at the school, we went to the market, enjoyed times of worship and prayer by the hotel pool, helped with a partnering ministry there, and ended the week with zip-lining through the rainforest. This was extremely hard on me physically, as each base required one step up to get reattached to the line and be pushed off to the next one. Step, push, jump, repeat. But once I was hooked in, I felt like I was flying through the unending, rolling green hills and trees, all the way to the bottom of the mountain we started on. I'll never forget that day, though my sore and tired legs paid the price for the rest of the week. Still, it was definitely worth it!

I left that week feeling refreshed from the powerful encounters with kids, the help that my team was able to offer the school, and the community I gained from my team. We pressed into God, into worship, into transparent conversations and sharing of our hearts, all while in another country. I knew that this was what life was really about and what truly mattered—connection and culture. It was one of the best weeks of my life, as I got to really grow with a group of people who became my family for that short week.

That trip morphed into bigger dreams of being a missionary to various nations around the world. I knew getting involved in overseas missions would always be a desire of mine because I couldn't even begin to describe how special it all was. A major prayer of mine has always been "Lord send me; I'm ready." I have a heart for Africa, India, and Israel, and to meet people in small towns in other countries. I want to go to share the Gospel with groups in other parts of the world who have never heard about Jesus. I want to go backpacking through Italy, stopping in little towns and villages along the way. My spirit wants to go to the nations, to go on constant adventures, to explore nature and the beauty all around the world.

As my physical challenges have increased over the years, along has come heartache and fear that while others have the freedom of mobility to go

Doubtless

anywhere at any time, I'd be left behind. I'm a dancer and a runner at heart. To have a body that doesn't align with those desires feels like being a prisoner in my own body. If I were to choose, I'd be hiking up a mountain or biking trails along the river.

My constant need for chiropractic and physical therapy feels like my life is one long doctor's appointment. The way I walk throws my hips and back out of whack pretty easily, and pushing a walker around causes a lot of neck and shoulder pain and stiffness. I feel like I'm eighty years old as I hobble around with my walker and crooked body sway. Taking care of my health seems like a full-time job and definitely is not the kind of adventure I had dreamed I'd be living.

I've tried it all—different diets, holistic and naturopathic medicine, massage therapy, acupuncture, laser therapy, light therapy, different gym memberships, various exercise bands and equipment, infrared saunas, hot and cold packs to help circulation, different kinds of socks… It's been both a journey and a battle. Through it all, swimming and the sauna at the gym have remained my main focus and have kept my body mobile and stretched out. I have gained a high regard for healthy living. I'm more particular about what I put into my body and prioritize taking care of my physical health each day. If I don't eat well or exercise, I feel the effects immediately. This internal "alarm system" has benefitted me, as I know it has fostered a healthier lifestyle and a passion for wellness.

How do we navigate deep desires for adventure and dreams of traveling or doing various activities when we have limits? Do we let our limitations in life break our hearts or can our boundaries be a good thing? My heart screams, "Let's go!" while my body says, "Sit down." I don't want to miss out on life! I don't want to face this feeling of disappointment in my situation while looking at what others are doing. This disease isn't who I am, yet it often keeps me under a label and reality that I still have to live with and accept. It's a lot of work.

Despite it all, I continue to seek out mission organizations, nonprofits, and people of other cultures to build relationships with. I want to experience other parts of the world, even though I'm only in Georgia. During my time in Athens, with the diverse group of friends that I had and the super small and intimate church I went to each Sunday, I started to find gatherings taking place in different houses.

As I mentioned earlier, I gained several international friendships through a family from Bolivia who hosted gatherings once a week and opened their home to anyone and everyone, which led me to meet a mix of people from different walks of life. Fernando and his wife speak both Spanish and English, and many of our Bible Studies were translated and involved both languages intertwined. Going to their house felt like visiting my second home, and they often shared stories of their times in other countries over exotic snacks and assorted refreshments.

Through them, I met a lady who invited me over for some Spanish lessons, as she didn't speak any English and was moved by my desire to communicate more with her. We didn't get very far with our conversations, but it was fun to try!

I started to meet Messianic Jews, Jewish people who believe Jesus is the Messiah, at their house and at my church, and they introduced us to all of the Jewish feast days. I got to experience Sukkot (the Feast of Tabernacles) and Passover celebrations and learn the significance of the different traditions and dinner table elements and how they each point to Christ. These holy days were extremely powerful and special to celebrate. A couple of them involved candlelight dinners under the stars, with a bonfire and wine with friends.

A married couple from my church, Josh and Amanda, also frequently had people over for dinner, and we would break bread and take communion, indulge in a homemade meal, and end with sharing our hearts and praying for each other. Other times we would sit around a fire or on someone's quaint front porch in an artsy neighborhood, and a friend would play guitar and serenade us with soft worship music. Another lady from my church, Josh's mom, Deborah, would often host a lunch at her house after church each Sunday, and my roommates and other people would come and go, enjoy the variety of foods she had prepared, and hear testimonies of her time with DFACS or while serving in the community.

All of these people had numerous connections to people from other countries and a fascination for other cultures as well, so it gave me insight into many stories and many different types of people. These memories from Athens are all interwoven in my heart as unique and special relationships that brought adventure to my life and made my heart come alive. I learned so much in my four years of being in that small college town, and I realized that quiet, country areas hold a lot of rest and a lot of meaning. I miss the small and vintage feel, the rare people, and the meaningful gatherings that took place among other believers I knew. My faith grew more in that magical and quaint little town than in any other place I had ever been to.

As much as I want to be traveling frequently, I have also learned to love activities around me that are more accessible and available. I live for front porch-sitting over coffee or a fire, bonfires under dangling lights in various people's yards, and celebrating life. I long to do life with people in these small moments while sharing a meal or a cup of tea. These things fill my heart with love and joy. As I often long for adventure and easily feel stuck in a place of comparison with others' physical abilities, the Lord has been bringing contentment to my situation by satisfying my wild heart in ways I wouldn't have expected. Life is what we make it and can involve daily variety when we look for it or create it.

People are created for community and for love. We may travel the

Doubtless

world seeing many amazing things yet feel totally alone and less than able to enjoy them. God has grown my compassion for the people around me and has given me a heart that thirsts to know them and do life with them. Walking with Him makes life more exciting and adventurous, knowing He is everywhere and in everything. What I've learned through Jesus is that every day is an adventure. No day has to look exactly the same when we are in tune with the Holy Spirit living within us, always speaking and guiding us.

As I listen to the still, small voice in my head or get random nudges to go somewhere or to talk to someone, something cool always comes from it. I've learned that God has us where we are for a purpose, and He has so much in store along the paths we're on. As long as we follow the small leadings of the Lord, we will end up right where we are meant to be. When we walk with God, He will always open doors and bring special people into our lives. Life will have a dynamic flow.

Every time we choose to follow Him, we can always trust Him to satisfy the longings of our wild hearts in unique ways. Maybe it's not being in an exotic place that brings fulfillment, but the people who are around us, and the moments and memories celebrated and created. I don't allow my wild heart to be tucked away and ignored, but rather, my heart has grown, softened, and now beats for the littlest things that remind me I'm alive. I've grown to appreciate the little things, whereas previously I wasn't able to do so while longing for more extravagant attractions. I've grown accustomed to making do with what's available and being content within my limits.

Psalm 37:4 says, "Take delight in the Lord, and He will give you the desires of your heart." This verse is a good reminder that God not only fulfills the desires of our hearts, but He actually places those desires there in the first place. He created us, so He knows our hearts and how we are wired. I used to be afraid that my disability would hold me back and that I'd never see my desires fulfilled, but actually, God strategically places certain desires in us that He intends to fulfill for His glory because of His goodness!

My disability hasn't hindered the desires of my heart as I feared, but rather I've seen God fulfill many desires in ways I wouldn't have expected. I've realized that God actually created me to have a wild heart because He has a wild heart! He is the Creator of all the abundance around us! My wild heart is simply a heart that wants to experience life in abundance—to embrace and enjoy all colors, cultures, countries, and various tastes, smells, and experiences.

Looking back over the years, I've realized that nothing has stopped me, and I have done more than I could have ever imagined. I've been on two international mission trips to Hawaii, Puerto Rico, and on family vacations to multiple countries, including Italy, Ireland, England, St. Lucia, St. Thomas, Aruba, and St. Martin, as well as several South American locations. I have seen a lot of major tourist spots in the US, including the Grand Canyon, have gone kayaking and canoeing, zip-lining, camping, visited lake houses and taken boat rides, gone on a jungle safari through the rainforest, taken multiple road trips to conferences and live concerts, attended multiple art shows, and festivals.

    I can say my life has been extremely full and active, even though it has required more help and support. There has always been a way, and people to help! Beach trip? Yes, I'm in! Camping? Of course. Road trip? Take me! I'm always ready. When first learning about my diagnosis, I thought international travel wouldn't be possible, yet despite my disability, I have traveled to many amazing places and have done so many fun things. Even though traveling takes extra effort, God has made a way every single time!

    Though I'm not currently a full-time missionary or constantly traveling the world, going backpacking across mountainous Italy, or hiking the Appalachian Trail, I'm discovering special things and people right in front of me. God has always brought neat opportunities and people into my life—people from other countries to share a unique cultural experience, people from various backgrounds who I can serve or share a meal or a meaningful tradition with. I've had multiple opportunities to hear people's stories and share their feelings of suffering or rejoicing. I've continued to learn that there is always a need in my neighborhood and community, and have partnered with my local church in many service projects to help feed the homeless, love the lost and hurting, and connect with those in need.

    Even when I'm not on some wild trip, I have learned to see different aspects of the world in a different light, often in the neighborhood next to mine or in someone's living room. My eyes have been opened to the reality that being across the world probably wouldn't mean as much if I can't even love my neighbor down the street... where I can often experience different ethnic tastes and smells, refreshing my senses and bringing a novel experience to my day.

    My mom and I go to local art and music festivals almost every weekend in the months of nice weather, and connecting with artists and creatives is new and exciting, breathing life into my soul and bringing fun into my life. I love seeing people's various gifts and talents and the neat opportunities the creative arts have to offer. Finding creative ways to get involved and try new things quenches my thirst for spontaneity.

    Wherever the Lord leads me and through whatever doors He opens, along come new opportunities and relationships, along with fresh revelations of who God is and what He is like, and there is always more to learn, explore, and discover. Through all of these things, I've realized that God gave me my wild heart, exploding with dreams and desires, and is still granting my heart's desires, despite my impediments.

    The reality is that the majority of people are not constantly traveling the world, though that's a common dream and desire. Initially, it was easy for me to believe that every able-bodied person was going on extravagant and

Doubtless

dreamy adventures and trips all the time, in the fear that a disability would be a blockage to that ever being a possibility for me. Yet, God has proven me wrong and has made a way in the numerous times I thought something would be impossible.

So now, whether I'm planning a trip or just sitting at the coffee shop, my wild heart beats the same for new faces and new places. And whether I'm in Africa (one day) or in my neighbor's kitchen, God knows my heart and brings the adventure I long for even if it comes in a different form. He has created me to have wild dreams and desires, and I cannot wait to see how He will continue to satisfy them throughout my life. He is the one who makes a way when it looks like there is no way, and I'm open to His leading. He has changed my heart to see and experience things in a different way!

18

A New Kind of Adventure

In addition to faithfully fulfilling the desires for exotic experiences and adventures He placed in my wild heart, God has also transformed my perspective on what adventure can be. For many of us, the thought of an exciting life involves traveling often, taking glamorous photos of breathtaking views, planning spontaneous camping trips with friends to the mountains—doing things that seem impressive and dynamic. I wondered how I'd be able to live the life I wanted with physical limitations making things so much harder.

As soon as I feel like I'm ready to go, I take a few steps with my walker and feel like I'm going to fall down. My legs are like heavy weights that are misaligned and crooked, with collapsing arches and knees. I am out of breath when I get a quarter of the way to where others already are. Add a slight hill or crack in the sidewalk, a curb, or some double doors... Can't everything be one straight and level path?!

I've had to accept a different kind of experience and a new view of what adventure can be. Adventure for me has been less physical movement and more sitting, meeting people where they are at, hearing their stories, and sharing in both their suffering and rejoicing. Adventure has involved serving through various church projects and seeing different aspects of the world in a new light, often in the neighborhood next to mine or in someone's living room.

It has involved trying unfamiliar ethnic foods at parties or themed gatherings. It has involved going to art and music festivals and being around people who are creative and fun, enjoying their gifts and talents. Adventure

Doubtless

has involved following the Lord's leading and discovering more revelation of who He is and what He is like. My desire for adventure has been fulfilled within the unique relationships I have formed and what transpires within them.

These things were not what came to mind when I thought of adventure, but they have brought a shift to what fills my heart in ways I never imagined. But I think the biggest adventure of all is living life with a disability, as just navigating the world around me can feel like a rugged corn maze with loopholes thrown in along the way! That may sound dramatic, but it can take a lot of creativity when trying to make an inaccessible place accessible, making many situations one big puzzle and obstacle course. I often have to make my own path and my own experience. But I keep going the best I can, showing up even if I don't know what the place will be like or who will be there. I refuse to be limited or make excuses and continue to give things a try.

Physical limitation is not who I am, and I will not let it hold me back, even though getting around and being on the go is exhausting for me. A disability has ripped me out of my comfort zone and placed me on a path of constant obstacles yet with opportunities for new delights and discoveries. I have an increased awareness of and sensitivity to those on the outside, and my time in Athens also fueled that in many ways as I discovered secret treasures within the people I connected to.

My heart now explodes for people who work unseen behind the counter, and I am open to a different path, a new opportunity out of the ordinary or against the norm, or a hidden place the "accessible" path would take me. Having limits has made me press into who and what's around me in more depth rather than moving on quickly to the next thing. I have become more sensitive to the hidden people and things in life that often fill my longing for adventure in so many ways. It has made me a magnet for people who are different and opportunities that require digging to find.

Through the early years of feeling disappointed with my physical limitations, I realized adventure is all in our attitude. The only things that keep us from doing something exciting and fun are negativity and fear. I've learned to just say "yes" as often as I can, and the details seem to always fall into place. It may take some extra effort to figure things out or go a different way than everyone else, but I do what I'm able to. I have learned how to ask for help when needed and how people generally want to help others when given the opportunity.

It can seem crazy that often people are not aware of inaccessibility until someone who cannot get in shows up. It challenges others to make changes and to also be in tune with inclusivity. If a coffee shop or restaurant is inaccessible, it frustrates me for a moment, but also leads to others catering to me or serving me well.

It isn't always that simple though, and there have been numerous times I've gone out of my way to go somewhere and have had to leave because there were no ways to get in or to maneuver once inside. But I can't help myself. I want to stay on the go and keep taking chances because, otherwise, I will always wonder what it would have been like. I'd say seven out of ten times, I'm glad when I take a chance and go somewhere new, despite the possible negative outcomes.

When hanging out with a group of friends, I may need them to assemble my scooter or only spend time with them when sitting over meals, since I am unable to join in on outings like whitewater rafting or hiking, and that can definitely be disheartening. Yet, times over a dinner table or around a fire are where the real conversations happen. That is when I can connect to people's hearts and share life with them, and, to me, that is adventurous.

When friends are planning a beach trip, a sense of dread can fall over me as I think about the extra work it will be for me to come along.

Will the people going wait for me? Will they be willing to bring my scooter and walker in their car? Carry me down to the water when my walker doesn't push on the sand? Help me carry my extra shoes when I take off my leg braces to get on the sand but then also have a wheelchair ready to get me when I can't go anymore?

What about where we are staying? Is there an elevator? A bathroom close by? How much walking will there be to where we are going and can they drop me close by? What if everyone wants to go bike riding or hiking? Is there a nice place I can sit and watch where I'm still a part of the group while not making anyone else have to miss out?

I need the right people with me who are willing to go the extra mile. It's an exciting opportunity when friends who invite me to go on outdoor adventures are willing and ready to help me, or when a group decides to hike along a paved trail that I can scooter on instead of through the rugged woods as they usually would.

I've learned who my true friends are over the years, and they were certainly hard to find growing up. I often felt like a burden when the extra effort to get me around added to the grumbling of my companions. I am still slightly hurt when I find myself with a group of friends who talk about how much fun they had on their hike to the waterfall and the whitewater rafting day or camping trip they all went on that I wasn't invited to. I act happy for them and ask them about how it went with all the stories and details that follow, yet I often end up crying on my way home, wishing that I could have gone too.

The pain and disappointment from situations like these deeply affect me to this day, but I need to remind myself that God isn't holding back on me when it seems that way. It's not fair to me. I often get a deep urge to break free from this body and run as fast as I can. A lot of sitting can make me feel trapped. Thank goodness for swimming where I can somewhat move freely and feel like my legs can get stimulation. I look forward to sitting on my bed

Doubtless

at night where I can finally take my uncomfortable and suffocating leg braces off, yet, even then, I feel trapped because getting up at all brings sadness again as my feet drag and cause pain or knee strain as they collapse under my weight. I have to remind myself of what I have to be thankful for, which is so much. But my legs and feet feel detached from my body.

Any form of physical ailment or sickness is hard to live with. It can be a daily battle reminding myself of the good out-weighing the bad and the reality that every single person has something going on in some way, visible or not. Yet, a disability comes with its blessings too because, though I have some extra equipment to bring in the car, I have the VIP handicap sticker to park close to everywhere I need to go, and I'll always be able to skip the lines at Disney World.

Though I cannot keep up with a crowd and need to go at my own pace, I often get more personalized care and better service. Though I often need to sit down, I usually get first dibs on a comfy seat when others need to stand at a gathering or event.

Yes, I may need to sit out while others hike or play sports, but just give me a cup of coffee and some nice scenery, and I'm thankful to be there without any pressure to do anything besides rest and be present. Yes, I may miss the long bike ride on the beach with everyone, but I can be at the lunch table conversation and the late-night bonfire.

Life isn't all physical. Life is relational. It is the beauty in the small, everyday moments and investing in a community of people to do life with. Having a disability has made life a whole lot more exciting as the struggles I've faced have matured and challenged me and others around me.

Waiting for the elevator line while everyone takes the stairs has grown my patience. Using the ramp and wheelchair lift on buses or planes has led to a ton of funny stories and given me more reason to slow down in a fast-paced world. Going slow has made me more aware and appreciative of my surroundings. It has given me a heart of gratitude to be alive and breathing.

I've realized that everything changes when we shift our perspective from what we don't have to what we do, and what we can't do to what we can. What if our sufferings are opportunities and our pains for a greater purpose? What if what we see as our disadvantage is our greatest advantage? Maybe the things that mark us the most can be turned into our greatest gifts.

I cannot help move furniture or do any heavy lifting, so I can do the decorating. I cannot carry things, but it's given people the opportunity to wait on me or bring me what I need.

My disability has led to hundreds of transparent and real conversations while being forced to go a different way with one or two people, against the grain of the crowd. Disability has forced me to look at life and people through a different lens—one of empathy, patience, and understanding. It has helped me press into difficult experiences with others who may be hurting by sharing

A NEW KIND OF ADVENTURE

in their suffering or rejoicing with them in their victories as well. Disability hardships have enabled me to press into difficult conversations, providing grace and advice to others who are struggling. It's easy and natural for me to go deep with people, share super vulnerable stories, and help foster those conversations with others.

It's often a neat opportunity for connection when I am the one who stands out in a room or crowd because it immediately draws people's attention and focus (even though I don't always want it). I get it, people can be intimidated or unsure about me and my abilities. They don't know how to relate or respond. But I can invite them into it. I can openly engage with them joyfully, and they quickly do the same and feel welcomed into my life.

I think our differences can give us the keys to other people's hearts, and I am so thankful for numerous opportunities to go deep with people quickly. I personally hate small talk anyway and want to get right into people's hearts and lives, and this disability has opened doors for that to happen. Although I find myself in circumstances I have not chosen, I have blossomed from an insecure girl into a fearless, confident, and bold young woman.

My perspective on disability has shifted because, though my body is weak, my spirit has become strong. My broken heart has softened with compassion. I have slowed down to truly see the people around me. Years of feeling lost have led me to truly find myself and God. What I thought were walls or barriers to opportunities or adventures were God directing me in different ways and protecting me from things that He probably didn't have for me. When I wanted to be like everyone else, He set me apart. Physical limitations have led me to art and music, reading and journaling, a passion for health and wellness, and a love for the hurting.

Maybe if we saw limitations as opportunities, we would look at the world differently and see that adventure is all around us, in many forms. Maybe the things that we think are limiting us are indicators of our callings and invitations into a new kind of adventure that is actually better than what we think we're missing out on.

19

Walk It Out

Every day I wake up, I'm greeted by my crooked, heavy legs and collapsing, dragging feet. I wheel myself to the restroom, crawl on the floor to try to figure out what I'm going to wear for the day, and attempt to stretch my constantly stiff muscles that feel forever locked into the wrong position.

Getting my morning tea or coffee is a challenge in a wheelchair since my options are to either scald my legs trying to prop a steaming hot drink in between them to wheel over to the kitchen bar stool, or try to walk with my mug and hold on to the counter at the same time. Standing barefoot is also uncomfortable due to my weak ankles and floppy feet. If I stand to make a drink, I then put it on my wheelchair or walker to wheel it to where I'm going, hoping it doesn't spill as I navigate corners and spaces.

I try to take advantage of some time being barefoot and letting my feet breathe before having to put my braces on for the day, yet it makes everything more difficult. Getting things from the house to my car takes pushing my heavy cart of a walker, luging behind it, and tripping along the way.

My walker has become like a giant purse that I throw everything into and hang things on, and though that seems convenient, it's never easy to get places or navigate spaces with. It hardly folds up small enough to fit in friends' trunks, gets caught on things I walk past, and often gets hair and other strange debris caught in the wheels. It's always something.

My legs are heavy, and it takes everything in me to respond when my brain says to move. My hips and knees turn inward, while my flat and

Doubtless

collapsing ankles turn outward, making movement awkward. I try to go about my day at a normal pace while dragging my bottom half along, usually lunging or falling over in the process.

Keep going Alyssa, I try to motivate myself. You can do it. Just keep moving. Don't give up. You don't have a choice but to keep going.

It's a daily battle to push through the discouragement and exhaustion it takes to get everywhere. But I'm not a homebody. I want to stay involved and active. I want to live full and fulfilling days. I'm not a TV or movie watcher or a gamer. I want to be out and about and busy. So I have to keep moving and not let myself get down.

I don't think people realize the gift it is to be fully able-bodied. Taking steps leading to any place that doesn't have a rail, forget it. Narrow pathways, scenic trails in the woods, docks, hills, curbs, uneven surfaces, sand, gravel, rocks, potholes, branches, cobblestones, long distances… all give me major anxiety. Yet, these things make up the world around us and are rights of passage available to most without much forethought.

When people complain about things that I wish I could do, it can be hard to have empathy. Their bike tires are low, their skis have a dent, their running shoes are getting old, their dance class was canceled, their wrist is sore from playing too much tennis, or they can't go hiking for a week because their doctor said to rest. Yet, they get to do these activities all the time.

All that to say, physical mobility is definitely taken for granted, and, of course, it's understandable if you have never dealt with a disability before. A friend told me that before she knew me, the topic of accessibility never crossed her mind. Since becoming my friend, she's now more in tune with what a lot of people are unable to do for physical reasons. However, she lives with a lot of personal fear and anxiety, making physical activities exhausting and not enjoyable. Sometimes I wish we could trade places, until I realize how fearless, mentally strong, and willing to take chances this disability has made me, whereas many able-bodied people may not be so. Perspective.

Taking care of my health is a full-time job in itself, it seems. It's a never-ending battle when you have an "incurable progressive nerve disease." The fact that my disease is both incurable and progressive is pretty discouraging. Words spoken by doctors, therapists, and parents can be really damaging and often are not what we need to hear. The medical field is all about research, facts, and repeating prognoses to patients. Doctors' offices and hospitals often have a negative energy about them because of the number of people in fear, panic, or hopelessness because of bad news. I hate that part of having a rare and life-long disease because even when I feel like I'm doing okay, no positive results ever come from a diagnosis or a doctor's test.

Through it all, I keep going and doing. I keep showing up. I have to work hard to break free from negative words spoken over me throughout my life. Doctor's words can be like powerful curses that easily become labels and identities—if we let them. I have learned I must speak life over my life and circumstances, not death. Even when life-giving words are hard to believe and not what we see or feel to be true, the more we speak positively, the more of a reality these words become in our lives.

Though it is never easy, I try to say that I am strong, I am able, I am more than a conqueror through Christ, and though I feel weak, He has made me strong! For most of my life, I've had extremely high standards for myself that I could never meet, leading me to criticize and condemn myself. I would constantly contradict any positive thoughts with negativity, always doubting myself and my abilities. I believe this came from the early years of being set apart and feeling different from everyone around me, causing me to always compare myself with others.

I have been convicted about the power of my words and have tried to form a new habit of only speaking positive things about myself and my disability, if at all. If I have a negative thought about myself or my disability, I try to not say it out loud. I try to fully give myself to where I'm at and who's around me, choosing to be joyful and finding the good in everything. We can't live in a constant state of disappointment from the life we do not have. The only option is to enjoy the life we do have.

Joy can be found everywhere and in everything. The most special aspects of life with a disability are the amazing people I have met and the ease it has given me to be transparent and open. Being "disabled" has made me more well-rounded and down-to-earth. There is nothing like a life of trials to bring you to a place of dependence upon God and humility that teaches you to appreciate the little things that are often taken for granted. And the "little things" are most often the people around us that we look past.

Having a disability has prevented me from looking past anyone and forced me to look directly into people's feelings, experiences, and lives. The people I have connected with over the years have made it all worth it because of the perspectives and insights I've gained from hearing their stories. Gaining new relationships in my life has made walking out my daily struggles more manageable because I receive so many blessings from their presence. I've gained friends who are therapists, doctors, coaches, teachers, leaders, ministers, musicians, artists, and parents.

I have been surrounded by adults when people my age were doing things I couldn't relate to. The connections I have made have given me the strength I need to walk a different path than many. Meaningful relationships have made daily physical struggles seem small. I honestly believe that God gives us what we need to get through hard things. Many therapists, doctors, and teachers have spoken life and encouragement into my life and have seen gifts, talents, and character traits in me when I didn't see them in myself.

Conquering the day when limitations and discouragement seem to push against us takes going at your own pace and pressing into the people

Doubtless

around you. Even when I feel like I'm not doing as much as others, I remember that we are each on our own paths and that life is what you make it. I don't want to overlook the person next to me at a coffee shop, the lady behind the desk at a doctor's office, or the cashier at Target. Even if I'm struggling to get around that day, there are people around me all living their lives too. All people are more similar than different, and I try to make a conscious effort to connect with every person I encounter in my day-to-day life.

Whatever you do or don't accomplish each day should not be the focus; effort matters most. I try to celebrate every step that I take and remember that choosing to show up and keep moving takes courage and looks different for everyone. We should celebrate every little step that we take and enjoy every stage of the journey, even when it seems small. Taking small steps forces us to slow down and regain knowledge of what we are living for.

We are all in a spiritual battle in a world that is mostly not following God. It is a fight to stay strong and hopeful instead of feeling beaten down and worn out. Life is hard and there are a lot of things demanding our attention, people around us going through different things, and this constant pressure to make something of ourselves. We have to renew our minds and fill our thoughts with positivity and hope. We focus on the person we want to be, and who God says He is in our circumstances (and all the time).

When there are things you cannot do, focus on what you can do. I have learned that while we often try to juggle many things at once or be good at multiple things, less is more. We only have the capacity to do one or two things really well rather than numerous things efficiently. If we live by that, it helps us gain focus and clarity on what our strengths and giftings are, or where our niche is. When we try to do everything at once, it causes overwhelm and stress.

A good reminder and powerful promise that Jesus gives is, "Therefore do not worry about tomorrow, for tomorrow will worry about itself. Each day has enough trouble of its own" (Matt. 6:34). We all have our daily struggles and crosses to bear, whether they are physical, mental, or emotional. The only thing we can do is the next best thing that is right in front of us, one step at a time. I have often tended to get ahead of myself, focusing on the large picture and everything I want to do and trying to figure out how it's all going to connect and come together all at once.

Trying to plan out our whole lives in this way only causes extreme pressure and anxiety, which leads to making no progress at all. Living most of my life with this all-or-nothing mindset about things I pursue has only led me to be overly self-critical and discouraged. Living with daily physical hardship is a lot to deal with in itself, so I've tried to remember to walk it out the best I can, one day at a time.

20

Beautifully Broken

As much as I've wanted to be like other girls with tame hair and really nice makeup, skinny jeans and cute flats or heels, and an outfit that yells confidence, it's always seemed harder for me. I've always bought baggy, boot-cut jeans because those are the only types that can fit over my leg braces. My hair is insanely thick and curly and quickly turns into a massive, frizzy triangle without regular styling.

I wear big glasses. I bang into things when I move about, and, when I'm out, people need to part like the Red Sea just so I can get through. I'm no model—I'm different. And it isn't a good feeling.

Growing up and trying to figure out my new life with a disability was hard to accept and navigate when I could not be comfortable with the way I wobbled around. To this day, insecurity can still arise every time I get up to walk, as I quickly grab everyone's attention, even if just for a moment. I think that because beauty and fashion always seemed harder for me due to my disability, I resorted to what was easy and comfortable, rather than stylish.

I didn't bother wearing colorful bottoms or different styles of jeans and instead wore blue denim shorts with everything. I had a few go-to shirts that were pretty basic in solid colors along with a plain fuzzy jacket from Walmart or Kohls, in case it was cold. Nothing was ever wrong with my clothes, but fashion and trends were never things I tried to follow.

Years and years of trying to figure out how to manage my thick, frizzy wild curls took trying out many different hair products, usually only resulting in a big, curly ball of frizz due to product overload. I would end up wearing a

Doubtless

puffy bun or ponytail that my mom called 'the librarian bun.' The librarian bun would make my face look rounder and give my head a large spherical shape; I would put in a strict middle part and make sure my hair always covered my ears. So then why wear makeup anyway? Who was I trying to impress when I was so plain all the time? I'd maybe wear a little mascara, but I didn't bother getting all dolled up. I didn't care. Who would notice? I didn't dress like a slob by any means, but, even as I entered my teenage years and beyond, I dressed more like a child than a young woman.

When I'm surrounded by other girls in heels or who are athletic, I can feel less than and out of place. Even on days when I wear a cute outfit, do my hair and makeup, and feel pretty good, I might see myself walking in a mirror or catch a glimpse of my reflection in a window and be shocked at how bad it looks on the outside.

Is that really what people see? I wonder in horror.

Or on a hot sunny day when people go for walks or hikes, play sports, and dance around in the grass or by the river, I sit and watch. I have the bulky leg braces and gym shoes and the walker or scooter and sit on the sidelines wishing I could be fully involved and seen rather than the one left out who's plain and wholesome.

Does sitting down all the time make me boring to others? I've often wondered.

While groups of people dance around and move freely, laughing and goofing off like I used to, I stay in one place, wishing people saw into my heart and personality before they saw my outer appearance. In those moments I wish they could see my fun side and what I have to offer, all that I've achieved and accomplished in life, and how I am just like them. I feel that my obvious physical challenges really intimidate some people, causing them to avoid interacting with me or wanting to get to know me.

And then whenever I *do* try to get around, I trip or stumble often, my knees collapse inward, or my stiff muscles tense up and lock, causing me to lunge or trip as my walker gets way ahead of me. It's not cute.

When getting together with a group of girls, and the conversation turns to boys, dating, or marriage, I don't have much to contribute because I haven't been a desirable choice for a lot of guys my age. I think that dating with a disability is seen a lot less frequently. Though marriage is a desire for most people, I think girls who have an obvious physical disability can feel left out of the dating game as they watch girlfriends around them being pursued and engaging in carefree relationships.

What makes people feel beautiful? Do disabilities come to mind? Definitely not. Is that something that men are looking for? Probably not. It's a packaged deal and takes more consideration, patience, understanding, and work. But is it worth it? Absolutely. It is a constant adventure that never gets boring and leads to many fun stories—for those willing to take the time.

There was a guy friend I had during my time in ministry that I fell hard for. We were friends, neighbors, and also in many of the same ministry areas together. He had all the traits of a solid Christian guy: attractive, nice, caring, sweet, loved Jesus—the total package. We prayed together and shared our hearts and emotions—all the things you do within a ministry setting.

I should have known that he, like most guys should be, was just a nice guy and a friend, yet at the time, I thought it was more than that. It wasn't often that I shared my heart and had transparent conversations with guys, which can become a slippery slope when neither person is communicating clear emotional boundaries.

The confusion and hurt it brought consumed me for an entire year and a half. I realize now it wasn't wise for me to be vulnerable and share my whole life story when talking to someone of the opposite sex alone, and without clarifying our intentions for one another. His sweetness, listening well, and relating to the hard things I was going through, brought a connection that trapped me on a roller coaster of emotions and heartbreak. I wasn't used to a guy being nice to me or giving me any attention.

He would send encouraging text messages, stay at our house late while hanging out with me and my roommates, wave and smile at me at work, compliment me, and share how he thought I had strong faith, was a fighter, and was encouraging to many. Was he flirting?

I kept thinking, *Well, he obviously likes me, and just is nervous or being careful because we work together. Or maybe he is just going through a lot and doesn't want to burden me. Maybe he is afraid I don't like him back so doesn't want to say anything.* I made up excuses and stories in my head.

I was sure God was saying he was the one and that all the signs were aligning. Unfortunately, when the balloon of false hope popped, it dropped me into a pit of heartbreak that I couldn't escape. I was so driven by my feelings that what I was feeling appeared to be reality—I truly believed he was falling for me. My time in that emotional space led to confusion and distraction due to the mixed signals I thought he was giving. Yet, I was the one who usually started deep conversations because that's who I am and I wanted to get to know him.

Halfway through the year, I found out he was dating another girl on staff. She literally appeared perfect: always with sleek, blown-out hair and impressive makeup, expensive clothes, and accessories. She also coached sports and loved working out—a man's dream. I should have known this was the kind of girl he would be into since he was way out of my league.
But even now, I have to wonder... If I didn't have a disability, would my chances have been higher? Would I actually have been a consideration?

Honestly, maybe. He was a good friend, said I was "inspiring" and "strong," like many have told me—but not someone he'd date. The "nice Christian guy" trap... Wow, did I feel dumb. There have been other times in my

Doubtless

life when I thought I was liked by a guy in return, only to find his interests were different. People often see me as someone they look up to but not someone they necessarily want to pursue.

Can I not be the one who stands out so much for once? Can I not have to keep missing out on physical things that are so easy for everyone else?

I've had to master being content with who I am. I think beauty has many characteristics, far beyond what you see on a magazine cover or someone's Instagram page. To me, beauty is the strength I see in women who carry themselves well, despite the suffering they have endured.

Beauty is uniqueness and aspects of someone or something that are special or rare. Beauty is birthed when scars are embraced and weaknesses become strengths. Beauty is out of the ordinary and refreshing, with spunky attributes that inspire awe and wonder. Beauty is all around us in numerous forms, yet not many take the time to truly appreciate or recognize it. The world's standards of beauty can often seem impossible to attain, probably because it means having it all together all the time.

An article from the British Psychological Society shares a study from The Mental Health Foundation that "50 percent of 18-24-year-olds and 20 percent of all respondents said they worried about their body image after seeing images on social media. And, shockingly, one in eight British adults aged 18 and over stated that they had been so distressed about their body image they had experienced suicidal thoughts or feelings."

The article also discusses the negative influence of body image on mental health and how social media and culture constantly bombard us with images of what idealized bodies look like. For women, it is being slim, flawless, and youthful, while for men it's about being muscular and toned. Though these images are usually digitally altered, they influence the way we feel about ourselves and set an unattainable beauty standard that we spend our whole lives chasing and comparing ourselves to.

And then there is the advertising and media propaganda of what a luxurious life looks like: having the organized, beautiful space, having all the new and fancy stuff, the trendy outfit, the group pictures in a cool location, and the label that shows everything is great in life. The truth is that no one really has it all together, and often the media drives us to live constantly feeling unsatisfied and discontent with what we have and who we are. There are the people who appear to be perfect, who have the perfect space and the perfect romance, and who always look perfect... and then there's the rest of us whose lives seem generally harder the majority of the time. All of these elements combined can leave us feeling inferior and with no possibility of measuring up.

But when I show up at the table with the fact that, yes, things are hard and, yes, I don't have it all together, it allows people to be vulnerable and real about what they are going through. Even though things can look close to perfect on the outside, I've never met someone who actually has it all together, and it's a huge lie when society says we need to be. Standards of perfection are not realistic. Our imperfections should be openly shared and celebrated.

I've had to learn to laugh at myself and just bring my whole, goofy, and lopsided self everywhere I go. It's much easier than trying to fit into a trend, a mold, or an assumed way of being, and it's a lot more fun to be myself without pressure to be like anyone else. I think that over the years, developing confidence in myself has looked like just showing up and being real about what's going on and where I'm at.

Embracing my beauty looks like pushing past my insecurities about my disability and just going, doing, and living while not caring what others think. I get a lot of encouragement from others while just being present in a place and going to things. People also notice when I refuse to let my disability keep me in a defeated and hopeless place. They see my determination as strength.

People I hardly know often recognize me because I stand out so much. Even when we are totally unaware, people are always watching how we live our lives and are impacted more than we realize. I have discovered the blessing that comes with being different and standing out. It puts you in a clear view of others, and it is a major opportunity to bless them and to set the tone of any environment.

If people look my way when I'm passing by, what better time to start a conversation or shoot them a smile? A smile is powerful and makes people feel welcome to engage. We are all broken people and everyone has something going on, even when things appear to be perfect on the outside. Having this disability has given me access to people's lives who also have disabilities, and I'm honored to get to be a part of many people's stories.

Going through trials forms an inner strength in you that nothing else can. People who have had to overcome many obstacles have an authenticity to them that stands out, making them more relatable to a wider group of people. I want to live a life making an impact and using what I can to help others. I don't just want to stay hidden and stuck inside of my own thoughts and insecurities but want to use them to be a light to others. Jesus calls us to be the light in a dark world and to those who are hurting around us.

What better way to be a light than encouraging others while going through your own trial? How beautiful it is to see people lifting each other up, fighting for each other, and doing life together. We really are all more similar than we are different, despite ethnicity, background, ability level, or status. Life would be a lot more boring if everyone looked and acted the same or if everyone had it all together all of the time.

Recently, the Lord started to reveal the beauty He has bestowed upon me and who I am as a child of God. He did this through exposure on social media groups and other circles of people, highlighting my art and story. I had art for sale at a few places, as well as a few opportunities to share my story through pictures of projects I had completed. I entered an art competition and an exhibition, and I got to have coffee with a girl at a local radio station who wanted to hear about the book I was writing. I realized more and more how God was using my story for a greater purpose and wanted me to be confident in who I am. My perspective on beauty and my self-image began to shift, and I began to embrace who I am instead of hiding.

Before I began to pursue self-care and put effort into my personal appearance, I realized there was a deeper reason why I had failed to do those things before. I learned that, for a number of reasons, self-care requires extra effort for individuals with physical disabilities, especially due to mental health issues that can arise as a result.

Individuals with disabilities can be up to five times as likely to struggle with mental health problems, according to CDC research from 2018 that found "17.4 million (32.9%) adults with disabilities experienced frequent mental distress, defined as 14 or more reported mentally unhealthy days in the past 30 days. Frequent mental distress is associated with poor health behaviors, increased use of health services, mental disorders, chronic disease, and limitations in daily life."

To back this up, Paul D'Amore, a personal injury lawyer who deals with many forms of disabilities, found that individuals with physical disabilities are more prone to neglect their mental health because they are so focused on their physical hardships. Major barriers that lead to poor mental health in individuals with disabilities include physical stressors, communication hardships, a lack of social relationships, transportation hardships, attitudinal, programmatic, and policy issues (including discrimination and prejudice, a lack of accommodation or needed equipment, and a lack of understanding of healthcare issues).

These individuals are also more likely to struggle with isolation, unemployment, poverty, and health risks, along with the stigma that comes from the mental health industry that labels those who do not seek treatment as fragile, weak, sensitive, or crazy. "Individuals with physical disabilities already have deep-rooted fears of being rejected and identified only for their disabilities. Seeking treatment for their mental health as well as their physical health can be difficult to accept, especially when the assistance could come with another label," D'Amore's research finds. So not only is taking care of mental health much more difficult for those with disabilities because of internal struggles, but there are many other factors that make daily necessities unreachable or hard to obtain.

Because having a disability makes taking care of yourself harder, physical beauty maintenance is even more work. I'm thankful to be able to use my hands to style my hair and put on makeup, but it does require standing to an extent. Shopping, trying on clothes, and maintaining my closet require extra energy and effort. And that's only a fraction of the daily necessities required to care for my health and appearance. Those with disabilities, who have daily barriers in place already, can lack confidence in and motivation for their beauty, as it all adds to the stress of daily self-care.

Not surprisingly, there is a strong connection between one's physical appearance and their level of confidence. In "The Surprising and Significant History of Red Lipstick" for Real Simple magazine, author Hana Hong shares how putting on red lips has been socially significant for women, announcing their independence from social stratifications that may have limited them.

"The concept of wearing red lipstick has always been a major social signifier that carried with it a multitude of meanings. Depending on the location and century, the visual statement was...an indication of confidence," writes Hong.

Lipstick is a small yet evident example of the sense of empowerment that can come from wearing makeup. Even if not for the purpose of looking nice for others, doing it for yourself can be freeing and uplifting as well. Looking good and feeling good go hand-in-hand, and it honestly feels good to look good. Dress up for yourself, and see how that elevates your mental state and confidence. It is so important to take care of ourselves and not hide the beauty we all have. Though it's not easy for those with mental or physical disabilities, the smallest steps can make a huge difference.

My feelings of being hidden for so many years led to my not putting much effort into bettering my self-image, but now I want to embrace who I am and work with what I have to work with. I no longer want to feel hidden or invisible. God began to take me on a journey of transformation with my skincare routine, hair and makeup, beauty, and style. I started to realize that He cares about all of it and wants us to take care of ourselves, carry ourselves well, and feel beautiful in the way He created us.

When all these desires started to increase, along came timely connections. A lady in my mentorship class at church has a Mary Kay business and offered to have a facial and makeup party at her house for some of my friends and me, where I got a lot of free skincare and makeup products. Next, I befriended a girl around my age who is a photographer who offered to take free headshots for my art website. She connected me with a personal style coach who helps people discover their ideal body shape and colors to refine their wardrobe. After that, I met a girl from church who is a professional makeup artist and hired her to do my makeup for my book cover photoshoot. God provided so many incredible women to help me on my beauty journey!

Around that time, I got my hair cut and thinned for summer, which led me to start straightening or curling my hair more frequently, giving me more control over its thick tangles and frizz. Not only was I finally stepping into feeling confident in my own skin for once, but my physical appearance

Doubtless

was coming together at a time when I was developing my personal brand. For most of my life, I felt disqualified from being as physically beautiful as others due to my disability, but the Lord started to put it on my heart to embrace my beauty despite my differences.

A sweet blessing came when I met Katherine Wolf, former actress, model, and author of *Hope Heals*, *Suffer Strong*, and *Treasures in the Dark*. Her ministry, Hope Heals, was birthed after a stroke that almost took her life and paralyzed half of her body, including her face.

Her powerful journey of perseverance and fighting to regain her life has brought her a huge platform to speak at churches and conferences, on TV and radio interviews, host her own podcast, publish two books, start Hope Heals Camp for families experiencing disabilities, and opened Mend Coffee & Goods to create jobs for disabled individuals.

She is such a powerful example of using brokenness for good and using weakness as her biggest strength. The number of people she is reaching and touching is more than she could have ever imagined. Having her as a friend has been a gift and encouragement when I forget that disability can also be a blessing in so many ways.

As a former model and actress, Katherine is also passionate about redefining beauty. In an interview with Southern Living Magazine writer Betsy Cribb, she said, "When women are dealing with disabilities, there is almost this unspoken rule that engaging fashion and style would be something they no longer have the right to do. That couldn't be further from the truth!"

She continued, "I try to be thoughtful about fashion because it is about much more than the clothes we wear. Everything is about so much more than it appears to be on the surface, and I think our personal style has the potential to show people what's important to us. As a woman dealing with disabilities and as a mother, I feel very strongly about the importance of presenting myself to the world in a way that allows others to see the dignity, read the worthiness, and feel the empowerment." What an incredible inspiration for me to connect with during this significant time in my life!

She wrapped up her interview with the following powerful words: "True beauty is walking away—running away!—from feelings of shame about your appearance. It is having a deep comfort level with yourself and not wasting what God has given you. It's choosing to cherish the life that you have. As much as I may want my face not to be paralyzed, because that would be seen as more traditionally beautiful, well, that's not available. So I'm going to love the face I have and choose to celebrate and cherish it."

For most of my life, I did not want to be seen in my wheelchair or scooter because it felt embarrassing and ugly. In photos, I'd try to stand up with everyone else, cling to them for balance, and push my walker or scooter to the side so it was out of view. I wanted to look like I actually fit into the photo and blended well with everyone. If I had a crush on a guy, I'd try to walk more upright and as normal as possible so he didn't think badly of me. If people had only ever seen me with my walker, I dreaded one day showing up in my scooter because I thought they would be caught off guard and not treat me the same. I wanted to appear strong and healthy, rather than weak or in need.

In Katherine's second book, *Suffer Strong*, she places an emphasis on how disability places us in seats of honor. How even people who don't need physical wheelchairs still have 'invisible wheelchairs.' My wheelchair happens to be visible, but other people's 'wheelchairs' may be social, emotional, or mental struggles. Everyone struggles with different kinds of weaknesses, but everyone is still beautiful. We are all beautifully broken. Our differences make us who we are. Being different attracts people to you. It sets you on a different path where you gain new perspectives. It sets you up to be a leader able to make an impact. Being different leads to a full life worth living, one that opens new doors of opportunity and deep self-discovery.

Living life with a disability has changed my view of beauty, especially with the number of people I've met who have different forms and levels of disabilities. Their differences make them truly unique and fascinating. Disabilities give people a certain superpower—a fresh awareness of life and people, a stronger level of perseverance, and a deeper sense of character. They are more in tune with who's around them as well as what is going on personally. While many areas of life may be off-limits for those with limitations, they have to make do with what they do have and accommodate accordingly.

I honestly believe that when certain areas are hindered or with ailment, other parts of that person are elevated and strengthened. My legs and feet may be damaged, yet my hearing is hypersensitive. So much so that I used to jump at every little cough, sneeze, or door slam. I have found that to be true for others I have met with disabilities, that their strengths far outweigh any hindrances. Some of the most amazing paintings I've seen were done by artists who could only paint with their mouths, while some of the greatest piano players were blind or deaf. What a neat reminder that everyone has something to offer!

We all have physical traits we are insecure about. Living with an ailment that has made me very self-conscious has sensitized me to how many women probably feel disqualified from being beautiful for numerous reasons. We are all uniquely beautiful, and no disability can disqualify us from true beauty!

In the beginning, "God created mankind in His own image, in the image of God He created him; male and female He created them" (Gen. 1:27). Every human being is physically beautiful because we are all created by God with a special and unique purpose. He wants us to embrace our inner and outer beauty.

My life has changed as I've put more effort into my appearance

Doubtless

and care into how I present myself. Having a skincare routine and dressing according to the kind of person I want to be and where I'm going has given me more clarity about and confidence in who I am. Feeling good about myself has impacted my creativity and calling as an artist and writer because it's put me in tune with who God created me to be—a creative with unique gifts. It has also made me love myself more, which has deepened my relationship with God because when we love ourselves, we receive His love and can therefore love others more openly and easily.

By not loving ourselves and embracing who God made us to be, we grieve God's heart. He created each of us so intentionally and specifically, and He truly loves everything about us! We are all meant to be unique and walk our individual paths, not compare ourselves to others or try to be like everyone else. Owning who we are and embracing where we are, with our weaknesses and differences all out in the open, makes us authentically beautiful. Our differences are beautiful, and our brokenness makes us beautiful. We are all beautifully broken.

21

Mended

Before the Lord began to really grow my confidence, I felt and lived like an outcast, which created a stronghold of disappointment in my life. Despite the many blessings around me, my heart held hurt that lingered and that I couldn't explain to anyone. Negative mindsets were the lenses through which I viewed myself and most situations.

I've always been a joyful and positive person, but I also frequently expressed doubt about myself and my abilities, comparing myself to others' intelligence, attractiveness, or pursuits. I saw my artistic calling as a bad thing because I wasn't in the corporate world, wasn't working a 9-5 computer job, wasn't experienced with numbers or administrative tasks, or was able to do many physical things.

I was always quick to turn positivity into self-doubt and hurtful self-talk. Deep down I still doubted God would be faithful to fulfill the promises He has given me as He would for everyone else. There was a problem with my thinking that needed to be mended by the Lord.

I knew I loved art and creativity, writing and helping others, encouraging and empowering people, and being in relationships.

Stop dreaming Alyssa, get a real job, I'd tell myself, always thinking something was wrong with me for not being in an impressive career or bringing in a stable income. I floundered in my double-mindedness for years.

Pursuing art and creative passions with some guilt, going on coffee dates with people, and doing things I love to do but not finding expansion nor seeing much fruit, I constantly second-guessed myself.

Doubtless

I'm just not that smart. I'm so behind in life, far from being a real adult. I don't have any job skills. I should be financially independent by now. I know I can't be an artist or just socialize all the time. I need to grow up, learn skills, and work hard. What's wrong with me? People who are artists or writers for a living have a large following and are well-known and talented. That's not me.

The problem was clearly in my thinking, and it had become a powerful stronghold. This way of thinking had to change. I didn't know how long it would be before it would all come together for me somehow. I didn't realize that what I enjoyed doing could actually be my calling and would be impactful to others, nor did I trust that God, who created me as an artist and writer, would use me in that way.

Even as I write this book, there can still be a daily battle to believe in myself while fully expressing my passions and having faith that it will pay off. God led me one step at a time, reminding me along the way that He is supporting me and guiding me. After a couple of years, my heart gained more healing and my mind started to change. He connected me with like-minded people and with those who encouraged and cheered me on. He opened doors in the art world and breathed fresh grace into my writing in a way I had never experienced before.

As a result, over the last couple of years, I've felt a new level of thankfulness for past hurts and have been seeing the blessing of being set apart. Pressing into my art and writing has been a powerful outlet to share my story, have a voice, and express myself. God has used art and writing to bring healing to my heart and tune me into who I am and who I was created to be. My heart has been mended because I've discovered the higher purpose the adversities I have faced have had for my life and creativity.

Standing out and sloppy walking once brought self-hatred, but now they are things about me that I just laugh at. Once others get past the initial meeting me and seeing that I have a walker and leg braces, it isn't something they see anymore. Having a disability has taught me a lot of important lessons and made me emotionally and mentally strong through the constant battle. I feel that these strengths have truly compensated for my physical weakness.

In the Bible, there are numerous examples of people who went through much suffering which eventually brought spiritual, emotional, and mental healing. Joseph was sold into slavery by his brothers but then gained favor with the Egyptian government leaders and saved many nations. Moses was given away by his mother at birth, but later on led his people, the Israelites, into the Promised Land. Job lost everything he had, but the Lord blessed the latter days of his life because of his faithfulness to the Lord.

God uses and allows hardship for our good, to make us powerful and strengthened people. Everything that we go through can be used for a greater purpose and to bless us. I can honestly say that the blessings that come with suffering are worth it. Hardships and trials develop a wholeness and healing in us that nothing else can. Churches today often focus on a prosperity gospel message, proclaiming God gives you everything you want if you ask Him and trust Him and will not allow you to suffer.

If He gave us everything we wanted all the time, we wouldn't ever need to have faith or turn to Him at all. We would all be entitled and spoiled people filled with pride, unwilling to go through any hardships at all. This is clearly unrealistic, as Jesus promises, "In this world, you will have trouble. But take heart; I have overcome the world" (John 16:33). I thank God for the trials because they have developed deeper intimacy with Him and a constant reminder of the hopeful promise of eternity. Earth is only temporary, and we tend to get too comfortable here.

When a daily struggle is in place, causing limitations and discouragement, God is sometimes the only One to turn to. Eternity is something that is longed for more deeply. People and things come and go; jobs, hopes, dreams, money, and physical abilities are all things that can be lost in an instant. We cannot hold onto anything in this life too tightly because everyone goes through loss, change, and the unexpected. I've had to learn to hold onto things lightly and keep open hands when nothing is promised except for God Himself.

We are not promised tomorrow. We are not promised our family to always be there. It sucks to think about it, yet all we are promised is the moment we are in. So why get caught up in the worries of the future when we have no idea what will happen in the next five minutes? I have had to learn to be present in every moment and remember that God has always gotten me to each next step, naturally. I realize I didn't have to worry so much over the years and live in rejection and feelings of being less than, left out, behind, or hidden. He was guiding me the whole way. He had a specific plan and purpose for me, but its timing wasn't revealed to me. His timing is always different but makes sense in the end.

I can confidently say now that though my body may be broken, my soul is secure, and He has made me strong in my weakness. Many people that I know who are physically able to do whatever they want are also feeling mentally hurt and emotionally broken. I find that I can help them through those kinds of hardships. The grass is always greener on the outside of one's life, yet suffering comes in many forms.

Turning to God for comfort, help, and guidance gives Him a chance to change our hearts. God wants a relationship with us and has so many sweet gifts to give us. Knowing Him has changed the way I deal with hardships, live life, and cope with tough times. Spending time with God brings peace and comfort and refreshes and strengthens us. He fills the voids in our hearts and minds and is the provider of all things. In an unstable and ever-changing world that can toss us around and wear us down, God is always stable and

Doubtless

sovereign.

Dr. Caroline Leaf is a Christian neuroscientist who is spreading information about the power of our minds and the effects they have on our bodies. Her book, Switch on Your Brain, explores the importance of the mind-body connection and the amazing neuroplasticity of our brains through healthy mind management.

Dr. Leaf writes, "You have an extraordinary ability to determine, achieve, and maintain optimal levels of intelligence, mental health, peace, and happiness, as well as the prevention of disease in your body and mind. You can, through conscious effort, gain control of your thoughts and feelings, and in doing so, you can change the programming and chemistry of your brain."

In her book, she compares the brain map to a tree, and the neural pathways stemming from it are the leaves. The patterns and shapes are dictated by the thoughts we think, the ways we strengthen our memories and exercise our brains, and the things we focus on. Through our thought patterns and lifestyle habits, we strengthen neural connections in our brains, either positively or negatively. Negative thinking can cause numerous damaging effects on our bodies and lives, while positive thinking nourishes our brains, creating a flourishing neuron network for the brain to operate at its fullest potential. What we focus on grows.

Joyce Meyer, one of the world's leading practical Bible teachers, also discusses the importance of positive thinking in her TV and radio shows, devotionals, podcasts, sermons, and books. She teaches that our minds are a battlefield and our thoughts control our future. The mind is the hardest thing to control because our thoughts naturally stem from our circumstances, which often cause worry, fear, hurt, and insecurity. She encourages people to think purposefully because we can choose the things we focus on.

According to Solomon, "Death and life are in the power of the tongue, and those who love it will eat its fruits" (Prov. 18:21 ESV).

Hebrews 4:12 NJKV says, "For the word of God is living and powerful, and sharper than any two-edged sword, piercing even to the division of soul and spirit, and of joints and marrow, and is a discerner of the thoughts and intents of the heart." What we speak and think matters and our words hold a lot of power.

If I speak negatively or complain all the time, I feed on and release negative energy, leading to harmful thoughts and attitudes. Speaking life-giving and positive words releases life and attracts good things into our lives. For example, Proverbs 16:24 says, "Gracious words are a honeycomb, sweet to the soul and healing to the bones." It is difficult not to speak about how weak I may feel, but I have started to realize that what I verbalize physically affects my body. When I begin to speak lies or insecurities I am believing, they seem more real and become more established in my life.

The words we speak and the thoughts we focus on can either help us or hurt us. Forming a new habit of thinking takes a minimum of 63 days, according to Dr. Leaf. It takes commitment to break a bad habit and form a new one. It is difficult yet important that we renew our minds and think and speak truth over ourselves and our situations. Even in hardship, we have a choice of how we react and what we believe.

Joy and hope are both choices. When we choose to handle hardship with joy and choose a hopeful mindset, we can remain joyful regardless of our circumstances. The world is filled with struggles and disappointments that can get us down, yet God's Word remains true forever. Renewing our minds with truth brings healing to our hearts, minds, and bodies. Even in the waiting, we can choose to have a steady, healed, and peaceful mindset, making our circumstances or physical hardships much more bearable.

If we have something in our lives that we cannot change, we must focus on what we can change, which includes our attitudes and mindsets. We are in a spiritual battle in the midst of a fallen and broken world with many competing voices, opinions, distractions, and hardships. To stay strong in the Lord, we need to fight the battle in our minds and learn how to renew them daily with truth. God's word has power and authority and reminds us who and whose we are. Without doing so, we forget and get bogged down and discouraged by the pulls and pressures of the world, the constant need to fit in, or the tendency to strive for a certain way of life.

I have struggled with thinking negatively about myself and complaining about how things are frequently hard and tiring. I have a generally joyful and positive disposition, but I've always had a lens of doubt and hesitation toward situations or personal desires and dreams. I want to be more confident in my abilities but often need a friend's encouragement to fully believe in myself or take action to pursue my dreams. I used to spend time overthinking every decision and quickly shooting myself down with discouragement or criticism. My friends would call me out for speaking negatively, or point out the good in me when I couldn't see it in myself. It took years of being reminded of the power of my words before I fully understood this reality in my life.

For me, daily implementation of a positive and hopeful mindset often leads to my reaching out to friends for prayer and encouragement. Calling a friend when we are down or burdened is necessary because they speak life over us and remind us who we are when we lose sight of it. As the Word says, "iron sharpens iron" (Prov. 27:17 ESV), and we are called to strengthen each other. We are called to fight alongside others in all our battles. No one is meant to face the challenges of life on their own.

At times when I may start feeling discouraged or bummed out, I try to change up my routine and get outside or do something creative. Painting or drawing, sitting on a bench under a large tree, listening to worship music, and reading Scripture help soothe my mind and refocus me. God brings us peace when we seek Him and when we take time to rest and surrender all the stress

Doubtless

we are carrying. It's a battle as the world can seem filled with heavy burdens and busyness. When these things don't always bring immediate relief, it can boil down to sitting, breathing, and assuring myself I can keep going by speaking positive declarations: "I'm seen, I'm known, I'm loved, I'm strong, I'm able." Inhale. Exhale. Repeat.

It's true that our past brings us to where we are in the present. God uses everything, and all pain is for a purpose. You don't always see the reason for things in the middle of the trial, but just keep moving forward, and watch all of the pieces morph into something truly beautiful. Constraints on us aren't to keep something from us but are often to protect us and bring clarity to His presence. He keeps certain things from us for our good. All the years I thought I was missing out, God had put certain people in my path that wouldn't have been there otherwise. He was writing a bigger story and painting a canvas along with me as I was just taking steps, living life, and doing everything I could.

Years of being different have refined my character and created a deeper insight into situations and a positive attitude toward obstacles and limitations. Suffering forces you to have humility when things are taken away from you that are given freely to others, and humility brings needed dependence on God. I have become closer to Him because I've had to rely on Him for strength. He is my only hope. I feel like I know Him well after forming complete dependence on Him to provide what I need and the strength to keep going. As our minds get renewed, our hearts heal.

Looking back over the years I see the ways God has truly mended my heart by giving me a sound mind due to the trials and the hardships I've endured. When I've felt physically weak, He has strengthened me emotionally and spiritually. I'm not fazed by much anymore, and I really don't feel any anxiety or fear when it comes to trying new things or talking to strangers. I have done a lot by myself over the years, and therefore I have learned how to appreciate time alone, discover new places and people, and take chances on new things.

I frequently find myself giving tough love to my friends who are on the sensitive side or experiencing emotional turmoil. Many find me to be very calm, chill, and go-with-the-flow, with a "just do it" kind of attitude. I'm so thankful the Lord has forged mental and emotional strength within me to get me through the hard times of navigating a disability. Time doesn't slow down for anyone, so we might as well keep moving with it, making the most of every day and saying yes to the opportunities before us.

MENDED

Lord, thank You for the story You've been writing. You see the bigger picture and have used years of hardships to grow and mature me. You've grown my understanding, my patience, my perseverance, and my appreciation of the littlest things. Having physical limitations, though often frustrating, has developed my ability to be still, be present, and be aware of the life rushing around me.

A disability has made me learn how to go with the flow and be open to new possibilities. Though my body may be weak, You have made me strong. You transformed me from someone who was negative and filled with insecurity to someone who has no fear and doesn't care what people think. You have taken my broken heart and mended it into a heart that explodes with love for those who are hurting.

After years of wondering where You were and if You'd ever answer, I realize You have been right beside me all along. You had sweet secrets along the way. What I saw as barriers or walls were You directing my path to greater things of deeper meaning. When I begged You for my life to look like everyone else's, You were setting me apart for a destiny so much better than I could have asked for or imagined.

Because of physical limitations, I've become a writer, artist, an advocate, and a public speaker. Lord, You have mended my broken heart. You are so, so good. I love the person I have become.

22

Royal DNA

When we have renewed minds and mended hearts, we can truly receive all that God has for us and step fully into who He created us to be, and it is indeed glorious. In 1 Peter 2:9, the Apostle Peter writes, "You are a chosen people, a royal priesthood, a holy nation, God's special possession, that you may declare the praises of Him who called you out of darkness and into His wonderful light."

I think we would carry ourselves a lot differently if only we knew that we were created and called by God for greatness and to be part of His Kingdom family. Unfortunately, circumstances of life or the upbringing we received cause many of us to believe lies about ourselves that keep us from the reality of our identities in Christ, making us feel insignificant.

The Apostle Paul writes in 1 Corinthians 1:26, "Not many of you were wise by human standards; not many were influential; not many were of noble birth. But God chose the foolish things of the world to shame the wise; God chose the weak things of the world to shame the strong. God chose the lowly things of this world and the despised things—and the things that are not—to nullify the things that are, so that no one may boast before him." In other words, God chooses ordinary people to do extraordinary things.

As I reflect on these verses, I am reminded of the transformation story that takes place in the movie, *Princess Diaries*. The main character, Mia, is a bit of an outcast and not into fashion, trends, or beauty. When she meets her grandmother and finds out that she is a princess and from a royal family, she is in much disbelief and shock. She embarks on a journey to step into a

Doubtless

new life of elegance and confidence.

Upgrading her wild and tangled curly hair, frumpy style, and untouched face was a frustrating and tedious process, but her makeover wrought a drastic transformation. Her stepping into an unexpected royal seemed unnatural and undeserved, yet she morphed into a beautiful princess and became her true self. She came to see her true beauty and worth and embraced her new royal identity and lifestyle.

Cinderella is a similar story of a young girl who was born to a wealthy couple. After losing her mother at an early age, her father marries a wretched woman. As the story goes, her father passes away shortly afterward, and all of his wealth passes into the hands of her sinister stepmother, who begins to treat her like a servant, rather than her stepdaughter. Cinderella feels hidden and less than as she is mistreated by her evil stepsisters who live a life of luxury.

Cinderella meets her fairy godmother, who grants her wish for a better life. She is transformed into a beautiful princess who then finds her Prince Charming and lives happily ever after. Royalty was in her blood, and it is also in ours as Children of God!

These two stories resonate with me as I have felt stuck in a place of unchosen hiddenness and unworthiness, yet God has been transforming the way I see myself and setting me free, often in the most unexpected ways. In many ways, they also remind me of the Gospel story.

In essence, the Gospel is the good news that while we were yet sinners, God sent His one and only Son Jesus to die on the cross to take away the sins of the world and give eternal life to those who believe in Him. Jesus rose from the dead and conquered sin and death forever.

Through His death and resurrection, as stated in Galatians 2:20 (ESV), "I have been crucified with Christ; and it is no longer I who live, but Christ lives in me; and the life which I now live in the flesh I live by faith in the Son of God, who loved me and gave Himself up for me." The price He paid to give us life shows our value and worth in His eyes. His blood makes us royal, and through His death and resurrection, we are no longer dead in sin but are brand new creations in Christ. God sees us all as reborn, complete, and perfect. He calls us His beloved sons and daughters.

When we know our true identity and who we are in Christ, we can fully receive God's blessings and tap into Heaven's resources. In Kris Valloton's book *The Supernatural Ways of Royalty*, he says, "People of royalty focus on who they are called to be. They have forgiven those who have hurt them, they have rejected the lies of the enemy, and they have embraced the truth. They don't live in the bondage of prison but in the wholeness of the palace."

When we agree with what God says, it empowers us to live differently, in the truth that we are worthy, loved, created, and seen by God. When we focus on the person He created us to be, what we fix our thoughts on becomes our reality. If we always focus on what we don't want to become, we can miss God's call on our lives. When we focus on the things of God, when we dream His dreams, we become His masterpieces and the people we were created to be.

It is so easy to focus on feeling insecure or insignificant and let that be what defines us, limiting our vision for our lives. I think many young girls grow up envisioning fairytales where there's a princess and a sweet romance, where the woman truly captivates hearts and is irresistible.

Though that fairytale hasn't been my reality on the outside, I've learned through intimacy with Jesus and knowing His heart for all of His children, that He sees me as a princess. He sees all of us as beautifully and wonderfully made (Ps. 139:14) and without any flaws (Song of Sol. 4:7). As I have gotten to know Him over the years, my heart and mind have been continuously transforming. I have a different revelation of God's goodness and faithfulness, and it has changed the way I live and see myself.

For those who believe in Jesus, we have an inheritance in heaven and are heirs with Christ (1 Pet. 1:3-5). Knowing that I was bought and paid for with a high price changes the way I see my worth. Rather than living in insecurity and feelings of rejection, insignificance, and invisibility, I know now that I am fully seen, known, and loved by my Father in heaven.

Over the years I have realized that nothing we do can change His love for us. Early on in my relationship with God, I tried to perform at a high standard and was often striving to earn His blessings, attention, and the healing that I longed for. I took it upon myself to try and be sufficient in God's eyes, and to prove to Him that I was working hard. Yet, the Gospel says that nothing we do or don't do changes His love for us, nor who we are in His eyes. We cannot strive for what we have already received.

I felt like I was doing most things right and kept believing for healing and blessings, and for my prayers to be answered in my timing. I felt rejected and unseen by God when He didn't do those things and blamed myself for not being good enough or not doing enough. It's a dangerous trap that is so easy to fall into. When I stopped striving, started resting more, and just focused on the tasks before me that I felt God was calling me to, things started naturally falling into place. God brought the blessings, the right people, and perfect open doors at the best times and in His way, and I did not have to do anything except just be.

Working in full-time ministry for two years gave me a special opportunity to saturate myself in these truths and share what I learned about finding identity in Christ. During this time, I mentored six girls weekly in their spiritual journeys and struggles in navigating college life. Many of them dealt with stress regarding their performance in various areas of life: getting good grades, spending time with God, keeping peace in the daily hardships of college, and figuring out what they wanted to do in life.

Doubtless

    I had the opportunity to directly speak into their lives with truth and encouragement and remind them that they didn't need to feel guilty or critical of themselves when they failed to do things perfectly. When they felt all over the place, worried about their unknown futures, and what they had to do to get the grade, major, or job they were hoping for, I reminded them there was no need to worry. God has the perfect plan for all of us, and we just have to rest in the fact that He will work it all out and provide for our every need. I took what I had learned about finding identity in Christ and reminded them who they are and how much God loves them. When most of them dealt with similar feelings of striving and perfectionism, I reminded them that God's grace and strength are sufficient.

    When we get the revelation of who we are as chosen children of God, we can live with our heads held high and confident that we were made on purpose, for a purpose. What would it look like to live like royalty? It would look like living as though we are created by God to be fully who we are and not like anyone else. It would look like knowing our gifts, talents, and dreams are given to us for a purpose—to give God glory and advance His Kingdom on earth. Nothing is by accident, but all things have a specific purpose. In the world, we may feel like we don't measure up or that God is holding out on us and blessing everyone else. This comparison is a trap and a lie.

    I often feel like I struggle more than most people my age who don't deal with physical hardships, but I know they have their battles in different forms. Though I often wish life was easier, I wouldn't trade any of it because of how it's grown and strengthened my character and has developed my relationship with Christ due to my essential dependence on Him. When we fully depend on God to get us through, we see Him truly provide and show His faithfulness to us. Being a believer sets us apart and brings favor, access, and to influence the lives of others in a positive way. God calls us to be set apart, in the world but not of it.

    Personally, my sense of identity has gone from being a chronic worrier living in a lot of doubt to someone who trusts God in the unknown. When I worried about how this disease would progress, I learned to trust God because He is my Father and has always given me what I needed and more. Trusting Him has given me more boldness and confidence to take risks. I always see amazing things come from the chances I take, and I believe God honors the steps we take in faith.

    I enjoy living outside of my comfort zone because the most special and rewarding opportunities emerge. He has given me His heart of compassion for the world. The way God has demonstrated kindness and favor to me has made it easy to naturally extend kindness and love to others. God has honestly transformed me from a hidden, insecure, and heartbroken lost soul to a confident, trusting, and beloved daughter of God who gladly receives His grace, favor, and guidance. This is how royalty lives—with an assurance that they are taken care of and a knowing of who they are. And not just a knowing—but confidence that they are truly seen and loved and an awareness that they matter.

Being in tune with His goodness and nearness has allowed me to receive the daily blessings and love He pours out on me. The Lord has shown me His love in unexpected ways, through my mom when she has bought me specific items that were on my heart at just the right time or when my dad took me to Indian Princesses or father-daughter-dances together when I was young, and he would make me feel like the most special girl in the world.

He has also demonstrated His love through the people He has placed in my life—the small group leaders, teachers, doctors, and therapists, the church families who pray for me and with me, and the ways He places me on others' hearts when I'm feeling down or discouraged. It often comes in the form of someone sending me an encouraging text message or someone buying one of my paintings when I feel like I lack skill or ability.

I'll never forget the time I was sitting at a Starbucks with my mentor friend Karen in middle school, eager to embark on my first mission trip to Costa Rica yet nervous about how I'd get funding for the trip. Suddenly, the cashier came over and handed me a little bag that was from someone anonymous. Inside was a note and a check for $100 "for Costa Rica" written on it. Someone nearby must have heard us talking about my concerns and wanted to bless me. It was a God wink that touched us both, bringing tears to my friend's eyes as she encouraged and rejoiced with me about how God loves me and has everything taken care of.

Little God winks have come over the years in the form of encouraging notes or gifts from people, like free coffee provided by someone sitting next to me at the bookstore or people at the gym pointing out how I motivate them to stay strong and keep moving forward even if it's hard. I can get down on myself for my funky, stumbling walk, yet in those moments people often call it out as my strength and gift to others around me.

A couple of years ago, I had the honor of being my friend Emily's maid of honor. The wedding day was a special time of being treated like royalty while getting our hair and makeup done, having snacks and coffee, and celebrating with music and girl time. It was easy to receive the royal treatment that day because it was such an honor to participate in a wedding. Rather than use my walker to walk down the aisle, I had a guy on each side of me for support. I felt loved and taken care of, especially after receiving an amazing makeover. I felt truly seen and beautiful that day, and will always cherish the way I got to be a part of my best friend's special day!

I think we can live more of a royal lifestyle when we know God places us in that seat of honor. The Bible starts and ends with a wedding because God loves celebration, and we are the Bride of Christ. When I think of royalty I think of glamour and elegance, propriety and prominence, beauty and grace,

Doubtless

joy and confidence.

Life before Christ looked like striving and heaviness, finding my worth in my accomplishments and performance, and living with the darkness of my sin or shame any time I messed up or didn't measure up. Yet, when we invite God into our lives and receive all that He died for us to receive, we are set free from our old selves, and He bestows these traits of royalty on us.

Following Christ and welcoming Him into my heart has changed the way I live daily and the way I receive love. I see life as a celebration and see His daily blessings in unexpected and surprising places, as He calls me a princess and provides my needs every time I feel lost or alone. We are royalty in His eyes.

23

New Authority

When we understand our royal identity through Christ, we are empowered to walk in the authority Jesus has given us. Finding the revelation of Christ's love for us comes from abiding in Him, spending time with Him, and discovering who He says we are because of who He is. When we understand our identity as beloved children of God, saved by grace through faith in Christ and not by our works (Eph. 2:8-9), we realize that His love is not contingent on our performance.

Nothing can change the amount of love He has for us. Even when we are far from Him or living a broken lifestyle, He loves us the same but waits for us to repent and return to Him. When we realize God is love, it should give us confidence that He is always waiting for us with open arms, ready to connect with us when we turn to Him and provide us with the good and perfect gifts we need to live an abundant life. God made us for a relationship with Him and wants to do life with us.

The truth is "While we were still sinners, Christ died for us" (Rom. 5:8) so that we can walk in freedom. Jesus says "Abide in my love…I am the vine; you are the branches. If you remain in Me and I in you, you will bear much fruit; apart from Me you can do nothing" (John 15:9, 5).

Therefore, everything we do stems from Him, the source of our lives. When we aren't connected to Him, attempting to do things in our own strength leads us to strive to earn the approval that He has already freely given us. We end up feeling discouraged and lost.

Yet, staying in relationship with the Father and Holy Spirit is a battle

Doubtless

as we live in a fallen world. We have an enemy, Satan, who showed up in Genesis, the first book of the Bible, as a serpent in the garden of Eden to tempt Eve to eat fruit from the forbidden Tree of the Knowledge of Good and Evil. That is when sin entered the world and all of humanity was doomed to mortality. Jesus said, "The thief comes only to steal and kill and destroy. I came that they may have life and have it abundantly" (John 10:10 ESV).

Scripture warns us to "Be alert and of sober mind. Your enemy the devil prowls around like a roaring lion looking for someone to devour" (1 Pet. 5:8). Satan was once an angel named Lucifer, who was cast out of heaven because he became filled with pride and rebelled against God (Luke 10:18). Though God has complete authority, Satan is still always trying to twist and destroy anything that God creates. He is sneaky in the ways he tricks, deceives, and distracts us through common things of the world. Satan hates God and hates us as God's children because we are loved and are uniquely created by our heavenly Father.

In 2 Corinthians 4:4 (NLT), Paul says "Satan, who is the god of this world, has blinded the minds of those who don't believe. They are unable to see the glorious light of the Good News. They don't understand this message about the glory of Christ, who is the exact likeness of God."

The whole world is engaged in a spiritual battle of good versus evil until Jesus returns and makes all things new. We all fall short of the glory of God through sin, and the evil one uses this against us to keep us in a place of guilt, shame, insecurity, lack of self-worth, fear, doubt, and lies about God's true character and who we are created to be. It becomes difficult to believe what God says about us when we live surrounded by distractions, fearing an unknown future, and doubting God's goodness in a fallen world.

The good news is that Jesus has authority over darkness and evil! And because of Jesus's death on the cross, God has given us His authority over all darkness. He died so that we can be restored to our original purpose and bring Him glory. Yet, many of God's people do not live in the fullness of all that Jesus died for because they don't have a true sense of their identities and destinies in Him. We cannot have the revelation of the power and authority we carry if we aren't connected to Jesus—the Vine, the source of our lives and giver of all things.

Sickness, disease, death, and all the other difficult things we deal with were never God's original intention for us. The tragedies and losses in life, poverty, sickness, relational issues, hurts, and pains are not God's doing but Satan's, or the result of human sin. God may allow the enemy to test or attack us in certain ways, but He will always use what the enemy intended for evil to work all things for the good of those who love Him (Rom. 8:28).

The *Oxford English Dictionary* defines authority as "the power or right to give orders, make decisions, and enforce obedience." We can see a glimpse of Jesus operating in His full authority in the story of the Roman centurion in Matthew 8:5-13. A centurion approaches Jesus concerned about his servant who is sick, asking for His help.

"I will come and heal him," Jesus says.

But the centurion replies, "Lord, I do not deserve to have you come under my roof. But just say the word, and my servant will be healed. For I myself am a man under authority, with soldiers under me. I tell this one, 'Go,' and he goes; and that one, 'Come,' and he comes. I say to my servant, 'Do this,' and he does it."

Jesus is amazed at his faith and sends him along his way, granting his servant complete healing because of his faith. This story is an example that we don't need Jesus to be physically present in human form to perform miracles. Believers have authority from Jesus and power from the Holy Spirit to cast out demons, heal the sick, and experience supernatural protection. (Mark 16:17-18). Jesus promised that believers would do the works He did, and even greater ones, to the Father's glory, because He was going back to the Father (John 14:12, 13).

Jesus performed countless miracles, including curing a man of leprosy (Mark 1:40-45), healing a paralytic who lived lying on a mat (Matt. 9:1-8), curing a woman with an issue of blood (Luke 8:43-48), opening the eyes of two blind men (Matt. 9:27-31), restoring a man with a withered hand (Matt. 12:10-13), curing a deaf and mute man (Mark 7:31-37), raising multiple people from the dead (Matt. 9:18-26 and Luke 7:11-18), and delivering afflicted people from demonic spirits causing sickness and insanity ((Mark 1:23-28), to name a few.

Jesus also turned water into wine (John 2:1-11), multiplied food to feed five thousand (Matt. 14:15-21), and calmed a raging storm (Matt. 8:23-27). Miracles are what He does! Because Christ died in our place to give us life, He is victorious over all darkness. In Luke 10:19, Jesus says, "I have given you authority to trample on snakes and scorpions and to overcome all the power of the enemy; nothing will harm you." He has authority over sickness and disease, over sin and death, guilt and shame, and everything else that we experience. Therefore we do not have to live with any of these things.

Authority is having the power to bring spiritual order and alignment into that which is in disorder or out of alignment with God's will and His Word. For many years, I lived with a victim mentality and a mindset of disappointment, fear, and worry. I didn't know what true freedom through Christ looked like or that it was available to every believer. I was anxiety-ridden and weak, and I could not overcome my fears on my own. Nevertheless, I kept showing up and kept moving forward, even though I felt wounded and hurt deep down.

I began to experience victory when I had a true revelation of what Christ died for. God sent His son Jesus to die on a cross for the sins of the world, and resurrected Him three days later, demonstrating His power over all darkness and even death itself. Through Jesus, we have received forgiveness from our sins, everlasting life, and new authority to live an overcoming life.

The areas of sin and weakness we overcome, become areas we gain authority in. I have seen many who have experienced extreme anxiety or depression effectively help others dealing with these issues because they have gained specific strategies and grace to minister to others in those specific areas. They can speak directly into certain situations because they are more familiar with them.

My heart's desire is for my story to bring encouragement to anyone struggling with a disability or feeling like an outcast. Because rejection has been a common theme in my life, I'm sensitive to others who may also feel that way. Walking through certain trials can bring you to a deeper level of freedom that you can then use to set others free.

Frequent testing of my faith has made me even more sure of my faith in God because I've had to learn to trust Him. He doesn't take us through the fire without leading us out of it. Living life with a crippling nerve disease has formed in me a passion to see others healed and whole. I feel led to pray for a healing miracle when I see sickness or disease around me, and it's so exciting to see people receive their healing. Though I'm still believing and waiting for my own miracle, I won't let that stop me from helping and encouraging others. I know God made me to be a healer because it's a promise in His Word and because I've experienced it firsthand.

During my time in ministry, everyone around me believed God would heal me. It was an environment where people frequently prayed for various needs and conditions. We all wanted to see miracles and moves of God, and that happened frequently. Despite the personal burnout from believing for my miracle and seeing nothing happen, others around me saw my persistent faith. I offered to pray for people with headaches, stomach pain, hurt legs—you name it. I saw God using me to pray for others and encourage them to believe in the Lord's miraculous healing.

The Word says that God's perfect love casts out all fear (1 John 4:18 ESV) and that He "has not given us a spirit of fear, but of power and of love and of a sound mind" (2 Tim. 1:7 NKJV). This is a good reminder for all of us when we feel fear rising up because God says that fear is a lying spirit and not from Him. We have nothing to fear! Exercising Christ's authority has made me more aware of the fears that I face and emboldened me to command them to go.

The Word says, "Whatever you bind on earth shall be bound in heaven, and whatever you loose on earth shall be loosed in heaven" (Matt. 18:18 ESV). If I am feeling heaviness, anxiety, or fear in a room or atmosphere I'm in, I use my authority in Christ to bind dark forces and loose—or release—light, life, and healing through the power of the Holy Spirit and His angels. We walk in and live with so much stress, anxiety, and fear that we could effectively banish if we understood our authority in Christ!

He is the one who fights our battles, protects and guides us, and opens the right doors at the right time. We just have to walk with Him and trust that His ways are higher. I've continued to learn God's will for all of us is to walk in confidence in who we are and in authority over anything that seeks to afflict us.

When we experience a struggle, weakness, or disability in our life that is a hindrance or that puts us in a minority, what if that became our greatest opportunity and blessing? Hard times grow and mature us, and God promises to never leave us nor forsake us (Heb. 13:5). If I didn't go through all that I've gone through, who knows who or where I'd be today? I'm so thankful for all that I've been through and how it has grown my faith and intimacy with Jesus.

He was often the one stable thing in my life when people and things came and went. He was always there. He created us and knows our every desire and thought. He gave us everything we have. He gives and takes away. He is sovereign over all things in the universe, and everything we own belongs to Him.

In 1 John 14:12-14, Jesus says "Very truly I tell you, whoever believes in me will do the works I have been doing, and they will do even greater things than these because I am going to the Father. And I will do whatever you ask in my name, so that the Father may be glorified in the Son. You may ask me for anything in my name, and I will do it."

One week at my church, a guest speaker came who had a strong prophetic gifting. The Lord told him the night before that He wanted him to give a word to a girl with a blue shirt and black shorts. He didn't know who it was for until I showed up in a blue shirt and black shorts. He called me out and said the Lord said that I was right on time and that God was using me exactly where I was and how I was. He said that I have a healing anointing, and if anyone in the room needed healing for something, to come to me.

After the service, there was a line of five or so people before me waiting for prayer. I witnessed two miracles that morning: one lady's migraine that had been harassing her for months went away completely, and another, who had scoliosis, had her back straightened out completely. I felt her back move with my hand as I was praying! That is only one of many times I've prayed for people and seen God bring healing to them. I prayed for many students in the ministry I was in who had pain, ailments, or broken legs and saw their pain improve or go away.

I will never stop praying for others, even though I'm still struggling with a disability. Throughout my life, God has given me such a heart for people who are hurting, and I immediately want them to feel a touch from God. I want to fight for them and with them. We are not meant to do life on our own. We need community and people to both hurt and rejoice with. We need to lean on the Lord for strength when we're weak and for peace when we don't understand. As we journey through this life, trials will come and go, but

Doubtless

we should press into those around us rather than do life alone.

1 John 3:8 says, "The one who does what is sinful is of the devil because the devil has been sinning from the beginning. The reason the Son of God appeared was to destroy the devil's work." God has given us the authority to join Him in this with our helper, the Holy Spirit.

Though Satan may be the ruler of this earthly world (2 Cor. 4:4), Jesus is preeminent over all creation (Col. 1:18) and is King over heaven and earth! Satan is filled with fury and hatred for God and all of God's people and knows his time is short (Rev. 12:12). Revelation 20:1-3 prophecies that Satan will be thrown into the bottomless pit when Christ returns. Until then, we get to operate in the authority Christ has given us to reclaim ground from Satan and destroy his works and plans through the power of Christ within us.

24

Way Maker

Following God and choosing Him, even when it has been a challenging journey, have opened doors that could only have come from Him. When we operate in authority that is beyond ourselves as children of God, the Lord opens doors that would be seemingly impossible for us to walk through on our own. As a follower of Christ, God has given me access to opportunities to share my heart, my creativity, and my passions, and for my voice to be heard.

Standing out physically has made me realize that I am seen and known despite being different. While I used to feel rejected and left out, I have realized that I am actually set apart, and that is not a bad thing. Deuteronomy 14:2 (NLV) says "You have been set apart as holy to the Lord your God, and he has chosen you from all the nations of the earth to be his own special treasure."

Being set apart is what brings favor, access, and influence to your life and to others. God calls us to be in the world, but not of it (1 John 2:15-17). The Bible warns, as "temporary residents and foreigners, to keep away from worldly desires that wage war against your very souls" (1 Pet. 2:11-12 NLV).

The joy of the Lord that I have isn't normal according to the world's standard, especially considering my current circumstances, and I truly believe people notice it. I've gotten to encourage and pray for many people who aren't aware that there's another way to live. There is a hopeful future for those who believe because we are eternal beings with God at work all around us. I see how many times He has protected me when I easily could have been hurt. He has put people in my path that only He could have.

Doubtless

When I talk to Him, thanking Him or simply acknowledging Him, He brings little blessings along the way and increases my awareness of things going on around me. God has made a way for me countless times and has recently opened doors I never thought would be possible for me.

My entire life, people have placed limitations on what I can and cannot do, as well as how long I would live. To live past 18 years with this disease is not guaranteed, yet I feel like I am thriving at age 26, and am considered a living miracle. God has given me faith to push past limitations that have been placed on my lifespan and lifestyle. Going to college, living on my own, driving a car, traveling internationally, tubing, camping, spontaneous trips with friends—God has provided ways and flung open doors.

Nothing is impossible until you believe it is. When others told me certain things would be too hard to do, I did them anyway. Nothing is easy, but it is possible when you believe in yourself and trust the One who created you to provide what you need. When we walk in our true authority, God pours out favor, blessings, and provision upon us, opening doors hardly imaginable.

As I mentioned earlier in the book, when I moved back home and was in a place of rest and pursuing my future career, I was granted the opportunity to paint a piano for Pianos for Peace, as well as a Little Library at a local park. These were large and exciting projects that came through people I met. I'll never forget interning at the Art Barn that summer in college and how Patricia believed in me and spoke encouragement, hope, and many prophetic words over my life and future.

The more I thought about Patricia's magical place from a few summers back, I knew I wanted something similar for my life. This motivated me to pursue that dream wholeheartedly. God gave me a glimpse into a kind of life and career that seemed like my wildest dream come true because He knows our hearts and is that good. Patricia kept affirming to me that the magical art barn that contained everything I love could be a reality for me and that I have a gift for art and working with others. It helped give more direction to my steps.

She taught me that when you cut unnecessary or unfruitful habits and activities out of your life and fill it with hopeful and encouraging ones, like painting, proper nutrition, and God's Word, you'll bring healing and transformation to your life. I knew I wanted to bring that healing and transformation to others as Patricia has done for me.

After I found BrewAble and Lionheart School, I was inspired to keep looking at similar workplaces that involved art, special needs, and advocacy, though they were hard to find. But I didn't feel led to settle for anything less because I knew the power of art and my love for those with special needs or disabilities. When I painted the piano for Pianos for Peace, I was proud of how well it turned out and the hard work it took, but what did it do for me or my resume in terms of a long-term career? I felt like I had a lot to offer people and places, but I just hadn't found my thing yet.

Pushing past the insecurity of thinking I wasn't doing enough and still pursuing my passions anyway, God finally started to open doors. He started to make a way for me as I was pursuing my passions and seeking His direction. My chiropractor told one of her patients about my art when she mentioned she needed help with painting. I got to paint a Little Free Library for a park nearby and received an opportunity to paint a second one soon. I freely donated a large, rainbow lion painting to a fundraiser at the Lionheart School, which sold for $250! I then sent two paintings to a lady who was putting on a fundraising dinner and auction for GAN to raise money for research. I entered a national Christian art competition as well as a rare disease art competition, realizing having a rare disease was also an opportunity to share my story and express myself.

As I started to gain more vision for this book, I began to build relationships with people at a few different local coffee shops. One of my favorites, Land of a Thousand Hills in Roswell, Georgia, became like my second home. As I got to know the manager, we immediately connected and became friends. I was first drawn to her British accent and learned about her former life in London and why she was at this small little coffee shop in the States, where she loved working at. She started to give me free drinks and offered for me to decorate the coffee shop with art to sell in whatever way I wanted to. I sold three paintings in the first week! She offered to sell my book at all three of their locations and set up a shelf for anything I wanted to sell.

Thinking back to the previous year, I got a chance to drive with a couple of friends to Orlando for a free, Christian stadium event called The Send. It was wild and amazing. However, the weather was intense, with temperatures in the high 90s and the sun beating down, and it was exhausting to get around. Walking inside the stadium was treacherous for me, and by the time we got inside and sat down, my legs basically gave out on me. We had to track down a wheelchair. Yet, the whole time, though I wasn't with the main group of people I knew from my church, I was pushed around by my good Athens friends. We went all over and encountered many people that day who prayed and prophesied over me, and it ended up being such a special trip.

A few months later, my friend, MJ, was putting on a big ministry event in Orlando called the Freedom March. Her ministry is formed of people who have been set free from the LGBTQ lifestyle and have found Jesus, and they now put on events in cities across the country to help others who are seeking freedom from same-sex attraction. I wanted to go to one to witness what exactly went on at this kind of event. I paid for a spot to be in their group Airbnb and drove down with a few of them. It was a wild few days.

My friend offered for me to sell some prints I had made of Jesus in watercolor. It was just a rough experiment that I had done in my sketchbook, yet she immediately saw potential in it. I took a chance and got a hundred

Doubtless

prints made, matted, and placed in sleeves with my personal bio on the back, and set them on display at the merchandise table for the event. I sold over twenty Jesus prints that weekend and even got the opportunity to pray and minister to ones passing by. I have always wanted to pair art and ministry together, yet I never expected it to take place in this way.

I ended up going to Orlando a third time that year to another conference that was taking place over New Year's Eve called Jesus Image. It was a powerful few days, with a group party in a nice Airbnb and a fun road trip. This was another event where God set me apart. While the crew I was with all sat in a certain row of seats, I had to be in the handicapped area on my scooter. I was alone most of the time. It made me sad to be by myself at a conference with probably a couple of thousand people, but it also gave me the freedom to scoot up close to the stage and move around however I wanted.

My leg braces and walker, as they usually do, made me a magnet for people to come up and talk, pray for, and encourage me. My journal is filled with prophetic words I received over that week, and though I was faced with the usual prayers for my healing and seeing nothing change physically, I know all the prayers from The Send and Jesus Image built me up and encouraged me, and they reminded me that God sees me and loves me and that I'm not alone.

All three trips to Orlando were exciting and powerful, and they were events I still cannot believe I got to experience. God made a way for me to go despite the travel challenges I commonly face with my disability and took care of me along the way. My Jesus prints are in the hands of many, and I have been told they have touched and encouraged people even when I didn't think they turned out well. I wasn't trying to make anything of the rough painting until my friend encouraged me to share it with the world. The prints are now in many friends' rooms and have even been placed in hospital rooms to bring hope and healing. I have prayed over them, and I think that God put a special anointing on them to touch people in the most unexpected places.

One morning, a few of my Athens friends came over for breakfast. One was in town, therefore bringing a couple of others over as well. As we were reflecting over the last couple of years and how our friend group had begun to really spread out and do different things, I was openly sharing how I wish I was doing something cool too. One of our friends had been traveling a lot to work as a chef at different resorts, another had joined the Navy, and the one at my house was about to embark on a new adventure of being in full-time ministry with the Circuit Riders, who go to college campuses all across the nation and share the Gospel.

What was I doing? Though I was very blessed, I still had this driving desire to go somewhere new and different. I have always felt that in me was a depth that called for more than a typical job or life. I wanted to see the world.

About an hour later, my two friends and I went to a Christian coffee shop called Crazy Love, named after Francis Chan's book. I got there before them and was waiting by the door, waiting for a table to open up. Two men offered me a seat and said they wouldn't be there much longer. They were very down-to-earth and friendly, welcoming me into their conversation and truly interested in who I was. I came to find out that they were in town visiting from Los Angeles and New Zealand, about to go to a meeting at a local ministry nearby. We started talking about what churches we went to, the times we were in, and our occupations.

One of the men had been involved in missions for over twenty years, which immediately piqued my interest. I was dying to know more about this guy, as I so badly wanted to travel too. He had been to Africa countless times and said it was the most amazing place he had ever been to in his life. He even met his wife on the mission field. He saw the excitement in my eyes and how I longed for those experiences too.

As we started to get into the mission talk, my two friends showed up and sat down. He said, "I tell you what, if you're serious about going to Africa, I will fully fund your trip."

My friends and I looked at him in awe...

Was he serious about fully paying for a stranger's trip to Africa? I thought incredulously.

Yes, he was definitely serious. He told me to pray about it and email him what I decided, for he had an amazing team that he would put me with who would take great care of me. He reminded me that no disability should be a hindrance because the proper accommodations would make it entirely possible.

My friend, Monique, was hitting me after they left and reminding me I was literally saying over breakfast how I wished I could go on a new adventure and how I felt behind compared to all my friends. It was an answered prayer within an hour, and she said she'd never let it go if I didn't act on it. I honestly didn't remember this until she reminded me.

Being offered a free trip to Africa doesn't just happen, right? After praying about it for two days, I knew it was an open door, and I had to take action. I emailed him that yes, I was definitely interested in going... He welcomed me with excitement. Apparently, I'm going to Africa. I still don't comprehend it and honestly feel kind of nervous, but I've always wanted to go. If God opened a clear door in such a crazy way and with such insane timing, I was going to say 'yes.' What a gift He gave me that morning!

Later on in the year, as my routine mostly involved going to coffee shops and writing, I started to feel guilty about my frequent lattes because I was not actually making a consistent income, even though I had decided I was going to fully commit to writing this book. Then I remembered that because of my new manager friend at Land of a Thousand Hills, I didn't have to pay half the time. And then the most recent surprise was when I went to pay at my

Doubtless

other favorite coffee shop, I found out the man who had left before I did had covered my tab for the two weeks remaining in the year. I came to find out that he was a well-known NFL player and had recently retired due to injuries.

Even after the new year began and I handed my credit card over to pay, the cashier told me the former football player had reopened a tab for me for an unknown amount of time. I shared this little sweet surprise with my friend, who reminded me how worried I had been spending money on coffees when working on this project, and how even now God was providing for me and blessing me!

While nearing the end of the writing process, more surprising doors opened. While in an antique mall with my mom, I met a vendor at one of the booths who had started her own creative arts ministry. Super intrigued, we immediately connected about art and ministry, and I shared my heart about wanting to use creativity to glorify God and encourage others. Her eyes lit up as she claimed those were the kind of people she was hoping to meet and be a part of her ministry! I've had the opportunity to sell art at her booth and regard her as a spiritual mother and friend.

During the first month that I was displaying work with her at the booth, I met my friend Corrie. I overheard Corrie sharing that she worked at Victory 91.5, my favorite Christian radio station. I had always wanted to meet the face behind the voice I heard every morning as I listened to "Coffee with Corrie." I went looking for her, but she quickly disappeared. After I found her, I basically told her I had overheard where she worked and had always wanted to meet her. We exchanged numbers, and I hoped to develop a new friendship with her. She texted me that same day, leading to multiple coffee and breakfast dates and then an interview on the radio talking about my book!

Meeting her was no coincidence, as nothing ever is. God is the one who makes a way and opens the right doors with perfect timing. After I became a part of a new creative arts ministry, a couple of months later I saw an ad for a soon-coming artist boutique mall looking for vendors in Roswell where I live. As I clicked the link and gained more info, I lit up with anticipation at the potential to be a vendor to sell art, which was a dream of mine. I found out there were other locations, and my mom and I made a day of it to go visit one of their older locations.

My jaw dropped right away as it was the coolest place! It was filled with booths by different artist vendors and businesses—an art show and boutique all in one. I asked questions about the pricing and found out there was a waitlist. Of course. Though it would require paying monthly rent and taking a big chance, I wanted this so badly. I would need to make sure to have enough paintings to fill the small space, or even consider starting my own business to take full advantage of the space. I applied with photos of the few projects I had done and a couple of pictures of my paintings, not sure I'd make the cut. They called me early the next day with an offer to have me as a vendor! They said my art was exactly what they were looking for. I was amazed and overwhelmed at the idea of a whole new business adventure with my art, something I'd only dreamed of my whole life.

As I was being faithful with writing and just showing up the best I could, God opened doors and directed my path. He is the One who makes a way when there is no way and transforms our dreams into realities when we trust and obey Him. Writing this book was so extremely pressing on my heart to do, even though I didn't know what I was doing. I just wanted to be obedient. I think about how many people have dreams that they never take a chance on because of fear or intimidation. I encourage anyone to write down their dreams, thoughts, and desires in a journal. Write a letter to God like I have countless times, and dream big.

In *Chase the Lion*, author Mark Batterson writes, "If your dreams do not scare you, they aren't big enough." He goes on to say, "At the end of our lives, our greatest regrets will be the God-ordained opportunities we left on the table, the God-given passions we didn't pursue, and the God-sized dreams we didn't go after because we let fear dictate our decisions." In other words, no guts, no glory.

According to Batterson, "The only way to tap your God-given potential, to fulfill your God-ordained destiny is to chase five-hundred-pound lions." God's plans and dreams for us are bigger than we can even imagine, and we just need to have faith that He makes a way because God Himself is full of creativity and imagination! Where we think there is no way, God makes a way when we trust Him.

Thank You, Lord, for where I've been and what I've been through. Thank You that my life hasn't looked like I would have ever imagined but has been truly a unique adventure. Thank You that You have carried me through every time I thought it was impossible, or I wouldn't make it. Thank You that You have always provided what You knew I needed to get through each obstacle set before me.

25

Hindsight 20/20

Two years after the initial idea and planning for writing this book, I showed up at the coffee shop every day with the deep conviction to write and work on it but not knowing how. I'd journal my thoughts, dreams, and ideas, but my book sat more in my head than actually making it onto my laptop. It was a daily cycle of frustration and procrastination, even though I had decided 2020 would be the year to do it.

Then, as I planned for an amazing year with exciting resolutions and goals, my sister died the first month in, followed by a global pandemic putting the whole world in lockdown for months. To make matters worse, the week Covid hit the US, my best friend lost her mother to a sudden stroke and heart attack. With all these things occurring simultaneously, it felt like a miracle that God was able to bring me through.

I believe 2020 will be a year that goes down in history and certainly the hardest year I have ever personally experienced. With a heated election year and a new unpredictable global pandemic, suddenly the world was filled with tragedy, global unrest, extreme political strife, racial wars, street rioting, and anger due to opposing viewpoints and constant media chaos.

With added lockdowns and mandates, churches, schools, businesses, and sports were either shut down for a time or generally handled differently. Many comforts were ripped away from people, as fun events or social gatherings, restaurants, and sports to watch on TV were unavailable. Vacations had to be canceled as airlines and cruise ships shut down, and suddenly people were stuck at home indefinitely.

Doubtless

Soon after Jaime died, two good friends of mine wanted to get me a gift, and both of them asked God what would bring me some comfort. Unbeknownst to them, they both felt led to buy me the book *Hinds Feet on High Places* by Hannah Hurnard. One of them sent me the book and the other sent me a devotional version. When they both realized God had prophetically told them the same thing, it was only confirmation that God wanted me to read it!

I had not heard of it at the time, yet I came to see a lot of myself in the heroine of the story. It highly impacted me during that season and gave me more hope for the future. The story is about a girl named Much-Afraid who sets forth on a treacherous journey to the "High Places," otherwise known as the Kingdom of Love, representing Heaven. She is desperate to escape her life of many troubles, doubts, and fears and step into a life of freedom and joy.

When the book begins, Much-Afraid is an orphan living in the Valley of Humiliation unwillingly with the family of Fearings. She meets a kind friend, The Great Shepherd, and longs to leave her unhappy life and go to live with Him in the High Places. The Great Shepherd leads her on a treacherous journey with two companions, Sorrow and Suffering.

The journey is filled with numerous, seemingly impossible obstacles for Much-Afraid, who has deformities in her feet and her face, making it hard for her to walk and feel beautiful, loved, or valued. Much-Afraid is afraid of many things, especially death and loss, and is constantly tormented by her Fearing relatives: Pride, Resentment, Bitterness, Self-Pity, and Craven Fear.

The Great Shepherd becomes a great friend who shows her much love and compassion and gives many precious promises to her, but He tells her that she must be willing to set forth on the scary path before her to get to the High Places, representing heavenly fellowship with Him. He also tells her that all who enter the Kingdom of Love must be completely whole, healed, and blemish-free, so her journey involves many purifications and testings.

On her path to the High Places, the Shepherd brings Much-Afraid through the Furnace of Egypt, the Forests of Danger and Tribulation, the Sea of Loneliness, the Precipice Injury, the Valley of Loss, and the Grave on the Mountains, where she must finally die to her old self and embrace the new identity the Great Shepherd created for her.

As she passes through these places, her Fearing relatives, Resentment, Bitterness, Self-Pity, Pride, and Craven Fear all show up to taunt her along her journey, hoping to sabotage her plans of escape. At first, Much-Afraid can call on the Shepherd to defeat these enemies, but eventually, she must rely on her companions and helpers, Sorrow and Suffering, to help her send them away. Along her journey, her heart starts to transform and change as she goes through and overcomes many trials, and she is given a new name, Grace and Glory. Her companions, Sorrow and Suffering, are transformed into Joy and Peace, and they all live in the High Places together.

Throughout the book, Much-Afraid shares her heart for wanting to be able to move with ease despite her deformed feet, and she fears the Great Shepherd would betray, abandon, or forget her. The journey set before her seems daunting and impossible, but it is worth it in the end.

The allegory is a reminder that God uses all things for a purpose and takes us through trials to bring us out of them stronger and more mature. It was a timely book for me because the obstacles and grief I had to walk through were frightening unknowns in my life, and I had no choice but to trust God and believe that He would work it all out for good.

Reading the book gave me new hope for the future and a new level of perseverance to walk out each day with confidence that God is with me and is leading me to hope and healing. Like Much-Afraid, I have many dreams and desires but feel held back because of my disability. I also know that the trials of that season were preparing me for the "high places" of my calling.

2020 brought a whole new dynamic and depth to my thoughts, desires, and revelations. As the months progressed, so did an urgency to write as I realized how many people were feeling hopeless, lost, and afraid. People yearned for hope and needed Jesus more than ever in a world filled with pain and constant unpredictable unknowns.

Though 2020 and the following year were uncomfortable and intense, at the same time they presented blessings, new opportunities, and open doors. I ate nutritious meals, went to the park every day, and spent time with my parents doing puzzles and watching movies, which gave me the necessary rest and quiet I didn't realize I needed. While no longer able to rely on worldly distractions to fill my days, I spent more time with the Lord and in His Word. Sometimes that was all I knew to do because the world was suddenly a scary and unknown place. The strong fear that was loosed into the world was heavy in the air. I came to learn that many others were also taking the time to rest and engage Jesus in quiet and simplicity.

I now look back at those months of quarantine as a divine reset. God renewed and refreshed both the global population and polluted the earth, which brought His people back to Him. That year helped many people slow down and prioritize what was truly meaningful to them, as everything was being shaken. I think that God allowed this shaking to awaken people from their comfortable routines, to remove idols and worldly distractions that constantly occupied their time and attention.

People said 2020 would be a year of clear vision. I think when people say "20/20 vision," they think of everything being great. But I believe 2020 was a year of finding clear vision by stripping away idols and distractions. The year brought a new focus, a simplification of life, and showed me what to prioritize in life. It involved hard, sharpening trials that served as wind in my sails and gave me new momentum to press into what lay before me and what God said to invest in.

Doubtless

Life is filled with constant noise and distractions, and we can get really bogged down and discouraged or fearful of things out of our control. 20/20 vision is about finding clarity in the blur. Fighting through tiredness, brain fog, mental funk, sadness or heaviness, confusion or doubt, it can seem like a war to push through and show up. That's exactly what writing this book felt and was like—a lot of warfare and having to keep showing up in faith while having no idea what the outcome would be.

But before I realized it, it was complete. God is faithful when we say yes. He is the one who sustains us, gets us through things we think are impossible, and is faithful to work when we think He is far away or not moving. Throughout my life, He has continually shown me His faithfulness and grace and has continued to give me hope.

Through all the testing and trials, He has healed my heart and mind, while constantly giving me hope for physical healing to come. Though I'm not sure what that will look like or when it will happen, I know God's plan is always so much bigger and better than we realize. I look to the future with expectancy for healing and breakthrough. I'm thankful for the hardships because I have awoken to what's important in life and how God will never leave us or forsake us. If you are struggling with being different and feeling like limitations are going to keep you from a good life, know that our limits are often our greatest blessing and truly hold the key to the most exciting adventure.

Moving into 2021 and beyond, I feel strengthened in my awareness of who I am and what my calling is, which is to write, speak, and create. I have gained a new fire and passion to finally step into these things after the hardships of 2020. In many ways, God used 2020 to give me a clearer vision of what matters and the urgency to pursue those things wholeheartedly.

The latest trials and hardships fueled this book more than I realized and gave a timely message to the theme of overcoming doubt. Just like Much-Afraid's daunting journey of escaping her fear-filled life and moving upward toward the High Places, she overcame a life of hopelessness, defeat, and sorrow and was transformed into a healed and whole person with joy and peace. Her journey involved receiving many difficult testings of her faith and enduring many challenging obstacles, yet the Great Shepherd used all these trials as lessons to strengthen and mature her to bring complete healing to her heart, mind, and body. It is a powerful reminder that God uses all pain for a purpose and is with us every step of the way.

When I flip back through the pages of this book, I see what God was preparing me for and how He truly does redeem things and make them into beautiful stories. 2020 was a year of loss, fear, and navigating a lot of unknowns, yet it also provided momentum to step into new things that I feared and broke the doubt that had gripped me for so long. I didn't believe I could be one to write a book until grief set in and seemed to shake me of mindsets that caused me to stagnate. I doubted my abilities, my voice, my gifts, and talents, and especially doubted God to get me through a painful season.

When I lost my sister, I believed for months that my family would never be okay again. When a global pandemic hit, the abundant blessings in the midst of the shaking brought about a new confidence and awareness of God's power. When my friend, Lauren, lost her mom, I witnessed how God heals broken hearts and strengthens people through loss.

My friend and I both stepped into a new level of boldness and confidence to speak up, pursue our dreams, and take risks. Loss made us press into our faith in a deeper way as we were challenged to know exactly why we believe what we believe about God, and that's when we most saw Him show up. Losing a loved one let me face death full-on and press into what I believe about eternity, which challenged and awakened me to live differently.

2020 was the year I started writing this book, when I started pursuing my own art business, and when I became more fearless and sure about my calling as an author and artist. Never would I have imagined that many of my life dreams would start to manifest during such a harsh year. The timing of it all proved God's ways to be higher and His timing to be perfect, better than what I could have chosen myself.

Through choosing to show up and say yes on a difficult path, I realized I'm more capable than I gave myself credit for, through Christ's strength and power. God showed me His nearness and grace, and He surrounded me with love and support in rare places.

I don't know how the year 2020 personally affected you or the specific types of suffering you may have endured, but I do know 2020 affected each and every one of us in both painful and profound ways. Like me, you may have lost a loved one. Or you may have been laid off from your job, suffered a mental health crisis due to stress and isolation from the financial crashes and lockdowns, or experienced estrangement from family members due to political disagreements. However, despite the trials you experienced in 2020, the Lord promises us that He will work all things together for the good of those who love Him (Rom. 8:28).

"How could that even be possible?" you are probably wondering. "How could God possibly work out all the loss and suffering I experienced in 2020?"

I completely understand your sense of incredulity. For many of us, 2020 challenged our faith in greater ways than many of us had ever experienced before. It presented new doubts about God many of us had never faced before. We had to endure greater levels of hardship and answer more difficult questions about what we believe about God and why. Before 2020, many of us undoubtedly believed and stood on God's word. However, after 2020, many doubts arose within us regarding the character and nature of God.

Is He truly good? Is He truly trustworthy? Is heaven real? Why did

Doubtless

God allow this pandemic to happen? Will life ever be like it was before? Do I really have a reason to hope?

If like me, you have continued to press into your faith and seek the Lord despite these difficult circumstances, I wholeheartedly believe you will come to the same conclusion I did: God is good.

The unprecedented trials of 2020 have forged unprecedented faith within many of us, unshakable and unquenchable. We've faced doubts about God we didn't know were buried deep within us, but only through facing these doubts have we been able to overcome them.

The early church experienced intense suffering and persecution while living under the harsh regime of the Roman Empire. During a time when many believers were being brutally tortured and killed, the Apostle Paul penned a letter to encourage them to keep going and never give up their faith.

He instructed his fellow brothers and sisters in Christ with the following words: "We rejoice in our sufferings, knowing that suffering produces endurance, and endurance produces character, and character produces hope, and hope does not put us to shame, because God's love has been poured into our hearts through the Holy Spirit who has been given to us" (Romans 5:3-5 ESV).

2020 forced us to face our greatest fears and overcome them so they would no longer hold us back. Like the members of the early church, may the trials we endure launch us into our callings and prepare us for our greater purpose—with 20/20 vision.

26

Doubtless

In the midst of enduring the trials of 2020, I suddenly had a new depth of understanding of how much the world needs a story of adversity and loss and who and where God is in the midst of trials. I had a new urgency to share, and a new level of compassion for those dealing with grief. It is all a call to be more like Christ when we can partake in the suffering of others.

While dreaming and planning with my friend, MJ, over coffee the previous year for the potential book I felt I had inside of me, the Lord gave a clear title to us: *Doubtless*.

I wondered why I felt such a strong nudge from God to use this as my title. *What does 'doubtless' actually mean?* I wondered.

According to Lexico Dictionaries, doubtless is "used to indicate the speaker's belief that a statement is certain to be true given what is known about the situation," or, in other words, "used to refer to a desirable outcome as though it were certain."

Synonyms include: "unquestionably," "positively," "seemingly," "absolutely," and "unconditionally."

2 Samuel 5:19 (KJV) says, "David enquired of the Lord, saying, 'Shall I go up to the Philistines? Wilt thou deliver them into mine hand?' And the Lord said unto David, 'Go up: for I will *doubtless* deliver the Philistines into thine hand.'"

And in Psalm 126:6 (KJV), the psalmist writes, "He that goeth forth and weepeth, bearing precious seed, shall *doubtless* come again with rejoicing, bringing his sheaves with him." God is showing us through these verses that

Doubtless

He will surely do what He says, without a doubt.

To me, *Doubtless* has meant overcoming adversity and trials with endurance and faith in God's promises. To embrace a *Doubtless* life looks like turning to the God of the impossible, inviting Him into our messes, letting Him fight for us, and asking Him to be our strength in our weaknesses. It looks like living life without fear, having courage and confidence in who we are—people who take risks and live our lives to the fullest, seeing every opportunity and situation as an adventure.

To be *Doubtless* means to not be double-minded but rather to live with peace and do things from a place of rest, hope, and joy, while remaining confident in decisions made with assurance of God's guidance and provision in every step. With a *Doubtless* mentality, limits don't block our dreams because Jesus is the lens through Whom we see how to live life abundantly. It is understanding that if He is for us, who can be against us?

As believers, we know that Jesus paid the ultimate price for us by dying so that we can live, and we are now citizens of heaven, children of the King, and free from the things that keep us in bondage. Jesus already has the victory, and therefore we can live from a place of victory, anticipating the amazing future He has for us and not settling for the mundane. We can live without fear, filled with faith, boldness, courage, authority, and the knowledge that our identity comes from Christ alone, through whom we can do all things because He gives us strength (Phil. 4:13).

God reminds us throughout His Word that doubt is the enemy of faith, and if left unchecked, it will quietly corrode our lives. To put it plainly, God hates doubt because He understands how destructive it truly is. That is why faith is a requirement for us to follow Him. In fact, "It is impossible to please God without faith. Anyone who wants to come to him must believe that God exists and that He rewards those who sincerely seek Him (Heb. 11:6 NLT).

When asking for wisdom from the Lord, James 1:6-8 (ESV) says, "Let him ask in faith, with no doubting, for the one who doubts is like a wave of the sea that is driven and tossed by the wind. For that person must not suppose that he will receive anything from the Lord; he is a double-minded man, unstable in all his ways."

In Mark 11:23-24, Jesus says, "Truly, I say to you, whoever says to this mountain, 'Be taken up and thrown into the sea,' and does not doubt in his heart, but believes that what he says will come to pass, it will be done for him. Therefore I tell you, whatever you ask in prayer, believe that you have received it, and it will be yours."

God wants us to live in faith and not doubt! He is so clear about how doubt can block His answers to prayer and keep us from receiving all that He has for us. That's why, to live a truly *Doubtless* life, we must walk in faith.

Sounds easy enough, right? If only it were that simple…

As God spoke clearly about that title, I had no idea what new trials were soon to challenge me and bring about a whole new level of doubt. Little did I know to what extent I'd have to journey through overcoming doubt to write this book.

Of course, as soon as I began to step into God's call to write my book about being *Doubtless*, doubt immediately reared its ugly head yet again. Doubt had always been the common theme in my life, always finding new ways to plague my heart and mind, even when I thought I was fine. I didn't fully realize how much doubt had tormented and crippled me until I began writing this book about overcoming it, which forced me to reflect on the years of its grip on me.

And yet, while limitations seemed even more pressing during this season, the words suddenly began to pour out of me as I began to face my doubts head-on and press into the writing process. As a new faith filled my wings, words finally began to flow after years of praying and striving.

While writing this book, I had to face the common questions that had terrified me for so long: Am I capable? Am I seen? Am I loved? Am I beautiful? Am I intelligent? Am I enough? Will I measure up? Will I have a good life? Does God know my heart and desires?

Since doubt has crippled me for most of my life, I think God was urging me to step through it and conquer it once and for all by embarking on a project that initially seemed to be too difficult for me to accomplish. Embarking on a journey of overcoming various forms of doubt has brought me full circle to a place of greater wholeness and awareness of who I am and where I'm going.

Writing this book forced me to reflect on the numerous times God had gotten me through impossible situations and made a clear path for me. Therefore, I realized that writing this book would create an opportunity for me to contemplate who God has always been and always will be, as well as provide powerful testimonies of hope and overcoming obstacles for readers facing difficult circumstances. Rising to the challenge of such a complex project— though it multiplied my doubt to an all-time high—was what ultimately delivered me from that sinister foe.

Writing this book compelled me to relive my most difficult experiences and press into still-tender memories, bringing up an array of forgotten emotions all at once, which was both painful and healing. All along, God has had me on a journey of transformation and growth, the puzzle fitting together one piece at a time, each leading me closer to freedom and confidence. Years of living in insecurity, rejection, low self-esteem, and defeat, have pushed me to stand up to these feelings and say, "No, that is not who I am. I am a child of God—chosen, called, loved, protected, strong, and worthy."

While completing this book, I danced through the seasons of my life, leaping past my old doubt-filled self in countless situations, laughing at each instance with a greater level of wisdom and strength. A disability thrown

Doubtless

upon me early on led me to doubt that God would be able to fulfill my many childhood hopes and dreams for the future. I doubted I was beautiful because I struggled more with beauty, fashion, and style. I doubted I could ever truly fit in when I was instantly different from everyone else. I doubted that I'd ever be able to participate in youthful activities again with friends. I doubted I'd ever feel freedom in movement or self-expression again. I doubted I'd have the dream college experience on a huge and hard-to-navigate campus. I doubted I'd feel known and loved by a group of friends when most of my life was lived feeling misunderstood and behind everyone else, always missing out and longing for different circumstances.

Adolescent years involved getting bullied at school and having to face difficult decisions like quitting sports, wearing pants when all the girls wore dresses and skirts, and missing out on basic kid activities like field day, relay races, and gym class. I'm still sometimes haunted by the memories of sitting on the side of the room at school dances and group activities. Coming home every day in tears from gym class as students stared me down on the track as they walked past me with their group of friends. A slow walk for them was like sprinting for me.

I'd try to be unseen when I changed class periods or chose seats because I didn't want people to see me walk or be in a place where I'd lose balance or fall. I had to visit my locker at strategic times when the coast was clear so no one saw me clinging to the lockers and railings for dear life while attempting to carry anything. Having to go to my school counselor when two girls ganged up on me, claiming I was faking it and only wanting attention. It was during the same time I had a year-long recovery from ankle surgery and was between a cast and wheelchair and constant therapy, feeling the need to cling to my teachers for extra assistance.

Then emerged the excitement of high school and hoping for happier teenage years, when along came another reminder that I was on my own path when I found myself hanging out in the art room alone or taking solo lessons of various kinds as friends talked about their boyfriends and group outings at the mall or soccer field. Girls were enjoying new trends with makeovers, skinny jeans, and cute shoes, while I had bulky casts on my legs and a new walker that everyone stared at. *I'm cool, I swear*, I'd think, yet few took the chance to get to know me.

When I found a group to hang out with, it wasn't long until I realized their friendship had a lot to do with my cool parents and open house, my mom's cooking, and my cool older sisters. Without those things, I can't say they would have been around. My best friend discovered another friend group that was considered the popular crowd, with cool parties, boys, and dabbling in forbidden substances, and suddenly hanging out with me wasn't fun anymore. While she went to prom with about fifteen people, all of whom had dates, I tagged along with others who weren't even my friends.

DOUBTLESS

Small groups, retreats, and mission trips were exciting opportunities yet were the loneliest times of my life due to friend groups and cliques that I wasn't included in. Was I weird? Did people not like me? I was super nice to everyone, a good friend (so I thought), with a witty, good sense of humor about me. But I fit in better with the adult conversations about real topics like genuine feelings and world events. I was clueless when it came to the trending gossip, cultural norms, who and what was popular, who was dating who, or famous celebrities. I couldn't ever relate, which brought a renewed sense of rejection from everyone around me.

College was bound to be my time, finally... only to find myself lonely yet again. I had to occupy the only single dorm room in my hall. No one wanted to share their college life with me, even after I knocked on doors to introduce myself, ready to have fun. I ended up having my mom pick me up every weekend for social interaction.

When I transferred to a large and sought-after university, wow was I excited! To then face an impossible-to-navigate environment for one with a disability. The rolling hills and spread-out town brought about a renewed sense of isolation and defeat, with the constant sense that so much was going on around me that I wasn't included in. I went to every club meeting and student event, crossing town in a disability van to try and find my place and my people, often having to navigate unknown territory that held unpredictable outcomes.

The dining halls especially came with a lot of stress as I had to navigate a tight line with a scooter and backpack, barely able to see what food was being served while sitting down, making it that much harder to reach for what I wanted. Forget trying to sit with anyone I knew because I often couldn't get to them. The most embarrassing moment was when I would prop my folded-up walker on the back of my scooter to have both with me so I had options to walk or ride throughout the day. It wasn't worth the effort. Half of the time my walker would spring open while I was riding, crashing into a door, or just creating this huge, awkward contraption.

When I landed in student ministry in late college, I thought being an intern would be the best time of my life, surrounded by life-long friends and memories. Yet, there I was again, on the outside of all the friend groups, even more left out than middle school and high school combined, at a place where "belonging" is supposed to be for everyone.

Then one day I met a guy, sweet and friendly, who actually saw me and seemed interested in who I was. He was a girl's dream. Could this be my Prince Charming?! A year of growing a friendship and engaging in deep conversations, praying together, and having some mutual friends... led me into a deep pit of heartbreak. A guy finally being nice to me and encouraging me in who I was, was just someone admiring my endurance to walk out my disability with positivity rather than actually seeing me as someone worth

Doubtless

pursuing.

Now, as an adult, I still can be regarded as "inspirational" and someone people admire, yet I still am often harshly reminded that I'm on a different path than everyone else. The hiking, whitewater rafting, beach camping, and weekend trips involving the outdoors are always coming up within my friend groups, and I'm never invited. People may be up for hanging out when it involves sitting at a coffee shop. I'm a pro at that. But I occasionally want to break free and run far and wide to explore the vast amount of the world that I don't get to freely tap into, as my boundary lines can get a bit boring.

Maybe if I could pursue a creative career path, a rewarding non-profit or ministry job that involved helping others, I'd be in my element. But I doubted I could find such a position. Just when I felt I had started to gain a little momentum in art, even though I wondered if it could compare to a "real" job, tragedy hit when my sister passed away. The unexpected devastation fed the heartbreak I felt was finally diminishing. While writing about overcoming, I was suddenly forced to add a new twist to my story with grief that I didn't know how I'd overcome. But I kept writing anyway...

After pushing through and reflecting, it all came full circle. My life all came to me in a slideshow that I wandered through like the closing scene of La La Land. Even though my life hadn't panned out the way I originally wished it would have as a little girl, the Lord has blessed me beyond my wildest dreams in the most special and surprising ways.

Being left out actually was a rerouting to sophistication and maturity. Being taken from sports was a redirection to art, writing, and quality time with others in real conversation. Being different has pushed me to embrace my differences and press into my identity as a child of God—who's uniquely chosen to not be like anyone else. Finding my identity in Christ has strengthened my awareness that Christians have the authority of Christ and that God wants us to truly know who we are and press into our gifts and talents that He gives us for His glory.

Dancing through the memories of living in crippling doubt that left me heartbroken and disappointed has helped me realize that all the doubt stemmed from fear and rejection. Being different, especially during adolescence, is hard to accept because it seems like the worst thing when young and wanting to belong.

Through the years I was left out and alone with the adults, God was maturing me and preparing me for a life of depth in relationships and ministry. He gave me wisdom and experience with a variety of issues and circumstances that I can now use to help remind others that all pain is for a purpose and to get us to where we're going. What we go through helps to strengthen us and refine our faith.

Because of the hard times, I have a greater appreciation for who I am today and for the many things I can reflect on. When doubt and insecurity attack me, I can also see the accomplishments with deep gratitude and amazement.

My best days are not behind me but lie ahead because God takes us from glory to glory. The years of frustration and heartache have forced me to live outside of my comfort zone and experience people, places, and things that are truly unique treasures along the pathway of an otherwise ordinary life. Having a constant thorn in my flesh has forced me to pursue my faith in a deeper way and depend on God as my strength when I had none, only to find that that's when He moves the most. My physical limitations have led me to express myself through the arts, an everlasting outlet of knowledge and depth.

Through art, music, and writing, I have learned the importance of rest and pursuing things for true, personal benefit rather than performance or competition, breaking my attempt to earn my place in this world. A disability redefined adventure, beauty, and personal worth, causing me to seek my identity in Christ alone instead of through popularity, ability, or status. Even in the midst of the loss of my sister and having to face my biggest fear in life during a global pandemic, God showed Himself to be near when my heart was broken and fearful, revealing to me blessings and love in surprising ways and strengthening my faith in His ability to give me a life even better than my dreams.

From my teachers nominating me for the top dog award in elementary school to being a spokesperson for the MDA boot drive where I spoke to groups of firemen about Muscular Dystrophy, to being in Advanced Placement art and music recitals, to mission trips and international travel with family, to going on weekend trips, having bonfires and dinners with friends, to graduating college, leading small groups, to mentoring college students in their faith journey, to selling art to support a nonprofit that supports individuals with disabilities, to becoming a job coach for young adults with intellectual delays, to doing art therapy with those in recovery and in nursing homes, to starting my own art business and writing this book, God has led me all along.

He was in every detail before I could even see it. He took me through some refining fires to truly define my identity and sense of beauty. I had to be left out and on the outside to see how I was chosen and uniquely woven by God for greater things with greater purpose. Because of my disability, I've had the chance to speak to a classroom of special needs young adults about believing in yourself and not letting anyone tell you you cannot do something because I never thought I'd be able to do most of the things I have done.

Because of my disability, I've gotten to choose my seat at concerts and performances, have gotten to park in the staff parking lot in front of college buildings, have gotten to have first choice in dining halls and events with long lines, have gotten a personal ride in a fire truck, a first-class seat on a flight, and personal tours on trips. A disability has been an automatic bridge to other

Doubtless

people's vulnerability with me and an open door to transparent conversations with others.

When people see me, they often feel led to open up about their struggles or offer support or wisdom. It has offered constant opportunities for connection. Not that I enjoy having a disability, but after laying aside the accompanying discouragement, a surprising invitation to influence and impact others who need hope has been presented to me. I'm writing this book to share my struggles and insights into a life of hardship yet deep beauty.

Doubt is both a choice and a lie. I can honestly say now that years of being on the outside, left out and on a different path, have strengthened me and made me more self-confident and self-aware than I ever would have imagined. I don't care what people think anymore. I don't think anything is impossible anymore. I've seen God do the impossible, always making a way, always bringing what I need, and providing the right help and support when things are challenging. I see now that what I thought were the sidelines and the outsides were the places where I was supposed to be all along—on a path uniquely designed and prepared for me to walk in,

I think it's significant that the Lord had me write a book about being free from doubt and overcoming a lot of adversity during one of the hardest years in world history. It challenged me to really live out what I was saying and fully depend on Him in a way I had never needed to before. He took me on a journey of refining and strengthening, as my writing flowed from my fingertips, bringing therapy to my grieving soul and a new understanding and clarity to everything I have been through. I came to see that writing my story was what would truly bring the healing and breakthrough that I needed.

I can honestly say that writing this book has broken off fear and doubt from my soul at such deep levels that I feel like a different person. I feel a heavy burden lifted, a feeling of rejection and hiddenness broken, and a sense of wandering and purposelessness silenced. Little did I know that choosing to push through doubt would deliver me so completely and free me to be my true self.

For anyone wanting to write a book or pursue a dream that seems scary or impossible, my biggest encouragement is to say 'yes' and to choose to come face to face with the self-imposed barrier called doubt, as freedom and confidence are right on the other side, pushing you forward into victory and God-given destiny.

Believe in yourself, believe that God is faithful and is our strength when we are weak. Choose to look doubt in the face, and say, "No, I will not doubt myself or what I am capable of." Even when things are hard, painful, or unfair, know that trials should not be wasted but can be used for our good. May the trials we endure launch us into our callings and prepare us for our greater purpose—so that we defeat our greatest doubts and become truly *Doubtless*.

EPILOGUE

Healing Awaits

Within the guardrails of physical limitations and a discouraging disability present daily from the moment I wake up, I've had to discover what God says about my situation and where He is in the midst of so many things that I wish I could change. The universal question remains for many—if God is good, why does He let bad things happen?

One of my biggest heroes is Joni Eareckson Tada. She is a quadriplegic with a worldwide ministry encouraging and helping those with disabilities. She has no ability to use her arms or legs and is only able to use her mouth to speak and paint (yes, she taught herself how to hold a paintbrush in her mouth!). Yet, she is more mobile than most with the impact she's making and the way she's living a fulfilling and meaningful life through writing, singing, speaking, and painting. She is one who truly knows what it's like to long for heaven with the daily suffering she endures.

In her book *Heaven: Your Real Home from a Higher Perspective*, she writes, "Most of the time, we scratched our heads and wondered how the matted mesh of threads in Romans 8:28 could possibly be woven together for our good. On earth, the underside of the tapestry was tangled and unclear; but in heaven, we will stand amazed to see the topside of the tapestry and how God beautifully embroidered each circumstance into a pattern for our good and His glory."

There are many things we will never understand, but it's crucial to remember that while we have an amazing God who created us and loves us, we also have an enemy, Satan, who hates us and constantly wants to destroy

Doubtless

anything good in our lives. Ephesians 6:12 says, "For our struggle is not against flesh and blood, but against the rulers, against the authorities, against the powers of this dark world and against the spiritual forces of evil in the heavenly realms."

This scripture shows us that we are in a spiritual war of good versus evil until Jesus returns. The daily battle we are all up against is over our identities, and it's rooted in our minds and what we believe about ourselves and about God.

But through trial after trial, I put my hope in the countless promises of God in His Word that are loaded with abundance and hope. He is a provider, a healer, a restorer, a redeemer, a comforter, and so much more. God always has a redemptive plan in mind. So in the midst of suffering and hardship, my only hope is in He who gets me through, gives me the strength I need, and promises a good future for me.

Hebrews 12:2-3 tells us to "fix our eyes on Jesus, the pioneer, and perfecter of faith. For the joy set before him, he endured the cross, scorning its shame, and sat down at the right hand of the throne of God. Consider him who endured such opposition from sinners, so that you will not grow weary and lose heart."

With his prompting us to endure and not grow weary, Paul writes in Philippians 4:8 "Finally, brothers and sisters, whatever is true, whatever is noble, whatever is right, whatever is pure, whatever is lovely, whatever is admirable—if anything is excellent or praiseworthy—think about such things."

In the midst of our suffering in a broken world, we can and should choose to think godly thoughts, focus on the positive, and stay in a place of thankfulness rather than defeat and negativity.

God isn't absent until we get to heaven. Rather, He is omnipresent, in every detail, always bringing heaven to earth through our prayers. The power and importance of praying "Your will be done on earth as it is in heaven" lies in inviting heaven to invade our lives and situations here and now.

In Luke 17:20-21, Jesus said, "The coming of the kingdom of God is not something that can be observed, nor will people say, 'Here it is,' or 'There it is,' because the kingdom of God is in your midst, (or within you)." On my most challenging days, with a body filled with aches and pains that seem to be decaying, I remind myself that "our citizenship is in heaven. And we eagerly await a Savior from there, the Lord Jesus Christ, who, by the power that enables Him to bring everything under His control, will transform our lowly bodies so that they will be like His glorious body" (Phil. 3:20-21).

Nothing that we endure in this life is greater than the promise of what's to come—His return that will restore and redeem all things for eternity. On that day, "He will wipe every tear from their eyes. There will be no more death or mourning or crying or pain, for the old order of things has passed away" (Rev. 21:4).

EPILOGUE: HEALING AWAITS

I want to see all things that happen on earth through the lens of eternity: that we are all running a race with endurance and overcoming trials with a God who already has the victory in all circumstances. God is always with us and He is "close to the brokenhearted and saves those who are crushed in spirit" (Ps. 34:18), and is filled with compassion. To see us hurting or struggling breaks His heart and is not His will for our lives.

Through living in a broken world, we are going to face loss and suffering. We are going to see our bodies decay and come down with ailments. We are going to lose people we love. And many things will happen that we will never understand. But He's in the midst of each and every detail, touching lives around us and bringing people near to His heart.

Walking out this life with a disability has actually given me insight into God's will and ability to heal. I've seen many healing miracles and believe when we use His Word in our lives and situations, He heals and restores what's broken. His Word is the ultimate truth and standard we should all live by, and it brings alignment to crooked situations or beliefs.

Suffering also reminds us to live with an eternal perspective. In the midst of pain, there is purpose. Our greatest challenges can be our greatest blessings too! I encourage you to let trials push you forward rather than keep you back. Let them be a platform to reach others and bring encouragement and hope to their struggles as well. Let's remember that though life is hard, we have the promise of eternity and our home in heaven awaiting us. In heaven, there is no sorrow, suffering, or death. There is no sickness, disease, or pain. We will all have glorified, whole bodies that are restored to God's original intent.

To quote Joni Tada again, "We pilgrims walk the tightrope between earth and heaven, feeling trapped in time, yet with eternity beating in our hearts. Our unsatisfied sense of exile is not to be solved or fixed while here on earth. Our pain and longings make sure we will never be content, but that's good: it is to our benefit that we do not grow comfortable in a world destined for decay."

She goes on in her book and says, "For me, true contentment on earth means asking less of this life because more is coming in the next. Godly contentment is great gain. Heavenly gain. Because God has created the appetites in your heart, it stands to reason that He must be the consummation of that hunger. Yes, heaven will galvanize your heart if you focus your faith not on a place of glittery mansions, but on a Person, Jesus, who makes heaven a home."

I will continue to believe God for healing here and now because He works miracles and heals people from sickness and disease. But even if I don't see that full healing on this side of heaven, I will still declare that God is faithful, loving, and good. He has used a disability for my good in more ways than I ever thought possible and has made a way every time I thought there

Doubtless

would be no way.

In heaven, I cannot wait to travel the world more efficiently, run marathons, hike mountains, frolic barefoot in a field, and ride a bike, but until that day comes, I will be faithful with what is set before me without fear or doubt, because God will be everything I need and more. Trust Him, for He is writing a story that exceeds your wildest dreams! He knows your every desire and is faithful to grant those desires in His time and in His way.

Through a journey of doubt, fear, and insecurity, I can truly say that there is nothing to doubt or fear, as God is in the midst of everything, using all things for a greater purpose and using our pain to make us into powerful people. In the midst of hardship, press in and press on, as this life is fleeting, and heaven lies just beyond the other side. Healing awaits, my friend!

Acknowledgements

During the writing of this book, two people I love passed away unexpectedly. I'm so thankful they were at least a part of my life when they were, but I wish they were here to celebrate with me and to read this book.

My sister, Jaime

Though I had the hope to write a book one day, I cannot say it would have happened if it weren't for Jaime. Losing her was a sudden shock and tragedy that I never thought would happen to me or be a part of my story, and it still seems surreal. I wish more than anything that she was still in my life and a part of my family. Years of memories forever flood my heart and mind, and it causes joy and also deep pain. I hate that it often takes losing something to realize what you had.

Jaime was always a huge encourager of mine, always seeing the best in me and loving me exactly how and where I was. She always spoke highly of me to all of her friends, saying I was strong and beautiful, fun and sweet. In my hardest moments, when I got down on myself or had a sob session thinking people wouldn't like me because of my disability or wishing my life was different, she would affirm to me that I was making a huge impact on her and everyone she knew and that God was using my situation to change lives. She was always amazed at how involved I was with my community and how I never let my disability stop me.

She'd often say, "I could never do what you do," and had a way of cheering me up through her sarcasm and sisterly advice. We had sleepovers and girls' nights at her place, would cook something fun, watch chick flicks, drink wine, and stay up all night talking about boys and our dreams for the future. She would do my hair and makeup when we went out, making me feel like the most beautiful girl in the room. When I felt left out or like I didn't fit in, I did with Jaime because she was always looking after me and taking care of me. She was my safe place during my hardest years of trying to find myself.

This whole book came to being because of Jaime. Losing her has reminded me that life is fragile, short, and unpredictable. She reminded me that we should never wait to take chances on something, even if we are afraid or filled with self-doubt. Jaime, more than anyone I knew, would assure me to never be so hard on myself and to embrace who I am. She constantly affirmed me in my strength, even when she was weak.

The whole time I wrote this book, I felt her presence cheering me on. I wanted to do it for her, while I was still alive and breathing. I wanted to speak up for those who have lost their lives too soon or for those who don't have the ability to speak at all. I never thought I was capable, smart enough, or strong enough...so I wanted to fully conquer doubt once and for all by taking a chance and not stopping even when I felt stuck or unsure of what I was doing and how I would do it.

This story is for you, Jaime. Thank you for being the best big sister and getting me through my hardest years growing up. If only you could see me now and how so many years of hurt have come full circle to launch me forward. Thank you for always believing in me before I believed in myself and for reminding me that what makes me different makes me beautiful. You are a huge part of my heart and my life, and I couldn't have done it without you. I miss you every day, but I know you'll always be cheering me on and smiling down on me.

My friend, Demaryius

As a regular at Ground and Pound Coffee by my house, I had started to see many familiar faces. In passing or while sitting down to work, I was often acknowledged by a particularly warm and friendly guy named Demaryius. He was known and loved by the entire staff. He sat with a crew of his friends in the same table corner every morning. He was quick to give hugs and talk to everyone in his path and was always filled with laughter. He would spend significant time speaking with each person he saw in passing. After only a couple of quick interactions, I came to find he had picked up my tab for the rest of that month.

"Oh Demaryius, he's a regular. He does things like that to bless people," his friends explained in response to my bewilderment at why he would do that for me.

As that month passed, and I went to pay for my drink, he ended up continuously paying my tab for at least a year! We became friends, and he would come to say hello and check in with me, offering help or support. He told me I could reach out to him anytime if I was ever in need. Sometimes he would just hand me a crisp $100 bill. I told him it wasn't necessary, but he always insisted because he loved and cared about me.

I came to find that he was a recently retired NFL player who played for the Broncos. He had won multiple Super Bowl championships. *What was he doing in this small suburban coffee shop? Why did a famous, successful guy like him notice a nobody like me?*

As I told him about the book I was working on, I eventually asked if he would write an endorsement for me. To him, it was an honor, and he assured me it would be done soon.

But, nearing the end of the year, I woke up to the news that Demaryius had a seizure in his shower and passed away. My heart broke, as spending time with him had become a major highlight of my days, and he had faithfully supported my book by covering the cost of my food and coffee while I wrote at the shop each day. He told me that he believed in me and truly saw me as a special person.

I'm so sad he will never get to read this book or see it in fruition. I wish I could thank him for providing such generous financial support and emotional encouragement throughout my book-writing process. He impacted my life and story more than he will ever know. I love and miss you Demaryius. Thank you for believing in me.

Bibliography

Adams, Rebecca. "How Lipstick (Yes, Lipstick) Can Instantly Make Your Day Better." *Huffington Post*, December 7, 2017, http://www.huffpost.com/entry/psychological-benefits-of-lipstick_n_4722612

"Adults with Disabilities: Mental Distress." *Centers for Disease Control and Prevention*, February 22, 2023 www.cdc.gov/ncbddd/disabilityandhealth/features/adults-with-disabilities-mental-distress.html

Cribb, Betsy. "How Survivor and Author Katherine Wolf Is Redefining Beauty and Sharing a Message of Hope." *Southern Living*, January 14, 2020 https://www.southernliving.com/culture/katherine-wolf-style

D'Amore, Paul M. "Mental Health Concerns for the Physically Disabled." *D'Amore Personal Injury Law LLC*. Accessed August 29, 2024 http://www.damoreinjurylaw.com/blog/mental-health-concerns-for-the-physically-disabled

"Doubtless English Definition and Meaning." *Lexico Dictionaries | English*, Lexico Dictionaries, https://www.lexico.com/en/definition/doubtless

Kuhlenbaumer, Gregor. "Giant Axonal Neuropathy." NORD (*National Organization for Rare Disorders*), 2013, https://rarediseases.org/rare-diseases/giant-axonal-neuropathy/

Hong, Hana. "The Surprising—and SIGNIFICANT—History of Red Lipstick." *Real Simple*, July 29, 2020, http://www.realsimple.com/beauty-fashion/makeup/history-of-red-lipstick

Mair, Dr. Carolyn. "The Influence of Body Image on Mental Health." *The British Psychological Society*, May 17, 2019, http://www.bps.org.uk/blogs/guest/influence-body-image-mental-health

Meyer, Joyce. "Win the Battle with Power Thoughts: Everyday Answers." *Joyce Meyer Ministries*, Accessed August 29, 2024, http://www.joycemeyer.org/everydayanswers/ea-teachings/win-the-battle-with-power-thoughts

"Peripheral Neuropathy - Symptoms, Types and Causes." Edited by Jennifer Robinson, *WebMD*, June 21, 2020, https://www.webmd.com/brain/understanding-peripheral-neuropathy-basics

Serani, Dr. Deborah. "Why Self-Care Is Hard for Depressed Individuals." *Psychology Today*, Sussex Publishers, February 6, 2017, http://www.psychologytoday.com/us/blog/two-takes-depression/201702/why-self-care-is-hard-depressed-individuals

Leaf, Dr. Caroline "Switch on Your Brain." *Dr. Leaf*, Accessed August 29, 2024 http://www.drleaf.com/products/switch-on-your-brain

About the Author

Alyssa Kumle is a writer, speaker, artist, and disabilities advocate currently residing in Alpharetta, Georgia. Living with a chronic, progressive nerve disorder since childhood has presented unique challenges in her life, but it also instilled perseverance and trust in God's grace within the limitations of her disability. Alyssa seeks to empower others to embrace their differences and share their gifts with the world. She creates meaningful messages through writing, art, and speaking to shift perspectives on hardship.

Alyssa graduated from the University of Georgia with a degree in Human Development and Family Science, including a certificate in Disability Studies. She has a passion for helping people through mentorship and advocacy. Her professional interests include healthcare, mission work, nonprofits, and the arts.

Alyssa is available for speaking engagements and welcomes opportunities to connect with individuals and organizations aligned with her mission. Please reach out to inquire about booking her.

Contact

- @alyssakumle
- alyssakumle.com
- alyssakumle@gmail.com

Milton Keynes UK
Ingram Content Group UK Ltd.
UKHW021028021124
450571UK00013B/166/J